African Safaris
Journey to Jabula

African Safaris
Journey to Jabula

Maggie Higginbotham

The Choir Press

ISBN 978-1-909300-22-4

Published by The Choir Press

For Beth and Louis, with love

Contents

Acknowledgements

It is impossible to thank each and every person who contributed to my experiences of Africa. The guides and rangers who introduced me to the incredible wildlife, flora and fauna that only Africa can deliver deserve my heartfelt thanks. I have been enthralled, frightened, exhausted and captivated, sometimes all of these in quick succession, and it is due to their skill, patience and good humour that I have learnt to love Africa. To all our safari companions, fellow travellers and friends we have met over the years, thank you for sharing some very precious times with us.

John Burdett of Africa Exclusive is in no small way responsible for me becoming an Africa addict. Thank you John for your patience and expertise in organising many of our safaris – each one was a delight. To Chris Breen of Wildlife Worldwide my heartfelt thanks, especially for the Eclipse Safari when you managed to join us. I cannot praise too highly these and other specialist safari travel firms for the professionalism and care they take to go that extra mile for their clients.

I owe Jean Charity a huge debt of gratitude. She persuaded me to write this book and her invaluable encouragement and praise helped me when I was in two minds whether to proceed. Thank you, Jean for your friendship and support. Christina Harkness worked tirelessly on the final edit, and her expertise, enthusiasm and professional skills were invaluable. She made hard work pleasurable. Many thanks for all your help and advice.

I struggled to find a title for this book. So did Louis van Rooyen who promised to come up with one! Thanks Louis for trying – I'm sorry I gave you some sleepless nights! And thank you, Sally Kay, who effortlessly came up with the title. Not only is it just perfect, but in a magical way it came from the new owner and custodian of Jabula, our beloved African home. Some things are just meant to be. The decade this book spans was a prelude to building Jabula, and each and every step we took in Africa created this journey to Jabula. Sally has assured us that she will keep the name Jabula – in Zulu, its rough translation means happiness and contentment.

Our sons, Shaun and Michael, together with their wives Caraline and Stephy, accepted our wanderings as the norm. Much to our delight, they have grown to love Africa. Thank you for putting up with all our absences and for encouraging us to build our own home in Africa.

Beth and Louis, our beloved grandchildren, have also grown to love Africa. Beth was only a baby when we first went to live in our African home, and she took her first independent steps there on African soil. As we explored, they grew up having 'part-time' grandparents. I missed them both more than I can say when I was away, and only hope they have forgiven my absences. On one occasion, whilst watching me pack for one of our journeys, Beth asked, 'Do you *have* to go to Africa, Granny?' This was heart wrenching and was one of the most soul-searching questions I have ever had to answer. Beth and Louis, now that you have been to Africa several times, and when you have read this book, perhaps you will find the answer.

Last, but by no means least, an enormous thank you to Gordon, my husband and fellow traveller. Without you, I might never have set foot on African soil. You have endured my catastrophes with bush showers; together we have survived a hippo attack, run after lions, and walked for mile upon mile in the scorching bush. We have travelled from the Cape in the south to the borders of Angola and Tanzania in the north, from the Skeleton Coast in the west to the shores of Zanzibar in the east, getting to know this magical, infuriating, beautiful and addictive continent. You have been the patient fundi who sorted out all the problems I frequently had with my computer and camera, and spent many hours preparing the illustrations for this book. Miraculously we are still friends and still together. Thank you for everything.

Thetford House – where we spent many happy hours at the beginning and end of several safaris in Zimbabwe. Overlooking the Mazoe Valley, tobacco was grown in its extensive grounds, followed by the rearing of ostriches. We were welcomed into this beautiful family home with open arms and generous hospitality. The spectacular views and birdlife provided a relaxing backdrop for us after an overnight flight from England and on return from our adventures into the bush.

Chapter 1

The Pioneer Trail

I watched dawn break over Africa. Most of the other passengers were asleep. How could anyone be sleeping when this most magical of scenes was unfolding below? The sky gradually lightened and the first rays of sunlight appeared on the horizon. Gradually, the midnight blue sky became tinged with a soft pink. Suddenly, the sun burst out over the far horizon, and a soft golden hue merged with light blue and orange, transforming the world below. At thirty thousand feet I caught my first glimpse of Africa. The dark green landscape slowly turned paler and the deep red earth became visible. Silver threads like tinsel on a Christmas tree caught the sunlight. Here were the rivers that brought life to the bush. Wisps of smoke twirled upwards. How I longed to experience the smells of the African bush again. Before I had even set foot again on its soil, Africa had worked its magic and I was entranced once more.

We landed at Zimbabwe's Harare Airport in the early chilly morning to be greeted by a welcoming driver who would take us to Thetford House for a night to recover and acclimatise before setting off on safari. Having safely negotiated the chaotic early morning traffic, we drove through the affluent suburbs of Zimbabwe's capital city and out northwards through the countryside. Everywhere, people were walking. Mothers strolled with their babies strapped snugly to their backs in warm blankets. Women pushed wheelbarrows full of plastic containers of water. Men sat in small groups chatting together, and small children played with sticks and balls, pausing from their games to wave energetically, their beaming smiles revealing snow-white teeth. Women tended small fires, roasting mielies for hungry passers-by. At last, I caught the smell of burning wood and knew immediately that I was back in Africa!

Our arrival at Thetford House was a truly colonial experience. The staff lined up to greet us in the driveway, and we were ushered to our bedroom up a magnificent staircase. We were not allowed to carry anything including cameras and hand luggage. Even my handbag was taken from me. Everything appeared safely with our cases in our enormous bedroom, furnished with beautiful antiques and vases of exotic blooms. The view from the vast balcony was stunning. As far as the eye could see the Zimbabwean countryside sprawled below us, with the Mazoe river flowing in the valley. This luxury was something we had never expected. In a small country hotel maybe, but not in such an incredibly lovely private home owned by a tall attractive lady, Jacqui, and her father, Mr Gulliver.

I read the information in the book left for guests and laughed at the wry humour. 'Don't put anything in the laundry bag that is remotely delicate. It will come back reduced to a size that fits nothing but a doll!' Jacqui obviously had a sense of humour. A potted history of her home followed the laundry information. It had been a tobacco farm, then an ostrich farm, at which point her husband had left her, and to keep things going, Jacqui and her father were taking in paying guests.

I lay down on the vast double bed, hardly daring to crumple the immaculate white cotton sheets edged with lace. I stretched out, easing my weary bones that seemed to be welded into the cramped sitting position of my aircraft seat. Never was such luxury so welcome after an overnight flight. I dozed and nearly drifted off when a squeaky gate started to disturb my rest. On and on it went with no particular pattern. Squeak . . . squeak . . . squeak. After half an hour I'd had enough.

'For heaven's sake, Gordon, please could you go downstairs and see if you can find the wretched gate and close it.'

My long-suffering husband got up with a groan and went out of the bedroom, only to return a few minutes later with a broad grin on his face,

'You are going to have to get used to Africa. Your squeaky gate is a bird called the boulder chat according to Jacqui. It lives amongst the slopes of the granite boulders and the locals call it the "squeaky wheelbarrow bird" as its sound is like a un-oiled wheel.'

Sleep was impossible, and not for the first time I wondered how I was going to adapt to two weeks in the bush with all its unknown noises if a small bird was able to prevent me from getting a much needed snooze. This confirmed my opinion of birds, as I am terrified of them, having been chased by a cockerel as a toddler and scared witless. Now I would do anything to avoid close contact with these feathered fiends.

'Well, if you can't beat them, you join them!' I announced. After a shower and a restorative cup of coffee, delivered with much style by a smiling man who I could only describe as an old retainer, Gordon and I decided to go for a stroll in the acres of grounds surrounding the house.

We met up with our travelling companions and close friends, Jo and Neil, who were equally impressed with the magnificent start to our safari. Together we strolled around the gardens, finding rampantly growing plants we could only grow in greenhouses in England. Enormous spider plants edged the borders; red and cream poinsettia grew as high as small trees, and cacti and euphorbia as tall as houses, provided dramatic structure behind rose beds. The most fragrant scent lured us to a bush, full of small flowers ranging from purple, through to lilac and white. We found out later that it is known as 'yesterday, today and tomorrow'. A beautiful name for a really lovely shrub.

After a delicious lunch served in the garden overlooking the pool, we retired for a siesta. I decided I could grow to like this way of life, but knew that for the next two weeks we would be roughing it, camping in the bush, so I would have to make the most of all this luxury while it lasted.

We gathered for tea and scones with clotted cream and home-made jam, and Jacqui suggested that we might like to go for a brief drive around the estate before it got dark. Setting off in a somewhat dilapidated Land Rover, we were entertained by a non-stop commentary on the problems of tobacco farming, ostrich rearing and errant husbands. Dusk approached, and a drinks hamper for sundowners miraculously appeared. A couple of stiff gin and tonics later, we watched the sun go down over the Mazoe valley, amazed at how quickly dusk turned into darkness. Frogs and crickets took over from bird calls, and the vast African night sky appeared in all its glory.

At supper, we were entertained royally by Jacqui and her father. It was the birthday of one of Jacqui's friends who helped with the smooth running of Thetford House, so Mr Gulliver produced a bottle of champagne, which he proceeded to open with a ceremonial sword, slicing off the top of the bottle and cork with a wild slash! We ate and drank, and drank some more, and were entertained by tales of the bush until we wondered if we would actually survive to tell the tale of our forthcoming safari. Everything in Africa so far seemed so much larger than life. I drifted off to sleep, fitfully dreaming of giant plants, noisy birds, wild animals and men with swords.

Breakfast was served on our balcony, and soon we were saying our goodbyes to Jacqui and her father. Jacqui offered to look after a superfluous dress and skirt until we returned to Thetford House at the end of our safari. I was not looking forward to the coming light aircraft flight, and wanted to be certain that my baggage was well under the limit of ten kilograms. A car arrived to take us all to the airport for a flight to an airfield at Hwange in the south of Zimbabwe's National Park, where we would begin our safari.

Arriving at Harare Airport, we were ushered into a holding area where there were numerous light aircraft parked. Our pilot introduced himself to us and we followed him to a tiny plane with our luggage. This was stuffed into the minute hold and we clambered into the plane. The door was shut and the single engine started up, making an unholy noise that made conversation virtually impossible. We taxied to the main runway and were just gathering up speed when the door next to me flew open. The plane came to a rapid halt, the engine turned off and the pilot jumped out and secured the door, apologising profusely. By now, I felt like jumping out too. Gordon took hold of my hand reassuringly. 'At least that didn't happen when we were airborne.' I was not reassured! If this could happen when we were still on terra firma, what else might be in store for us?

Thankfully, the flight was uneventful, and we were soon arriving at Jijima Camp, situated on the border of Hwange, Zimbabwe's largest National Park. We were shown to our tented chalet – a large tent with a bathroom attached, with a thatched canopy over the tent, which apparently helps keep the tent warm in winter and cool in summer. A sitting area at the front under the thatch looked over the green lawn where an impala was delicately nibbling at the lush grass. This was camping in luxury. We went for a walk in the grounds after a buffet lunch, and found that the impala was tame enough to be hand fed – apparently, it had been orphaned at birth and had been reared by the owners of Jijima.

I soon found out the reason why the grass was so green. Suddenly, a green snake started to hiss, followed by a stream of water drenching us before we had time to realise that the watering system had been switched on. After a change of clothes and assurances from the staff that our dripping apparel would be dry for us in the morning, we retired to sit on the sun-loungers overlooking a waterhole. Being mid-winter, this was not weather for lounging about in swimming costumes. It was just about warm enough to sit out as long as we kept our anoraks on. Having left England in a rare heat wave, it seemed strange to be in Africa wrapped up against the cold. The grass outside the watered area was parched and like straw. At least the game would be easy to spot at the waterholes, as there had been no rain for four months.

At supper, we were introduced to our guide who would be taking us on a full day safari into the southern area of Hwange the following morning. He explained that the guide who was going to look after us for the rest of the walking safari in Hwange was making his way back to Jijima, having just finished guiding another party. We would meet up with him the following evening. In the meantime, we would explore part of Hwange and be back in time to be fully briefed on our walking safari.

I drifted off to sleep, wondering if the tents we were going to have during the camping part of our trip would be as luxurious. We were woken up just as dawn was breaking and downed a hearty breakfast, being warned that when camping we would only get tea and rusks. I thought that maybe we were being gently broken in to the idea of camping in deepest Africa. Inner man satisfied, we climbed up into an open Land Rover from a landing stage that made getting up into the seats easy – something else we would not be having in a day's time! Off we went and were soon tucking blankets around our waists to keep the chilly wind at bay.

We drove along a railway track that stretched in a straight line as far as the eye could see. This was part of the proposed Cape to Cairo line, the dream of Cecil Rhodes to link the whole of Africa from south to north. Crossing this historic piece of engineering, we entered the Park and settled down to a day of game spotting. We soon spotted large herds of buffalo, elephants and giraffe not to mention wildebeest, impala and a pair of white rhinos in the distance. We talked together about how we would feel when walking on foot with such an amount of game around.

Bird life was spectacular and I started to appreciate these sightings – something I had previously thought was rather overrated. How could anyone fail to be impressed by the wonderful colours of a lilac-breasted roller, the vivid purple, blue and lilac hues flashing when in flight. Two jackals trotted briskly past us, but these were the only carnivores we saw. We stopped at a picnic area for lunch, and then slowly made our way back to Jijima. At last, I felt we were really back in Africa, all my senses fully satisfied after a long day in the bush.

Back at camp, Shane, who was to be our guide for the walking part of our safari, introduced himself. He was a slightly built young man with a shock of brown hair, dark friendly eyes and a warm smile. With him was a trainee guide, Ben who would help Shane look after us all. Over a drink before supper, we pored over a map Shane had produced, looking at where we would be exploring, and during the meal he and his father regaled us with stories of the safaris they had been on together. Shane's father had lived and guided in the Zimbabwean bush virtually all his life, and declared he could spot a lion a mile away, just by the dark tips of its ears or a twitch of a tail. I hoped fervently that Shane had his father's talent, as walking into a pride of lions was not on my agenda.

We were up at the crack of dawn and after breakfast our bags were loaded into the trailer hitched behind our Land Rover. Having clambered inelegantly into the vehicle we set off, only for Neil's hat to fly from his head before we had travelled little more than a few yards. 'The strings should be tied under your chin to stop your hat flying off, Neil,' announced Shane, laughing as he leapt off to retrieve the offending item. I'm sure he was wondering if we would ever get to our destination without having to stop every few yards for a group of disorganised tourists. We settled down, and clung tightly onto anything that might possibly fly off the Landy – the local terminology for the vehicle that was to be our only means of transport for the next few days. The adventure we had been looking forward to for many months had now started.

Elephants have always played a significant part in our safaris. Our first close encounter on foot was when we were crouched below a dam wall with a large bull feeding over our heads. Over many years, these encounters have been thrilling, emotional and sometimes frightening. I have nothing but respect for these awe-inspiring animals.

Chapter 2
Detema Dam

After a bumpy, windy, and chilly few hours we arrived at the camp where we were to stay for three nights. Everything was already set up for us, and we were greeted by the sight of a row of three small tents overlooking a valley, which spread into a plain of dry bleached grass. A larger mess tent and a minute tent that enclosed a bush shower stood at either end of the tents that were to become our homes. The kitchen area had been set up to the back of the camp and five smiling men, who were already busy lighting an open fire, waved a friendly welcome to us. Up a small hill was a brick-built shed, which apparently contained a loo. Rocky outcrops surrounded the entire small area, with a somewhat dilapidated wire fence marking the boundary between us and any wild life.

I looked at it dubiously, and wondered how a thin bit of wire would deter a lion or leopard, let alone an elephant. Inside our tent, I looked at the two camp beds made up with sleeping bags, and couldn't help but smile at the thought of our luxurious double bed at Thetford House and the large tented chalet at Jijima. This was what we had come to Zimbabwe for – an authentic bush experience, not five star luxury accommodation in a safari lodge filled with tourists. We had experienced this in South Africa, and now we wanted to experience the *real* Africa, walking all day, and sleeping under the stars at night with only a thin bit of canvas between whatever wildlife might chance our way and . . . us.

Shane showed us round the camp, and introduced us to the staff who would look after us. Meals would be served in the mess tent, and if we needed any drinks, we were just to help ourselves if no one was there to serve us. If we left our laundry out on the floor of our tent, it would be ready for us on our return from a day's walking in the bush. On no account were we to venture past the wire fence, and there were whistles in our tents if we wanted help at night for whatever reason.

Lunch was served, and we realised that this was camping in style. A delicious quiche and salad, followed by a fruit salad, washed down with wine or beer. Content and replete, we retired for an hour's rest before going out for a brief walk before dark. I was much too excited even to snooze, so spent the time sorting out the few clothes we had brought and made certain that cameras and binoculars, plus insect repellent, anti-histamine tablets, sunscreen, tissues, paracetamol, anti-diarrhoea tablets, a basic first aid kit and a bottle of water were safely packed in my rucksack. I was fully prepared! It was only later that I realised Shane carried a much more comprehensive kit, together with his rifle and a belt of bullets!

First came the all important safety briefing. The four tourists from England gathered around Shane and Ben, looking and feeling like first formers standing before their headmaster.

'The most important rule of the bush is – never run,' Shane intoned, looking around his attentive group. 'Remember, everything out there can run faster than you, and if you run, the chase reflex will be activated in any predator, resulting in an easy meal for them! Always walk in a straight line behind me. Ben will bring up the rear and keep an eye open for anything behind us. The last thing I want is to have four people scattered around the bush if we should come across an animal. I need to know at all times that you are close behind me. Follow my instructions at all times, even if you cannot understand why I ask you to do something. I might well have seen something that you have not noticed, and your safety is my first priority. I never want to be put in the position of having to shoot an animal, let alone fire a warning shot, because of your actions. Remember that we are visitors in the animals' environment and not the other way round. Keep an eye on me and any hand movements I might make. My hand up means stop. My hand waving you down means crouch, or even lie down on your stomach. Look where you are putting your feet and try to avoid dry branches and twigs as they make a lot of noise and scare game away. Talking about noise, keep this down to a minimum – no chattering please. Remember also that we are not on a photographic safari. I will try and get you as close to animals as is safe, but you will not be as close as maybe you are used to in a vehicle for obvious reasons. We will pause frequently for photo opportunities, but most importantly, I want to give you experiences that will bring the bush alive for you, and that you will remember for the rest of your lives. Have you any questions?'

I looked at Gordon and saw the serious expression on his face. What had we got ourselves into? So – I might have to lie down in the bush – but would I ever be able to get up? No running suited me just fine, and at the moment, I didn't want any animal nearer to me than half a mile. As for questions, I had a hundred, but was struck dumb and shell-shocked, as it seemed were the rest of the party.

'Right, let's set off!'

We followed Shane out of our camp, past the safety of the wire fence and into the bush. We went down a small hill, trying not to slip on the dry earth and loose stones. The next obstacle was a small river bed with reeds. Over we went and reached a wide open plain with the occasional bush and tree. It was midwinter in Zimbabwe and the grass was crisp and dry. Termite mounds towered amongst the straw-coloured landscape. It seemed amazing to me that any animal could survive in this parched wilderness. Shane's hand went up and my heartbeat and blood pressure soared. 'I can hear a strange noise that sounds like a metallic click. Have any of you got a loose buckle or something similar?' I was mortified to find out that the metal zip tag on my rucksack was the culprit. Now I had to hold on to the wretched thing to prevent it making a noise, stop my camera and binoculars clanging against each other, look at Shane at all times, watch where my feet were to avoid twigs and branches, and try and enjoy the experience!

'As we've now stopped, let me give you a hint as to how to walk in the bush quietly. Always put your heel down on the ground first, then the ball of your foot. You'll find you make much less noise.' Suitably chastened, we set off again, only to stop in another few hundred yards. I started to get a fit of giggles, trying desperately to stifle my laughter. Stopping was proving to be a bit of a comedy show. If just one of us failed to see the signal to stop, then they would plough into the person in front, sending them flying. Why have we stopped?

'Now I'm going to teach you all about dung, and what you can learn from it.' Shane grinned. In front of us was a heap of elephant dung. 'Who wants to put their finger in it? We can tell the approximate time this elephant was around here.' He promptly put his finger in the pile and pronounced that it was probably produced early this morning. Solemnly, we all put our fingers into the dung, finding it moist and faintly warm.

'Tomorrow we'll search for some elephants. They'll probably come down to the nearby dam to drink as this is the only good waterhole for several kilometres.' On we went, looking rather like a clip out of *Dad's Army*. We stopped for another pile of dung, this time, white. We stooped over it trying to look intelligent. 'Never put your finger in this – they are hyena droppings, and contain enough bacteria to make you very ill. In fact any carnivore's dung is bad news, but a herbivore's is pretty harmless.'

After an hour's gentle stroll, looking at dung, insects, birds and animal tracks, thankfully not coming across any of the latter, we stopped for a well-earned drink by a pile of bleached bones. The temperature was still hovering in the twenties although the sun was sinking lower on the horizon. Shadows lengthened and the plain started to take on a glow of early evening. Shane turned over the bones and explained that these were the remains of an old elephant. How did he know it was old? He showed us the jawbone. We learnt how an elephant has six sets of teeth, each new set moving into place when the animal outgrows or wears out the previous set. This old fellow was around sixty years old when he died, having got through his last set of teeth, and unable to eat the one hundred and fifty kilograms of food needed per day to keep himself alive. No wonder there was so much dung around, and there were signs of tree damage everywhere.

'Right,' said Shane. 'We'll set off back to camp now. An extra drink at supper for anyone who can tell me where our camp is!' We all looked around, absolutely clueless. 'Now come on you lot!' Shane laughed. 'What would you do if I had been knocked unconscious, and Ben had gone for help and he didn't return? How would you get me back to camp?' We then had a lecture on remembering where we were, taking in trees, bushes, boulders, where the sun was – in fact anything that was a pointer to our whereabouts, and where our camp was. We were amazed to find out that we had simply walked in a circle and that our camp was just a few hundred yards away behind a small rise.

Back at camp, a canvas bowl suspended on a wooden tripod and filled with warm water awaited us. After a quick wash, we gathered around the campfire and had our first sundowners in the bush. Never was a drink so welcome as we mulled over the experiences of our bush walk. Over a filling supper of steak, roasted vegetables and a sticky toffee pudding with custard, we talked about what we were going to do the following day, and then retired once more to the campfire. We sat on canvas chairs with mugs of coffee and iced Amarula, and gazed into the hypnotic, leaping flames of the fire whilst listening to Shane recount some of the stories about his safaris and life in the bush.

The evening chill descended and we drew our chairs closer to the fire, content to listen and watch the 'bush television' throw up sparks as another bit of wood was carefully placed on the fire. We exchanged our own experiences of being on safari in South Africa the year before. We had visited Londolozi, the world renowned safari lodge in the Sabi Sands Game Reserve adjoining the Kruger National Park. Here, Kathy, a wonderful ranger stimulated our love of the bush. She had the amazing gift of making everything interesting, whether great or small, and after a magical three days, we were determined to 'get Africa under our feet' and go on a walking safari.

Whilst at Londolozi we decided to go on a bush walk with another ranger. Jo, Neil, Gordon and I, together with two Italian men, set off in the heat of the day. Our ranger motioned us to stand still and explained that there was an elephant in the tall grass in front of us, close to the river bed. He asked if any of us wanted to crawl any nearer. Gordon and Neil decided to be brave. Jo and I, and the Italian men decided to stay put in the tall grass, on the understanding that we were not to move. We would be collected on their return. Slowly, Gordon and Neil crawled towards the hidden elephant, and disappeared from our view. Jo and I sat in the shade of the long grass, nervously whispering to each other and wondering if we would ever see our husbands again.

Time passed and suddenly there was the noise of something coming towards us through the bush. Was this the elephant or was this the men? A sudden noise behind us distracted our attention. We looked in amazement to see the two Italians running back towards the camp. So much for chivalry! Here were we, left alone in thick bush and the two Italians nowhere to be seen. Eventually, the ranger appeared, followed by our two Englishmen, the latter with grins from ear to ear. Apparently, they had got close enough to see the legs of the elephant but the ranger decided that this was close enough. He was not best pleased that his other two guests had fled back to camp.

That evening, we came across the Italians at supper, dressed to the nines with gold medallions adorning their chests, entertaining other guests with their bush tale of how they had gone on a bush walk and had a close encounter with a wild bull elephant. They noticed us listening to their macho tale, looked somewhat embarrassed, and promptly retired to their room!

Shane laughed with us, but also reinforced the strict rule of the bush that we were never to run. Slowly, the tales of the bush faded with the dying embers of the fire and we were escorted to our tents for our first night of camping in the bush. I had asked if my hot water bottle could be filled and there it was in my sleeping bag, together with another one. Each of us had a hot water bottle to keep us warm, but I had two, one for my feet and another one to snuggle up to. Gordon had been very scathing that I insisted on packing my 'hottie'. I refused to leave it behind as it always comes with me regardless of where we travel. It is my very precious security blanket. I climbed into bed, making sure the whistle was close by and settled down to go to sleep, warm and snug in the chilly African winter with just a thin piece of canvas between the bush and me.

I woke up suddenly to the noise of the kitchen utensils being tossed around. The sound was horrendous. What on earth was happening? I tried to wake Gordon. This was a somewhat fraught operation, requiring me to aim a shoe at him to bridge the gap between our two camp beds. He had managed to sleep through all this crashing and banging!

'Probably hyenas going after the scraps of left-over food,' he mumbled.

'Great,' I replied. 'How am I to get any sleep?' The only response I got was more tins being rattled on the granite boulders. I dozed off to sleep, only to wake up with my tummy rumbling and the urgent need to go to the loo. That's all I need, I thought. The only loo was past the kitchen area and up a slope of boulders. No way was it going to be possible to negotiate my way there by torchlight with hyenas out there. In fact, I wouldn't even attempt to open the flap of my tent. If I had only wanted to wee I might just in desperation, have squatted outside, but this was not just a need to empty my bladder. I cursed the fact that I had drunk more than usual round the campfire. The change of drinking water and extra alcohol often seemed to have this effect, and I hadn't considered the consequences.

Was this enough of an emergency to blow my whistle? How could I justify waking the whole camp and drag Shane out of his sleeping bag just to escort me to the loo block? I lay back and tried to ignore the calls of nature. Miraculously, the first twitters of bird life heralded the coming of daybreak. Never was a dawn chorus so welcome! I heard the sound of human movement around the camp and rapidly scrambled out of bed, grabbing the nearest clothes I could find, shoving my feet into my trainers, after rescuing the one I had thrown at Gordon, from underneath his bed.

'I hope you remembered to shake your shoes – remember scorpions like to hide in them,' murmured a sleepy husband.

'B . . . the scorpions! This is a real emergency,' I replied, and ran up the hill as though being chased by a herd of elephants. The kitchen staff looked on in amazement at this mad English woman who was supposed to be in bed for at least another half hour! Thankfully, I made the loo just in time, swearing to myself that I would never again have so much alcohol whilst camping. On my return, the canvas washbasins were again full of hot water, and I joined the line of fellow campers washing their faces and cleaning their teeth. We were finding out that privacy was virtually non-existent on a camping safari, but somehow as the days wore on it never seemed to matter.

The embers of last night's fire had been rekindled and steaming hot coffee, tea or chocolate with teeth shattering rusks awaited us in the cold dawn. A thin mist hung pearl grey over the bush, and sparkling drops of dew lay everywhere. I could see my breath whilst I stood huddled near the fire, warming my hands on a mug of hot tea whilst dunking a rusk. Gradually, I shook off my somewhat disturbed night's sleep before preparing for another day's walking.

Shane and Ben had apparently slept through all the pots and pans doing an imitation of a bad rock band. Apparently, hyenas or honey badgers often came into camp hunting for food. Jo had experienced a bad night as her back hurt on the camp bed struts and she decided to sleep on some extra blankets on the floor for the rest of the safari. I asked about going to the loo in an emergency in the middle of the night, and learnt that it was quite safe just to go close to the tent – spades were always available. That was a relief!

We set off in the grey African dawn, trying to remember all the tips about walking quietly. I realised that walking in the bush was so much more rewarding than driving around in a vehicle, and taking photographs was no longer my first priority. Gordon was recording our safari by video, but it soon became obvious that he too was more intent on enjoying the experience first-hand rather than through the lens of a small viewfinder. There was the odd mutter from him when he realised he had forgotten to turn off the recording, and we have long stretches of film picturing his size eleven feet walking through the bush. Some serious editing would be called for when we got home!

We concentrated on learning to read tracks. As the sun was low, the shadows on the sandy ground made it easy to see what had passed in the night. Shane excitedly showed us the tracks of a leopard and we followed the trail for over an hour, meandering around the bush. We stopped at a large hole and I made the mistake of going to peer into it. Shane immediately pulled me back.

'Never go in front of any hole – you don't know what might be hiding inside it. There might be a warthog denning there or even a leopard with cubs.' We were on a steep learning curve, and the more we got to know Shane, the more we appreciated his knowledge and love of the bush.

'Remember that we are in the animals' habitat and we must respect them at all times and allow them their own space. They will usually never attack unless they feel cornered or threatened, especially if they are protecting their young. My task is to ensure we never encroach into their individual space or get into a situation where we surprise an animal. This is why we are *reading* the bush. Every track tells its own tale. After all, animals are like human beings in some respects. We all know what it is like to have our own individual space threatened by someone. Our reaction is similar. We either retreat or attack just like animals.'

We noticed this with the plains' game we came across. Impala were numerous, and we could approach them quietly and get within a few hundred metres. Any closer than that, they would stop grazing and adopt a wary, alert look. If we walked any closer, they would stamp and sound the alarm by snorting, before scattering in all directions.

After a couple of hours walking, we stopped for a drink of water. The cold dawn had given way to a perfect sunny winter's day, the temperatures rising to the mid twenties. Jo and I sat down on the nearest small log, only for it to collapse under us, sending us sprawling. Shane quickly hauled us up with yet another warning. Scorpions and snakes apparently hide under logs. The last thing he, or we for that matter, wanted, was a painful if not fatal bite on our backsides. Another lesson quickly learnt!

We hunted for tracks of the elephants we wanted to see, but there was nothing fresh. We decided to wend our way back to camp as it was now approaching eleven o'clock. I was amazed to realise that we had been walking for nearly four hours. Shane was certain that we would find the elephants at the dam later on during our afternoon walk, so we trekked back to camp for a well-deserved hearty brunch. The camp staff had prepared cereals, fresh fruit, a full English breakfast, toast and muffins, and copious amounts of freshly brewed coffee or tea. We certainly were not going to go hungry, and were astonished at the quality and quantity of the meals – all cooked over an open fire.

It was now time for an introduction to the bush shower. Large buckets of hot water had been heated up whilst we were doing justice to our brunch. I volunteered to go first and examined the small canvas tent, which was placed on a gentle slope so that the water would drain away. I stood on the wooden duckboard and turned on the tap at the bottom of the water container, which was strung over the branches of a tree. Never was a shower so welcome to wash off the dust of twenty-four hours in the bush. I soaked myself with the warm water and started to wash my hair with copious amounts of shampoo. I then attempted to turn off the water while I washed the rest of the dust from my body, but found that the water container, now lighter, had risen higher than I could reach. I tried jumping to turn off the water, but soon found that jumping on a slippery duckboard on a slope was a recipe for disaster – a broken leg at the very least. The water above me trickled to a halt, and there was I still covered with shampoo and shower gel with no way of rinsing it off.

'Gordon,' I called softly, hoping he was within hearing distance. No response. 'Gordon,' I shouted, and Shane arrived at the outside of the shower. 'Are you OK, Maggie?' he enquired solicitously. I explained my predicament, that I was stranded, covered with soap and the water had run out. I felt so stupid, and vowed never again to volunteer first for anything. Shane went off, chuckling to himself, and another bucket of water was delivered to the shower tent by one of the camp staff. I then had to explain that someone would have to come into the shower and adjust the bucket so that it hung a bit lower. His lack of English meant that I was reduced to asking him for my 'baas' to come and help. A somewhat bemused husband, who had been busy looking at his video shots then appeared, and adjusted the height of the shower bucket so that I, and future shower users, could reach the tap more easily. Being six foot four inches tall, he did not seem to have much insight into my problem.

'Why does everything seem to happen to you?' he asked a now cold, wet, soapy wife. This was not a well-received question. I was rapidly losing my sense of humour and knowing me well, he retreated quickly to the peace and quiet of his video camera. I rinsed myself down and, draped in a large towel, somewhat shamefacedly, stalked back to my tent.

'Nice shower, Maggie?' asked Jo. I related to her the perils of the shower tent, and to use the absolute minimum of water, shampoo and shower gel so that she did not repeat my mistake and run out of water when rinsing off. Jo decided that she would shower with Neil, who was a little taller, and would be able to turn the tap off for her. This was not a great success, as one bucket of water between two was not enough. Gradually, all of us finished our ablutions. There were no more shower disasters, apart from Gordon managing to slip on a piece of soap and landing on his backside on the sandy slope, much to my amusement! Over the next three days, we all managed to sort out our showers with a minimum of fuss, and soon became experts on the art of showering in the bush. I had a great sense of satisfaction getting mine to a fine art and managed to save at least three quarters of a bucket of water with which I could have a good rinse.

One of the most pleasant times of day on safari was the quiet time spent after lunch, doing one's own thing. It was hot and the entire bush seemed to be having a siesta. I found a bit of shade and wrote up my diary, looking up every so often to see if anything was happening on the plain in front of the camp. Writing completed, I retired to my camp bed to have an hour's snooze before being woken up to have a cup of tea and a large slice of cake, everyone else having also recharged their batteries ready for the next walk.

Shane decided to give us an easy afternoon, and we set off in the Land Rover, parking it at one end of a large dam. We left the security of the vehicle, walking with a bit more confidence now that we had two bush walks under our belts. We soon came across fresh tracks of a herd of elephants just as Shane had predicted. They were going down to the dam to have a drink after a hot day.

On the horizon, we saw a group of around twenty elephants slowly meandering towards the dam. We were told to sit down. Shane did not want us to break up the horizon with our outlines. If the elephants saw us they might well go off in another direction. We watched these ambling giants gradually come nearer until Shane told us to crouch down low and follow him. After a couple of hundred yards we came to a dip in the ground, surrounded by trees and, at the far end of the dip there was part of the rocky dam wall, built waist high. We clambered over the rough ground strewn with large boulders until we reached the dam wall. Here we rested, hidden from sight by the trees and boulders, and waited for the elephants to come down to water in front of us.

Jo and I leant over the small wall with Shane standing next to us. Gordon and Neil were further back, concentrating on taking photos and film of their respective wives looking over the dam wall at the elephants. Ben stood at the back, making sure nothing surprised us from behind. Gradually, the elephants came down to the water, increasing their speed when they neared the water. We watched entranced as they poured water into their mouths with their long trunks. When they had satisfied their thirst, they went into the water and splashed around like children, sinking into the water until only their trunks were visible – the perfect snorkel.

Soon there were over thirty elephants enjoying the now muddy water. Calves of no more than a few months old played together, hauling themselves over each other in the mud, and generally behaving like children at the seaside. When they got a bit too boisterous, their mothers reprimanded them with a warning thump over their backs with their trunks. Stroppy teenagers tested their strength against each other in noisy mock fighting. If this got a bit too serious, they would retreat to be closer to their elders, who would reprimand them with a short trumpet of sound. Everywhere I looked, there were elephants swimming, drinking, playing, floating, diving and just enjoying the cool, refreshing water after a long, hot day foraging for food.

Eventually, their thirst slated, their bodies washed and cooled down, the herd began to leave the water and started to fling dust over themselves. Shane explained that this was to get rid of ticks and to protect their skin. The matriarch of the herd led the calves and their mothers away from us, leaving a few larger bull elephants to enjoy a few minutes of peace and quiet before they too left the water. Instead of following the matriarch, these bulls started to climb up the shallow incline towards the dam wall and . . . us.

I looked across to Shane who motioned to us to keep quiet and still. When they came within a few yards of where we were, Shane motioned to Jo and me to crouch down and smiled at us reassuringly. He stood beside us in full view of one elephant, which was now standing on the dam wall. I very slowly glanced up a fraction of an inch, only to see the elephant's foot and toenails within touching distance just above my head. I heard Shane move very slowly and then, out of the corner of my eye, saw him get a couple of bullets out of his belt. What on earth had got me into this situation? Who in their right mind would ever go on a walking safari? Who would tell our children that we had been killed by an elephant? All these thoughts flashed through my mind in an instant.

Shane very gently knocked a bullet against the barrel of his rifle. Click, click, click. Slowly the elephant retreated a couple of steps; his trunk came over Jo and me, and he started to feed on the branches over our heads. Click, click, click went the bullet against the rifle butt again. The elephant retreated another step, withdrawing his trunk. Shane motioned to Jo and me to crawl back slowly and quietly to where Gordon and Neil were standing. Jo, crawling alongside me on all fours, muttered, 'And we're paying good money to do this!' I decided that I would save my stifled, near hysterical laughter for a later moment if I actually managed to survive the next few minutes. We reached our husbands, trousers filthy and knees bruised from the rocky ground, and looked back to see Shane still standing there virtually face to face with the elephant towering above him. With a toss of his head, the magnificent beast ambled off to join the rest of the herd.

Shane signalled to us to join him back at the dam wall and we gingerly made our way back to him. 'Well done all of you! Now I know I can trust you to do what I say!' This was praise indeed. He then explained that the reason he had told Jo and me to crawl backwards away from the elephant was that if the elephant had decided to ignore the warning sounds of the bullet being tapped against his rifle, and had continued feeding above our heads, it was possible that some branches might have fallen on us.

There was I thinking Shane was going to have to shoot the elephant and the only danger was, in fact, falling branches! Shane continued, 'The elephant was well aware that we were all there and saw us as no threat to him at all. All he wanted was the leaves above your heads, but he was a gentleman and decided to leave us in peace!'

'Why the bullet tapping?' asked Gordon.

'I've found that this is a sound that warns animals as it is a sound that is out of the ordinary in the bush. Well, at least I now know that none of you will have a heart attack on me!' joked Shane, and we gradually returned to normal, laughing and joking about our experience of a close encounter with the world's biggest land mammal. I was going to have fun looking at Gordon's video footage and Neil's photos when we got back home.

We had a much needed drink of water and then Shane guided us up to the top of the dam wall. There in the distance was our Land Rover we had left a couple of hours ago. We started to walk along the bank of the dam when Shane signalled us to stop. Far in the distance, he pointed out another herd of elephants coming towards us.

'Sorry folks. We are going to have to go back and round the other side of the dam.' I looked at the small distance between us and the Land Rover, which we could have covered in a few minutes and asked why we had to go round the long way.

'You might be able to cover that distance in a few minutes, but when elephants smell water they could cover that distance rapidly and be there very quickly. Charging or fleeing elephants can move at nearly forty kilometres an hour, which is faster than any of us can run. Besides which, if one of you fell and injured yourself then we really would be in trouble. Never get between an animal and water is a safe rule to follow.'

I glanced at the vehicle. Never had something looked so safe and so near to get to, but back we trekked, past our hideaway, round past the end of the dam and on to the far bank. As we walked briskly, we saw the herd come down to water. There was no time to stand and stare. Shane wanted to get us back safely to the Land Rover as the herd might decide to come across the water to where we were. After forty minutes of rapid walking, we reached our transport and Shane produced sundowners from a cool box. This man was a marvel! Not only had he saved us from a browsing elephant but he also produced life-giving gin and tonics just when we needed them!

We sat on some rocks on the shoreline and toasted each other. There is nothing like sharing a life-changing moment to bond people into a close group. Dusk was approaching when we saw an elephant come towards us. 'Just sit quietly and let's see how close he comes to us. If I tell you to get back into the Land Rover, just move slowly with no noise,' whispered Shane. Maybe it was the gin and tonics, the proximity of our vehicle, or the fact that I had learnt to trust Shane implicitly, but I was more relaxed this time.

Gradually, in the deepening dusk the gentle giant walked past within a few metres, completely ignoring us. I marvelled how something that weighs up to 6,000 kilograms makes virtually no noise at all. The only sound was the deep, soft, rumbling he occasionally made, his way of contacting his fellow elephants by infra sound. I wondered how much more he was transmitting that we, as mere humans, could not hear. He disappeared into the night and we sat silently, not wanting to break the spell.

Almost reluctantly, we climbed back into the Land Rover, and Shane drove us back to camp where the fire was burning brightly and our supper was waiting for us. Around the fire after supper, we talked over the events of the day before climbing into our sleeping bags complete with hotties, each of us recalling a very precious day we would never forget.

Taking a break when we were walking in the bush.

This tent was our home for our first few nights under canvas in the bush. I was hooked for life after this experience. There is nothing quite like camping in Africa, knowing that the only thing between you and the wildlife is a thin sheet of canvas. Initially, every sound is a wake-up call, guaranteed to alert every sense, but having survived the first night, I had some of the best night's sleep ever. To hear the roar of a lion or the sawing sound of a leopard is a dream in itself!

Chapter 3

Life in the Bush

The next couple of days sped by, following the same pattern. Bush walks early in the morning and later in the afternoon; siestas and delicious meals, ending with nightcaps around the campfire where we put the world to rights and became entranced, listening to stories of the bush. I fell asleep each night to the sounds of untamed Africa – a lion roaring in the distance, a leopard making its unmistakable sawing sound, a hyena whooping and a Scops owl purring. All this lulled me into a deep contented sleep. I was in an infinitely beautiful and wild environment; one which nurtured me in a way that I never knew was possible.

The care our camp staff took to ensure that we had every possible comfort enhanced this sense of nurture. Freshly washed and ironed clothes appeared as if by magic, neatly placed on our beds each afternoon. I decided I had to see how this was done, so went up the rocky slope to investigate. One of the camp staff was busy ironing some clothes on top of a flat rock covered with a thick blanket. He was using an old-fashioned flat iron, which he would heat up every so often on the glowing embers of a fire. He carefully tested the temperature of the iron before applying it to our clothing, flicking some water onto stubborn creases. Through sign language, we tried to communicate and bridge the gap of two continents. He took me over to his friend who was working in the camp kitchen. Large water containers were always simmering over a large open fire, hot water instantly available for drinks, showers, washing-up and cooking.

Hot coals filled a hole in the ground and, inside a tin covered with a cloth, our bread was being cooked for the next meal. A stew was gently bubbling in a pot suspended over some more coals. Ice blocks were kept in an enormous insulated container, run by a petrol driven generator, which came to life when we were away from camp. On our return, this was switched off to ensure that the peace of the bush was not disturbed.

The infinite care and pride these five men took in their work impressed me deeply. My ironing with an electric steam iron at home could not produce such immaculate results. As for making bread, my attempts had always failed miserably. Yet here, out in the bush, these men produced fresh bread any master baker would be proud of, with delicious meals appearing three times a day, and cooked to perfection. I thanked them all for their hard work, attempting to convey how impressed I was, and went back to my tent contemplating how much we, in the so-called First World, could learn from these gentle people.

One evening, round the campfire, Shane told us how he and his father used to go out into the bush and spend the night sleeping beside a fire. No tent, only the African sky above them. One such night, they had gone to sleep and in the morning, they woke up to find lion spoor all around them. A lion had come up to them, walked around their sleeping bodies and settled down close to the embers of their fire to keep warm! Shane's tales of such experiences kept us spellbound for hours around the campfire at night.

Soon we came to the end of this part of our safari. Our last afternoon bush walk produced some lion tracks, so, with mixed emotions, we followed these for a couple of hours. Of course, I would dearly love to have seen lion whilst out walking, but only in the distance! Unfortunately, we were not in a position to determine how far away we would be when we came across them. I found out a lot about myself in these four days, learning that I could not control what happened in the bush. All I could do was follow Shane's instructions to the letter, as my very survival depended on him and his knowledge gained over many years out in the wild.

Remembering Shane's story, I wondered how close he would get us to lions. Suddenly, he signalled to Ben to lead us back quickly. We turned round and followed Ben at a brisk pace. I focussed on keeping up and not tripping over, realising that Shane needed to get some space between us and whatever he had seen. I was expecting the roar of a lion and doubted whether we would ever see our ranger again. I desperately wanted to look back and see what was happening, but realised that I had to concentrate on following Ben. Five minutes later, Ben halted and we were able to get our breath back.

In the distance, we saw Shane walking briskly towards us, every so often looking behind, rifle at the ready. I had learnt over the last four days that when Shane was relaxed, he carried his rifle down by his side. When something was obviously concerning him, the rifle came up a little and his other hand reached towards the bullets in his belt. He explained that he never walked with a loaded rifle because there were more accidents caused by a loaded rifle than by charging animals. As he approached, I saw him slotting two bullets back into his belt. We all breathed a sigh of relief.

'Sorry about the brisk retreat, folks,' he said with a grin on his face. 'I heard a low growl coming from the bush in front of us, and then saw the spoor of several lion cubs. They were obviously denning there and the cubs must be very young and not venturing far from the den. That's why we didn't see any sign of them before. Coming across a lioness with small cubs is definitely not a good idea, hence Ben having to lead you away rapidly.'

Once again, I marvelled at his skill at reading the bush. No one else had heard the low growl. Thank heavens for his expertise! Having to shoot the lioness would not only end her life but also the lives of several cubs whose survival depended on her. I was glad we didn't get to see them.

How my attitude had changed in such a short space of time. When I first came to Africa a year ago I was intent on seeing absolutely everything, but mainly the so called 'Big Five' – lion, leopard, buffalo, rhinoceros and elephant, and take as many photographs as close as possible from the safety of a Land Rover. Now I was content to hurry away from a lioness with cubs and absorb as much knowledge as I possibly could, getting Africa into my soul and, totally and utterly into my blood.

Reluctantly, we walked slowly back towards camp, each footstep bringing us closer to the end of our walking safari. Groves of bare bushes grew in thick clusters all around us. We learnt that these bushes are young mopane trees, also called butterfly bushes due to the shape of their leaves. Piles of dried leaves were scattered over the ground. These are shaped like a butterfly's wing and, when green, open and close with the heat of the day. The leaves are not very palatable but elephants eat them, so we wondered if we would see any more elephants before we reached camp. As if on cue, a large lone bull appeared over the brow of a hill. We paused and watched it amble slowly towards us, its large, dusty ears flapping when he shook his head slowly from side to side. Faint clouds of dust floated up into the sky, the fine particles illuminated by the red setting sun. Shane spoke quietly, requesting us to follow him in the opposite direction, leaving the elephant to continue his gentle ambling.

He asked us if we noticed anything special about the elephant. We all agreed that he had only one large tusk; the other seemed to have been snapped off. Through our binoculars, we could see that the injury appeared to be a recent one. We also noticed that the temporal glands in between its eyes and ears were weeping.

'Well done!' he said. 'Your observations are really improving no end'. We all looked pleased with ourselves. 'Now, why did we walk away from him?' Silence. We tried to make sense of what we had seen. We knew the elephant was under stress because his temporal glands were weeping. Maybe it was the heat, as he showed no other signs of being in musth. Shane explained that he might be coming into musth, but the most obvious sign was the recently snapped-off tusk. 'He could easily have the most awful toothache and if he came across us in his favourite feeding area, he might be very bad tempered!'

We walked back to camp, ruminating on walking away from a lioness with cubs and an elephant with toothache. We did not mind that we had no photographs of either. A few days walking in the bush had brought about such a change in all of us.

Our last evening round the campfire was a reflective one, each of us sharing our thoughts about getting Africa into our souls. I could hardly bear the thought of leaving this magical place and saying goodbye to Shane who had become our friend and protector, and had shared his love of the bush with such enthusiasm and expertise. My life had changed completely in four days and I vowed I would return and walk again in the bush. Shane talked about the long journey we would take the following day, motoring virtually the length of Hwange National Park in the open Land Rover. It would be an early start in order to reach the lodge on the banks of the Zambezi River where we would stay for a couple of nights for a bit of comparative luxury. Shane's family ran this lodge, and we would be able to take a boat on the Zambezi or visit Victoria Falls before setting off for another two lodges in the south of Zimbabwe. My spirits rose with the thought of unlimited water to shower in and the prospect of boat safaris on the mighty Zambezi.

Before we turned in, each of us gave Shane a wish list of anything we wanted to see en route. Mine was very simple, but apparently the most difficult. I longed to see the elusive wild dog, also known as the African Hunting Dog or Painted Wolf. I also wanted to see a dung beetle rolling a ball of dung! Shane was adamant that I wouldn't be lucky in seeing a dung beetle as it was the dry season and they only came out during the rains. He was also very hesitant about the chances of seeing wild dog. Hunted to near extinction, there were now only around 4,000 left in the whole of Africa so the chances of coming across a pack were remote. This made it even more important for me to go on another safari with the express brief of seeing wild dog sometime in the future. Gordon and I chatted in our tent about where this next safari might be before I drifted off to sleep to the sound of a lion roaring faintly in the distance. Smiling to myself, I recalled how we had walked away from the lioness and her cubs.

Another close encounter with a pachyderm! Rather than being on foot, we were in the open Land Rover, which tended to give me a false sense of security. However, this time the elephant kept strolling towards us. I lost my nerve and slipped down onto the floor of the vehicle, until re-assured by our guide that it was safe to return to my seat. This resulted in a picture of me eye to eye with this large bull when he halted a couple of yards from the vehicle. After a stand-off, he tossed his head and meandered away.

Chapter 4

Journey to the Zambezi

We were woken by the now familiar get-up call 'Knock knock!' before the sun had even started to warm up a crisp winter morning. It was so cold that it was a race to get some layers of clothing on – not an easy task for two people in a very small tent! A quick wash of face and hands in the steaming water waiting for us in the canvas bowls outside our tent, and then we rushed over to the campfire for the now customary mug of hot tea and home-made rusks. After warming up a bit, I returned to our tent to pack the remaining bits and pieces of our luggage and said a silent, fond goodbye to this minute tent that had become our home in the bush. It had served us so well, and I wondered why I had ever had any doubts about camping in Africa.

The camp staff lined up ready to say their goodbyes to us, so we all went along the line shaking hands in the African way with the double handshake. I would love to have given each of them a big hug, but didn't want to embarrass them. They had all worked so hard behind the scenes to keep us in real luxury. Water for showers and washing appeared whenever we wanted; delicious meals were set before us three times a day; our clothes washed, dried and ironed ready for us each day – all done with broad smiles and a real desire to please. We were delighted to hear from Shane that once they had packed up our camp, they would be returning to their families for a well-earned holiday.

We were given closely woven thick woollen ponchos to put over our sweaters and padded anoraks. We looked at each other and tried to remain straight-faced when Shane explained that they really were necessary as the wind chill factor meant that we would be very cold without them. Jo and Neil were the smallest and found that they had to tuck up their ponchos to avoid tripping over when they walked. My poncho came to just above my ankles, so at least I could walk about with little danger of coming a cropper. Gordon, being six foot four, found that his garment came to mid thigh, so he looked the least ridiculous of us all. Unable to control ourselves, Jo and I collapsed into hysterical laughter. Why is it that whenever women start to laugh together, men never seem to think it is very funny? They stared at us in utter incomprehension, probably not wanting to admit how utterly ridiculous we all looked in our flowing woollen robes. Ben added the finishing touch – a knitted balaclava for each of us – although he seemed somewhat hesitant to produce anything that would set Jo and me off into more peals of laughter. Gordon gave me a husbandly look, which I pointedly ignored, as I interpreted it as, 'For heaven's sake, pull yourself together and behave yourself, woman!'

Once Jo and I had mopped away our tears of laughter we proceeded to try and climb into the Landy. This was a difficult enough procedure at the best of times, as it involved hauling ourselves up with our arms until one leg was safely up on the running strip ... Then we had to climb over the side to get ourselves into the vehicle. If it was someone's turn to sit on the back row of seats, it was a question of either clambering over two rows of seats from the inside, or else edging one's feet along the narrow running strip and climbing onto the back seats from a height of around five feet off the ground. Given the added problem of being dressed in long ponchos to hinder our efforts, this took some time. I decided that in future, by far the easiest thing to do was to only dress in all my finery once ensconced in the Landy!

Off we set, waving madly at our lovely camp crew who were by now grinning from ear to ear. I like to think that they really had become fond of us, but I am also sure that our travelling wardrobe had something to do with their grins. I quickly donned my balaclava, putting my sun hat away in my camera bag. Shane had been right about the wind chill factor. Here we were, in the middle of Africa, with a clear blue sky promising a lovely sunny day, and within half an hour, we were all windblown and cold. I mentally counted the number of layers I had on under my poncho – cotton T-shirt, shirt, pullover and padded anorak, and still I was cold. I pulled my sun hat out and pushed it onto my head over the balaclava, tightening the strings beneath my chin. Tears were starting to stream into the balaclava due to the bitterly cold wind, so out came my sunglasses. Not an inch of bare flesh was anywhere to be seen.

I thanked my lucky stars that our travel agent had told us to pack gloves. We heeded the firm's advice and had prepared thoroughly, noting the comprehensive list of items to pack, plus the instructions that our luggage should not weigh more than ten kilograms per person due to the internal light aircraft flights. I had hesitated to pack gloves – why on earth would I need warm gloves on a trip to sub Saharan Africa? Gloves weighed nearly as much as a swimming costume when I was trying to decide what to leave out of my small canvas holdall. Now I knew why a swimming costume was totally superfluous on this trip!

On we travelled, bumping along a faint, dusty track, the dust flying up behind us, and swirling around sometimes as the wind veered round to hit us in the face. Occasionally, we would slow down for a herd of impala to cross in front of us. Zebra and giraffe grazed on virtually non-existent grass. As far as we could see, the landscape was parched and dry. Sometimes we caught a glimpse of green trees lining a dried-up river bed. Somewhere under that dusty sand was moisture to enable the trees to keep their leaves throughout the six months of the arid Zimbabwean winter. I snuggled up to Gordon for extra warmth. Conversation was difficult, as the noise the Landy made going over the rough ground made communication, other than by sign language, virtually impossible. Shane had told us that unless we saw something absolutely spectacular we would only stop for food, drinks and comfort breaks.

After an hour and a half of hard driving, we finally came towards a waterhole and slowly came to a halt. 'OK folks, time for a break,' declared Shane as he jumped out of the vehicle, stretching his limbs. Gingerly, I climbed down from my perch up at the back. I was seized – solid and frozen. 'How are you all doing? I told you it would be hard going and a bit chilly!' *Chilly* seemed the understatement of the century!

As if by magic, large thermoses of hot water appeared, and Ben began taking orders for tea, coffee or chocolate. When I had thawed out a little with the help of two full mugs of delicious hot chocolate, I realised that what liquid went in must eventually come out! When walking in the bush, it had become second nature for Jo and I to ask Shane or Ben to find us a bush, and to inspect and make certain that there was nothing lurking either behind it or in the dried out, flattened grass before we squatted. Here however, there were no bushes anywhere.

'Men to the left and women to the right of the Landy,' Shane instructed. The ponchos came to have another use apart from protection against the cold. When arranged like a tent around us they provided Jo and I with a degree of privacy! For once, Gordon and Neil were at a disadvantage trying to cope with long ponchos with no convenient gaps when answering the calls of nature. Now they knew something of the trials women have to put up with!

We walked nearer the waterhole to get a photo of some enormous crocodiles warming themselves in the sun with their mouths open wide, displaying vicious teeth. 'Not too near please,' warned Shane. Crocs, we were told can move very rapidly, and there might well be some still in the water. These submerged reptiles could easily leap out and grab anything within a yard or so of the bank. We retreated to the safety of our vehicle, bracing ourselves for another couple of hours of dust, bumps and rattles. I was relieved that the sun was now up and at least seemed to be warming us a little, although all our layers of clothing were still absolutely essential. When we were enjoying our hot drinks Shane had told us that he'd come across a ranger who was driving a group of Americans on safari in the winter. They had not been so well prepared for the cold, and one poor man had been evacuated to hospital with hypothermia.

The next two hours passed in a haze of some discomfort, but we all decided we were British and certainly would not moan! Gordon recalled the journeys his grandfather had made, up through South Africa and into Zimbabwe at the turn of the last century. He had been one of the earlier adventurers, and he fell in love with a young chorus girl on the stage in Cape Town. They eloped, and were married close to the Modder River in South Africa. A daughter, Gordon's aunt, had been born out in Africa during the time that his grandfather was wheeling and dealing both with, and against, Rhodes, and she had the dubious distinction of having both Rhodes and Jameson as her godfathers. 'They must have been a tough lot, trekking with an ox wagon all these distances!' mused Gordon, trying to keep warm under some blankets Shane had fished out of the trailer to give us yet another layer to snuggle under.

We eventually pulled in to a fenced-off camping ground. There were several groups of campers there and it was a shock to the system coming across people from the outside world. Not once in the last four days had we seen any trace of the human race outside our own tiny community. We dashed to the loos and on our return found Shane and Ben busy lighting a fire. I had expected a few sandwiches to keep us going, but soon we were tucking into a feast of bacon and eggs, toast and marmalade, all washed down with freshly brewed coffee. I had never welcomed a meal more.

By now, the sun was high and I even thought about taking off one layer of clothing. I decided however I would rather be warm than frozen, so settled down to another couple of hours in the Landy, only to start getting cramp in one leg. It would not go away. Eventually, Gordon called down to Shane that we had a bit of a problem, and we stopped to let me ease my leg. Ben suggested that I might be better sitting in his seat at the front, as there was more room for me to stretch out my legs. I was reluctant to change my seat, as I believed that game viewing was better from the back of the Landy, but my cramp was agonising so I climbed into the front seat, and we set off again.

Within ten minutes, I was nearly passing out with heat stroke. I wondered if this was the first sign of malaria or some dire tropical disease, only to realise that there was a very efficient heater supplying warmth to Shane and Ben, added to which, the large windscreen protected them from the vicious wind. I roared with laughter and relayed the information back to my fellow poncho-clad, balaclava-helmeted travellers. Shane and Ben were not the macho, weather-hardened men we had thought them to be – their secret was now common knowledge! There we were, commenting how they were clad only in thin fleeces and shorts, and admiring their fortitude! They both looked rather shamefaced and from then onwards we all took turns at warming up in the seat next to the driver!

I also realised that sitting next to the driver had another advantage. When photographing an animal, I got a much more exciting shot, as I was nearer to the ground, not five feet up in the back of the Landy. Shots of elephant taken at a level below their body produced wonderful photos, and other plains' game photos taken at their eye level were equally impressive. The disadvantage was that only photos taken side-on were worth anything, as the windscreen got in the way. Standing up was forbidden unless Shane told us it was okay, as standing in the Landy meant that the outline of the vehicle was broken. Animals were used to these noisy, smelly machines and considered them to be no threat. However, once the outline was broken by anyone standing up, they saw this human being as a potential threat and either fled or charged. Shane was always very aware of providing us with as many good photographic opportunities as possible when we were out in the Landy, and invariably managed to position the vehicle with the sun in the optimum position and the vehicle angled correctly for good shots.

We had another stop at a high lookout point, where there was a hide overlooking a dam in a valley below. Shane parked the Landy and we walked up to the hide. He slung his rifle off his shoulder and his hand went to the bullets in his belt. 'Just stay where you are with Ben and I will come back and collect you in a moment.' We waited, wondering what might be happening now. Shane soon called us into the hide and explained that a few months ago a woman had walked into the hide where a leopard had been resting in the rafters of the roof. Unfortunately, she was badly mauled, and the leopard, wounded by the accompanying ranger, had escaped. The Park Authorities were notified and rangers sent out to see if they could track the leopard down and shoot it. Sadly, a wounded leopard that had also attacked a human was not an animal that could be allowed to live. This was one of the very few circumstances where man had to intervene with nature. As far as Shane knew, the leopard had not been found, hence his extreme caution.

I looked warily around the hide before sitting down on the rocky wall. Below us, a breeding herd of elephants had come down to drink. The calves played around in the water and a herd of zebras came down to satisfy their thirst. Five giraffe gingerly approached the water, taking an age to settle down and have a drink. They slowly spread their front legs, enabling their heads to reach down to the water, taking a quick drink before jumping up, spraying water everywhere. They are always in such a vulnerable position when they are drinking, as any predator could easily knock them off balance when their front legs are splayed so wide.

Suddenly, what looked like a large grey cloud appeared. This turned out to be a flock of red-billed quelea and the cloud was, in fact, tens of thousands of these tiny birds, swooping and turning. We watched mesmerised by the patterns they created. They resembled columns of smoke, twisting and spiralling over the water, the noise of twittering filling the air. It seemed incredible that so many thousands of these birds never collided with each other, but Shane said that he had seen many impaled on sharp acacia thorns when coming to rest in trees; the weight of a flock of quelea has been known to break tree branches.

We left this amazing spectacle as we had another hour of driving before arriving at the lodge on the banks of the Zambezi. My excitement rose as the kilometres sped by. All the discomfort of our long journey across Hwange faded into insignificance, and we all peered into the distance for the first sight of this mighty river. A herd of elephants crossed in front of us, and we watched as they increased their speed, almost running to keep up with us. This was a sure sign that they were moving towards water.

We rounded a bend and there in front of us was a shimmer of light. We had arrived at the river, which marked the frontier of Zimbabwe and Zambia. After nearly a week in the parched bush with only pans and dams providing water for the wildlife, here was an enormous stretch of water flowing swiftly in front of us. It was a shock to the senses to see green grass and reeds bordering the river, and tall majestic trees, which spread their leaves to provide shade, season upon season. We motored along the bank and there in front of us was a small oasis. Thatched roofs covered the stone built bungalows, and a neat lawn led down to the river. At last, we had arrived at Imbabala. Shane sounded the horn and several men, smartly dressed in black and white uniforms, rushed to welcome us.

Some tourists relaxing by the pool looked with utter amazement at the spectacle of four dusty, tired visitors, clad in long robes with balaclavas hiding their faces, clambering down from a vehicle covered with dust. What on earth had arrived to disturb their peace? Jo and I looked at their expressions, and again our sense of the ridiculous took over. Here were some immaculately coiffured women staring at two females who appeared to have never had a wash or a visit to the hairdresser in their lives. Our taste in fashion didn't seem to meet with much approval either. Once more, we collapsed in a fit of giggles and I thought about the holiday these elegant women were no doubt enjoying. Regardless of any luxuries they might be savouring, I knew that absolutely nothing could have been more enjoyable or exciting than our four nights spent camping and walking in the bush.

Giraffes on the alert at a waterhole, before having a much needed drink.

There were two sights I wanted to see on this walking safari. The first was a dung beetle rolling a ball of dung and the second was wild dog. As it was winter and towards the end of the dry season, unfortunately, dung beetles were not going to materialise. On the final evening of our walking safari, we were relaxing on a pontoon on the Zambezi. All thought of wild dog was long gone when suddenly, out of the bush, two wild dog appeared before trotting off in the dusk on their evening hunt. This was the beginning of my lifelong fascination with these rare, endangered 'painted wolves'.

Chapter 5

Hippos, Elephant and Wild Dog

The staff showed us to our bungalow where our small dusty holdalls awaited us. I looked at the invitingly large double bed, two sofas and the low coffee table with wildlife magazines and a vase of flowers placed on it. The bathroom boasted a Victorian bath, separate large shower and a loo. What absolute luxury to have these to ourselves, and all within a few steps from our bed! I stripped off my layers of clothes and stood in the shower, streams of refreshing water flowing over my hair, washing away the dust of the previous twelve hours. At last, I did not have to ration the flow of water and I revelled in the warmth cascading over my tired body.

All too soon my impatient husband appeared, desperate to get into the shower. I promptly got out and ran a bath, putting in several times too much bath gel. For the next half hour, I lay back in the soothing foamy water, closing my eyes and remembering the small buckets in the bush shower. Those were a real pleasure after a morning of tracking animals, but this was luxury personified! I vowed never again to take such simple pleasures for granted.

Drinks were the next thing on the agenda, and we met up with Jo and Neil, who were feeling equally refreshed. We walked over to the small bar to order some long cool beers and rock shandies – a drink I had come to love – half lemonade, half soda water, a large splash of angostura bitters and lots of ice. We were reluctant to join the rest of the tourists staying there. It felt as though this would break the spell of the last few days, but dinner was soon served and gradually, we started to mix with the other guests who were eager to hear of our experiences and what we had seen. They listened with amazement at some of our stories, and I realised that, in sharing our adventures, maybe sometime in the future they too might choose to go on a walking safari and enjoy similar encounters. Now was the time to be generous and open, just as Shane had shared with us his great love and respect for the bush. He had gone off to Victoria Falls, only a few kilometres away, to have a well-earned rest and an evening off with his family. Before he left us, we had made plans for our next couple of days. There were to be no stories around a bush television tonight. The prospect of a large double bed with soft cotton sheets and duvets was much too inviting. I fell asleep listening to the hypnotic sound of the Zambezi gently flowing past our bedroom window.

After a substantial breakfast, Jo and Neil departed to spend the day at Victoria Falls. Gordon and I had seen the Falls the previous year in a brief stopover before travelling on to South Africa, and so wanted to do something different. Shane suggested we spend some of the day on the Zambezi, and organised a large motorised pontoon for our use. We walked down to this strange contraption where we found David, the ranger, attempting to start the motor. Time after time, he pulled the starter motor and gradually the battery became weaker and weaker until it gave up and died.

Thankfully, there was a plan B. He asked if we minded going out in a small boat with an outboard motor. *Minded*? We were delighted! The large pontoon was usually the preferred option for guests as it enabled them to walk about, and enjoy refreshments on board. Added to which it floated higher in the water so was less liable to hippo attacks! As we were keen sailors and loved the water, a small boat was much the more attractive option to us, even if we had to take our chances with hippos. Some bottles of beer and water were hastily put in a cool box, and we climbed on board. A small Jack Russell dashed down to the water's edge and jumped into the boat, settling himself at the bow, his paws dangling over the side. David tried to get him back onto dry land but the dog was having none of this. Not only do we love boats but also dogs, so

Tigger came too. David told us that this African pooch regarded the boat as his own, and if he wasn't allowed on board he would run backwards and forwards along the bank barking furiously and disturbing the peace and quiet for everyone at the lodge until the boat returned home.

Off we set, the three of us plus Tigger, happy to spend the next few hours motoring on the Zambezi. David showed us where pods of hippos usually congregated, and we were soon looking at heads of hippos surfacing from the dark water, their small eyes taking in where we were. It was apparent that Tigger did not like hippos as he barked furiously whenever a head appeared. Thankfully, he was well trained and a sharp 'Quiet!' from David was enough to silence him, only for another bark to warn us when another head appeared. He was an excellent early warning system, as he somehow managed to sense when a submerged hippo was about to surface.

Occasionally, large hippos surfaced, confronting each other in displays of dominance, their huge mouths opening wide and displaying fearsome tusks. No wonder these animals are known to cause more deaths in Africa than any other animal. David frequently turned off the motor and we gently floated downstream. Only the grunts and wheezes made by these enormous animals disturbed the peace of the river. They sounded like old men laughing over a risqué joke. We learnt that they weigh anything up to 3,200 kilograms, and leave the river at dusk to forage on short grass before returning to the water before dawn. This was not an animal to come across when walking back to our bungalow at night!

As the morning progressed, it got warmer and we welcomed the gentle breeze coming off the water, especially when we motored along. Tigger stood on the bow of the boat, his balance obviously perfected over some years. Apparently, he had only once fallen overboard and this once was enough as far as he was concerned. We had only to look towards the bank to see enormous crocodiles basking in the sun to realise that this was not a river in which to take an unplanned swim!

We floated gently past a group of elephant coming down to drink. When the current took us too close, David started up the outboard motor to give them more space. A few hippos were resting on an island in the middle of the river, and the sound of the motor disturbed them. They got up and dashed into the safety of the river, the resounding splashes disturbing the smooth flow of the river. We had now to estimate where these huge 'river horses' were and hoped that they would not surface underneath the small boat. The wash they created rocked the boat violently, prompting Tigger to jump off his lookout point on the bow, and retreat to the relative safety of Gordon's knee. After a few minutes, a warning bark, quickly silenced by David, heralded first one and then the other hippos surfacing just a few yards away. David rapidly swung the steering wheel round, and we veered off in the opposite direction towards the bank. The middle of the river marked the boundary between Zimbabwe and Zambia, and we had to keep on the Zimbabwean side even though there were no patrol boats about.

As we drifted closely to some trees, their overhanging branches nearly touching our heads, we spotted a waterbuck quietly grazing. A few minutes later, we heard the haunting call of an African fish eagle, and then more calls. If ever a bird sound evokes Africa this is the one which brings back the most memories. We floated silently towards a pair of fish eagles perched on a dead branch, their necks and throats extending backwards and then forwards when they called to each other. Never before and never since have we been so close to these magnificent birds. So engrossed were they in their courtship ritual that we came within a few feet of them before the current carried us past.

David started up the motor and we slowly motored back to the lodge. He talked about the wonderful trips he had made to another National Park in Zimbabwe. He had noticed how relaxed we were in a boat and thought that we would enjoy visiting Mana Pools. Here one could walk freely as well as canoe down the Zambezi. Gordon and I looked at each other. In an instant, we had decided on our next safari!

After a lunch served beneath the shade of trees, we retired to have our now customary siesta, talking together about how wonderful a safari that included walking and canoeing, would be.

Jo and Neil appeared in time for tea, having thoroughly enjoyed their excursion to the Falls. We wished that we could have been in two places at once, but our morning had been a most fantastic experience, and we talked about maybe going to Mana Pools together some time in the future.

When Shane appeared to hear about our day, he suggested that we went out in the Landy for a drive and sundowners. We didn't need any persuading, and collected our anoraks before jumping on board as though to the manner born. The quietness of drifting on the Zambezi contrasted strongly with the rattling and bumping of this, by now, well-known vehicle. We came across a large herd of buffalo grazing on last season's grass, and stopped while they slowly came past us. They gradually surrounded the Landy, ignoring us completely, and the only sound to be heard was the rhythmic chewing and tearing up of small clumps of parched grass.

In the distance we heard another sound – an elephant trumpeting, and we decided to go and investigate. A few minutes later, we spotted a breeding herd of elephants. They had obviously been down to the water as they were still wet. Again, Shane turned off the engine and slowly they ambled towards us. 'Just stay still and keep quiet,' whispered Shane. 'We'll see how close they get to us!' I eyed the rifle slotted safely into a bracket in front of the steering wheel and reminded myself that we were now in a vehicle and not quite so vulnerable as we had been when on foot. We sat in a frozen tableau as they came close and closer. The sun had now set and night was rapidly approaching. A large female elephant with a tiny calf on her far side stopped to browse on the leaves of a nearby tree. Occasionally, she would pause and lift her trunk towards us, sniffing at the air, making sure she knew where we were. The calf started to suckle and we could hear the sound of greedy sucking of milk.

Night came and still the elephant and her calf stood in front of us, barring our way back to the lodge. All we could see was a large dark shape. After about twenty minutes, Shane gently tapped on the side of the Landy and immediately the elephant stopped browsing and quietly ambled off into the night, her calf following. We set off with the spotlight flicking backwards and forwards, illuminating the rest of the elephants in the distance. 'I didn't want to disturb the mother and her calf by using the spotlight on them,' explained Shane. There seemed to have been a mutual sense of trust between the elephant and us. She perceived us as being no threat to her and her precious baby, and allowed us to witness a very special, intimate scene. One more magical, and treasured memory!

The next morning we decided to be utterly lazy and do absolutely nothing. After all, we had experienced a week of pre-dawn starts and days filled with excitement, and so felt we deserved a restful morning. We settled down for a morning on sun loungers to watch the Zambezi gently flowing in front of us, and peer through our binoculars at the animal and bird life. We decided that we wanted to go on one more trip with Shane in the late afternoon, this time on the pontoon. He also suggested that before this, we should walk with him to the nearby hide where we might be lucky enough to spot some elephants coming down to the river.

I looked with horror at the hide. It stood over six metres high and the only means of getting up to it was by climbing a rickety ladder. I have never been good at heights, so started to climb very cautiously. The real trial was actually getting onto the platform. This was indeed an obstacle course. I hauled myself up by my arms, swung off the ladder and up a good half metre over a gaping space of absolutely nothing, and then onto the planks of the platform. I landed like a beached whale, and wondered how on earth I was ever going to get down. The view was stunning, overlooking the Zambezi and a mud pan. Gordon strolled up and down the platform, hanging over the few bits of wood that provided the so-called safety fence around the platform. My warnings went unheeded, and I was accused of being an over-anxious worrier. We were balancing on a precarious platform high over the African bush, and short of having a full domestic, there was nothing I could do to dissuade him to stop behaving like a middle-aged Tarzan, so I ignored him, and tried to concentrate on taking a few photos. It was as much as I could do to stand still and take in the magnificent view; even standing still was difficult with the whole platform swaying slightly whenever anyone moved.

Soon enough a breeding herd of elephants came down to the Zambezi, and several small calves started to play in a nearby mud pan, rolling around in the glutinous liquid. Their mothers, having slaked their thirst, returned to collect their offspring, and soon there was only one calf left in the mud. We watched intently as it attempted to climb up the slippery slope. The mother, together with several other females, gathered around to watch its efforts. Time passed, and it was becoming obvious that the calf was getting tired and distressed. Each step it took resulted in it slipping back into the thick sticky mud and its calls for help became more frantic. One young elephant got into the mud and attempted to push the calf out.

By this time, around twenty elephants had gathered round, their trumpeting and rumbling adding to the unfolding drama. Shane told us that it was by no means rare for a small elephant to get permanently stuck in such a situation, resulting in a slow, painful death. We watched with bated breath as a potential tragedy unfurled. Eventually, the matriarch of the herd climbed down into the mud and tried to haul the calf free. Her trunk furled under the belly of the baby as she attempted to lift it out. Several agonising moments later, the strength of the matriarch's trunk broke the suction holding the calf in the treacherous mud and she lifted it up onto the firm dry earth. The calf shook itself and started to walk off, only to receive a big thump from its mother's trunk, as if to say, 'You've been very stupid, never do that again!' The calf squealed and we roared with laughter and relief at this all too human display of elephant behaviour.

As we waited for the herd to move away, we discussed elephant behaviour and how their life span was very similar to a human being's. Eventually, they had moved far enough away for us to climb down that rickety ladder. By now, Gordon had realised that I was really scared at the thought of the descent to terra firma. We decided that the best thing to do was for him to go down before me and guide my feet onto the highest rung, whilst Shane would hold on to me as I launched myself off into space. Crouching within inches of an elephant feeding over me was nothing compared to the terror I felt getting down that wretched ladder, but the scene I had just experienced made it all worthwhile. I was learning new things about my capabilities and myself all the time whilst on safari, which sometimes felt like a survival course!

I sat back on the pontoon, just floating peacefully along with drink in hand, watching the sun sink lower as night began to gently wrap its cloak around us when suddenly Shane pulled me to my feet. 'There you are, Maggie, at least one of your wishes has come true!' There on the bank were two African wild dogs, slowly trotting off into the dusk! I wiped away a few tears of joy. It was too dark to take any decent photographs, but the most important thing was that I had realised a dream. I had seen fleetingly two of the most rare and – in the past – much maligned, canines on the African continent. Gordon gave me a warm hug, and we all had an extra sundowner to celebrate!

We continued our celebrations over supper, remembering all our incredible experiences with Shane and Ben. I felt sad at the thought of having to say goodbye to them, but we focussed on potential future safaris. As elephants had played such a major part in our safari, Shane suggested that we might think of going on an elephant-back safari. His family had rescued several orphaned or injured elephants and nursed them back to health. It was impossible to release these elephants into the wild, as they had no family structure to enable them to exist safely in the bush. They were also used to humans, and would be at risk from poachers as they regarded man as no threat to themselves.

A few kilometres away, a camp had been established where it was possible for people to spend a few days with these gentle giants, riding through the bush on their backs, feeding them, washing them and accompanying them on walks through the bush. Shane assured us that they were trained humanely with no cruelty and they were able to follow certain commands. It was one of the first places in Africa to train African elephants as it was previously thought that they were unable to be domesticated, unlike Indian elephants. I was somewhat dubious about going on such a safari. As far as I was concerned, elephants, and indeed all wild animals should remain wild in their natural environment, but having got to know and respect Shane and his love for the bush, I realised that he would never be associated with anything that could be of harm to an animal. Something else to put on a short list for the future, together with camping in Mana Pools.

We all said our goodbyes to Shane. It was impossible to thank him enough for such a life-changing experience, and we promised to send him some video footage of the highlights of our safari. It was sad to see him leave, and I was envious of the next group of tourists he was going to pick up in two days' time. I wondered whether they would soon be crouching at an elephant's foot, and if our experiences would be shared over a campfire, and become a little part of safari history in Zimbabwe!

In order to reach far-flung destinations in Africa, light aircraft, the workhorses of the African bush, is the best mode of transport. Flying has never been my favourite occupation, whereas Gordon always remained entirely and sometimes infuriatingly, relaxed. Here he is asking me if I intend to get into the aircraft or prefer to be left on the tarmac. So far, I have never been left behind, but looking at my luggage still by my feet and not in the hold, I seem to be seriously considering the matter!

Chapter 6

Exploring the Past

We were up with the dawn the following day, as we had to get to the small airport just outside Victoria Falls for our flight to Bulawayo. On arrival at the airport, we were instructed to place our bags on a giant weighing scale out in the open, close to numerous small aircraft. That done, we were subsequently told that each of us had to be weighed too! This was a first, and I was pleased to find out that I hadn't put on any weight, thanks, no doubt, to all the walking. We sat on a low wall waiting to be collected by our pilot, who turned out to be a very attractive young woman. She led us out to the tiny light aircraft, its tail propped up by a support, and Gordon explained that this was to stop the tail dropping onto the tarmac when our bags were loaded and we boarded. Heathrow seemed a million miles away!

Eventually, our baggage and the four of us were installed in a plane that seemed to get smaller by the minute. No wonder we were instructed not to take more than ten kilograms per person. The propeller started to whirl and we waited to begin taxiing to the runway, but nothing happened. After a few minutes, the pilot turned to face us and explained that the engine was not developing enough power. Off we got and went back to the wall to sit down and await developments. Half an hour later, a mini bus arrived to take us to the larger international airport twenty minutes away. Here we would be able to board another aircraft to get us to Bulawayo. As we travelled up the long straight road, lined with stalls selling wood carvings and stone sculptures for tourists, I felt we were well and truly back to so-called civilisation.

On arrival at this airport, we were ushered to a holding area where our female pilot was waiting for us. She escorted us to an aircraft, which Gordon then recognised as the one we had left an hour ago. He asked if she had managed to get the fault fixed, only to be told that the fault was minor and she had flown the plane up to the main airport as it had a much longer runway, enabling us to take off in safety even though the engine was a bit down on power!

Nothing daunted, we repeated the exercise of loading ourselves into this tiny space, our luggage being stuffed into the hold. I held my breath on take-off and tried to relax. Flying has never been my favourite pastime, in fact, I hate it, and the thought of being up in the air in an underpowered light aircraft was my idea of sheer torture. Gordon tried to distract me by talking about the scenery, and pointed out that we were following the railway line straight down to Bulawayo; he gave up when I curtly told him I would much rather be in a train. I mused over how the loss of power would affect our landing, but decided I did not want to have a technical answer from a husband who had by now decided I was not worth talking to. I looked at Jo who was catching up on her holiday reading, Neil being fast asleep, and I envied them their composure.

Half an hour into the flight, just when I was beginning to think it was safe enough to relax, the engine gave a loud cough. Our pilot quickly fiddled with a few dials and the sounds of terminal coughing gave way to a smoother sound. I noticed Gordon was looking slightly more pallid than usual, and trembled as the pilot turned around and announced she was just changing fuel tanks ... 'Nothing to worry about.' If only she knew how I was feeling! Eventually, we landed safely and I was able to clamber down on to Mother Earth, breathing a heartfelt thanks to the blue sky we had just left.

A mini bus was waiting to take us to our next lodge outside Bulawayo, and soon our host, for the next three days, was greeting us. We had chosen to stay here so that we could see some of the sights around this area, including the place where Rhodes was buried in the Matopos Hills. Richard, our host, turned out to be very knowledgeable in the history of the area, and he and Gordon got on like a house on fire when he discovered some of the history of Gordon's grandfather. He offered to take us to where the early pioneers had trekked and where some skirmishes had taken place. No doubt, Gordon's grandfather had passed along these trails during his travels.

After lunch, we were introduced to the extended family, including a warthog that had been orphaned at an early age. It had been hand reared and its best friend was a Labrador. Richard said he was sure the warthog actually thought it was a dog, and we spent an amusing half-hour watching the two of them play together, before the warthog went off to graze on some grass. As I watched it, I realised that although we had seen many on safari, I had not noticed how they knelt down on their knees to feed. Every so often the Labrador would come up to us for a nuzzle and a bit of petting, only to be shoved out of the way by the warthog. Its coat was as coarse as a scouring pad, with bristles as hard as fine needles, and its emerging tusks would soon mean that cuddles might be a bit fraught. Off it went into the bushes, only to emerge with a half eaten melon – its favourite food – and nothing would persuade it to give up this tasty bit of fruit to the Labrador!

Not only was Richard the source of extensive historical knowledge, but he was also an extremely talented photographer. After supper, we relaxed in the family's sitting room and he presented a most beautiful slide show of some of his photos, accompanied by glorious classical music. Thoughts of the nights spent camping in the bush faded and I was transported into another world of beauty accompanied by the sounds of Mozart.

The following morning we set off for a day in the Matopos Hills. Enormous boulders dominated the area, and formed incredible formations, with smaller boulders balanced precariously on the summit of larger ones. Green, orange and yellow lichen coloured these massive natural structures. Large strangler figs grew up rocks and host trees, their massive root systems even splitting the rocks and boulders over which they had grown. We stopped frequently to take photos and examined some beautiful paper bark trees – their lovely grey bark with large papery cream flakes fluttering in the breeze and falling to create a thick carpet.

As we walked on our guide turned over a large dead log, asking us to stand back. A scorpion was hiding under the wood. Stretching itself, it started to move, the tip of its tail revealing a bulbous sac full of venom. The guide picked up a twig and gently touched its back, causing it to immediately turn and attack the twig with its vicious sting – a sting, which would certainly land one in hospital. 'I hope you always shake out your shoes before putting them on!'

Gordon looked thoughtful and retorted, 'I think I'll shake out my trousers too.

Jo and I remembered the log we had sat on, only for it to collapse and send us sprawling on the earth, and Shane's concern over scorpions. Now we had seen for ourselves the dangers lurking under any stone or log.

An hour or so into our journey, we stopped for cold drinks and the inevitable loo stop. For Jo and me it was again a question of climbing over a boulder and crouching down behind it to preserve a fraction of modesty – and what should we come across when we squatted, but a tiny mouse-like creature, which eyed us doubtfully and scampered off into the undergrowth. Thankfully, neither Jo nor I have hysterics when faced with mice, so when we rejoined the men folk we told them what we had seen, and we all set out to investigate. Soon enough this tiny creature reappeared, and we found out that it was an elephant shrew – one of the smallest mammals to be found in the bush and one of the 'Little Five'. Obligingly, it posed for photographs and kept us captivated by waving its long nose around like an elephant foraging for food with its trunk.

Eventually, we reached the site where Rhodes was buried. We walked up the mountain formed from enormous smooth boulders, and at the summit found ourselves looking at the resting place of the controversial explorer, marked only by a plaque: 'Here lie the remains of Cecil John Rhodes'. A simple statement for a complex, extraordinary man. The view was absolutely stunning – a three sixty degree panorama of the Matopos Hills lay below us. Rhodes called it the View of the World and it seemed fitting that he had chosen this place for his burial – it reinforced everything we knew about the man and his often described love of both grandeur and simplicity. A little further down the rock to one side we saw Jameson's burial place. Geckos and lizards lazed on the weatherworn surface in the warm noonday sun, only to scamper away when we got too close. It was a strange feeling to visit the place where the godfathers of Gordon's aunt lay for all eternity. This was part of our family history too, whether we liked it or not. Knowing his elderly mother would be interested in seeing this historical site, I took some photos of Gordon standing near the graves. His mother had been born when her sister was already in her early twenties. Her parents left Africa where two fortunes were made and lost during the wheeling and dealing with Rhodes, and settled down to a life of genteel poverty in England. Somewhat subdued and full of our own thoughts, we made our way down the rocky slope to our vehicle.

The following day Richard took us out to look at former battle sites and we came across a monument commemorating the track where missionaries, hunters and traders passed on their travels. The inscription on the monument read: 'Honour their history. They revealed to those who followed the bounties of a country they themselves might not enjoy'. How true. Richard suggested we might think about visiting the battle sites in KwaZulu Natal, especially Isandlwana and Rorke's Drift as they were very special. We were collecting enough ideas for many years of visits to this fascinating continent.

On we went to look at some Rock Art sites, painted by the Bushmen, now known as the Khoisan, some thirty thousand years ago. Most of these paintings are situated on rocky overhangs and caves with a northerly aspect, and being interested in art I found them very moving. Some had obviously been painted with a finger, others with quills, feathers or small bones. Many colours were still vivid – red, black and white, and I marvelled at the artistic skill of these ancient people. I gazed, enthralled at pictures of hunters stalking antelope, men with bows and arrows, and groups of figures appearing to dance. These talented artists even made use of the contours of the rock on which they were painting, and stomachs of elephants and antelope appeared swollen and lifelike. What incredible sights we were seeing on this very different part of our journey, but all too soon it was time to pack our bags for yet another new experience.

The following day we returned to Bulawayo Airport, where we were to fly south to a lodge where we hoped to see the rare black rhino. The area we intended to visit has the highest concentration of black rhino in Zimbabwe. I waited anxiously for a pilot to come and collect us from the waiting area where all the private aircraft were parked, and whispered to Gordon that I certainly hoped it wouldn't be the elderly man who was inspecting his tiny light aircraft with a cigarette in one hand – a sure candidate for a heart attack, I felt. When the very same man came up and introduced himself as our pilot, Gordon merely smiled wanly at me. We then had a choice to make. His plane could only take two passengers, and he had arranged for a farmer friend to fly two of us in another plane. Jo and I decided to toss a coin, and Gordon and I were soon being taken to the aircraft owned by the smoking pilot!

Despite his addiction to nicotine, he turned out to be an absolutely charming man, and invited Gordon to sit in the vacant co-pilot's seat as there was more room for his legs there. I huddled in the back listening to the non-stop chatter between the two men, whilst we waited for permission to take off. Jo and Neil's plane took off first and shortly afterwards we too were airborne and flying between two small, scenic mountain ridges, catching sight of their plane a couple of hundred feet below us. The flight was only a short one, much to my relief, and before long, we were circling around the dirt airstrip where we were to land. I peered out of the window to see that Jo and Neil had already landed and were waving to us. Our pilot then asked Gordon if he would like to see the lodge where we were going to stay, and before I could say anything, the men had decided that we were going to make a brief detour. The engine revved up and we soared once more into the sky, banking sharply, and there in front of us was the lodge, perched on a hilltop. We banked sharply again and flew over it – Gordon laughing when the pilot told him that he could almost dip a wing into the small swimming pool!

We landed with a series of bumps on the rock-hard red earth, and were greeted by Jo and Neil asking us what we had been doing. 'Just seeing if we could dip the plane's wing into the lodge's swimming pool,' replied Gordon, whilst I attempted to stand upright on legs that were still trembling.

Before long, a Land Rover arrived to take us up to the lodge along a rough and very steep track. Magnificent views greeted us – rolling countryside with the occasional game pan as far as the eye could see, with ranges of impressive granite hills in the far distance. Our bedrooms were chalets built of local stone with thatched roofs, and a natural cleft in the boulders provided an entrance to the lounge and bar area. Further up there was a gazebo and a 'cuddle puddle', where we could apparently sit and soak in warm water and watch the sunrise or the sunset with a drink, according to our host Pieter.

Once settled, the four of us decided to go off for a walk before lunch, having been advised by Pieter that we would only come across plain's game – leopard were there but were secretive and would avoid us. As long as we kept to the paths, we would be safe, as the conservancy area of over 160,000 hectares that held the black rhino, buffalo, elephant and hippo was protected by electric fences. We set off, hoping that any leopard, which might be lurking would give us a wide berth! It was a real treat to feel the African soil under our feet again, and in a couple of hours, we spotted warthog, zebra, giraffe, not to mention baboons and vervet monkeys. To walk out in the bush by ourselves without a guide made us realise that we had come a long way since our first walk with Shane.

That afternoon Pieter took us to a large dam, as he wanted to introduce us to a friend of his – Harry the hippo! Harry was orphaned soon after birth and was hand-reared, but was released back into the wild when he started to turn into a rather stroppy adolescent! Pieter and Harry had formed a somewhat precarious working relationship – Pieter would feed him once a day with grain husks, and Harry would allow Pieter to bring guests to watch him come out of the safety of the water and amble up to Pieter. So far, Harry always behaved himself and there had been no disasters resulting from with close encounters with a beast renowned to be responsible for more human deaths in Africa than any other animal.

We assembled by an old dilapidated shack on the banks of the dam, and watched whilst Pieter called for Harry, rattling the grain husks in a metal bucket. In the middle of the dam, a head appeared and Harry proceeded to swim towards us, snorting loudly as he clambered out of the water. Pieter put some husks on the ground and then retreated towards us. Harry soon hoovered up his snack and Pieter threw more food to him. I managed to get some wonderful close-up photos and Gordon was busy with his filming when Harry decided to venture closer. Pieter decided that we had better retire behind a low wall in front of the shack, and my final photo was of Gordon making a rapid retreat, tripod slung over his shoulder, with Harry close on his heels.

We left Harry and went off in the Land Rover to another dam, where we climbed into a small boat and motored along the length of the dam, enjoying the birdlife and waterfowl. Gin and tonics appeared from a cool box and we sat in silence with the engine turned off, watching the sun set in the west and a full moon appearing in the east – the warm reds and oranges of the sunset contrasting with the dark blue sky framing the ice cold moon.

The following morning we were up early as Pieter wanted to take us on a walk. He had told us about the 'Grain Bin Kopje', which we had seen from the lodge, and thought we might like to climb up to the top of it. Some friends of Pieter also wanted to come on the climb, and we were assured that it would not be too difficult. I looked at the so-called hill, which seemed to be taking on the appearance of a miniature alp the more I looked at it, and I wondered if I would ever make it. Nothing daunted, we set off, our rucksacks filled with water.

The initial ascent was not too difficult, but we were soon scrambling over rocks and through thorn and prickly pear bushes. The ground was sandy and full of loose stones and boulders, which meant that every step was fraught with difficulty and heralded a potential fall. Pausing for drinks half way up, Pieter reassured Jo and me that it really would be worth the effort. No doubt, he had seen the expressions on our faces and the potential beginning of a mutiny. Higher and higher we clambered until we reached a rocky overhang. 'What now?' Jo and I asked in unison.

'Up and over,' replied Pieter.

'You've got to be joking – I'm not a mountaineer!' I stated firmly, my heart in my mouth at the very thought of it, and butterflies starting to flit about in my stomach. Even Gordon and Neil were looking a bit dubious by now. Pieter explained that he would go first to show how it was done, and with no more ado, shot up with the agility of a mountain goat. Gordon managed to follow, his long arms and legs being a distinct advantage, and then it was my turn. I flung my rucksack up to my athletic husband – more in temper than anything else. A theme was starting to emerge on this holiday of exploration – moments of wonder and awe were regularly interspersed with those of terror, physical hardship and danger.

'You realise our travel insurance probably won't cover any mountaineering activities, don't you? I hissed under my breath.

Gordon grunted. 'Just get on with it and stop moaning. Give me your hand and I'll haul you up. You'll be able to do it, you know.'

Somehow, with the help of Gordon hauling and a few shoves from heaven knows who behind me, yet again, I landed like a beached whale past the overhang and onto a narrow ledge. Picking myself up with not a shred of dignity left, I looked up and there in front of me were the grain bins – tall, mud-coated storage utensils, some as tall as a small adult, some complete, others showing the reed structure which provided the basic shape before the mud was plastered on. Shards of pottery lay stacked at the bins' bases. What a sight!

Jo arrived in an equally undignified way on her knees and looking shell-shocked. 'For heaven's sake don't tell my daughters what we've been doing – they would never let us go abroad again!' she gasped. 'I hope it's worth it at the summit.' Like me, she then looked up and saw the grain bins, and the discomfort of the last hour's climb was forgotten. Pieter sat us all down overlooking the magnificent view of the rolling veld, and explained to us that this kopje was a natural fortress, most recently used by the Shona people in the mid 1800s whilst protecting themselves from the Ndebele impis. The Shona people consolidated their positions by choosing well protected natural fortresses. This hill was very obviously a difficult climb, and attack from above was impossible. I wondered what life would have been like living where we were sitting. The thought of having to climb down to get any water in the dry season was sobering. The grain was safely stored away in these large bins so that if there were a prolonged siege, there would be enough food. We carefully examined the shards of pottery and Pieter told us that each time he comes up here, he makes more discoveries.

He then guided us to the very top of the kopje – a spacious plateau of nearly flat granite. The view was unbelievably spectacular. This one hill stood by itself, surrounded in the far distance by many other granite kopjes. Below us, the Zimbabwean countryside spread itself and in the distance, several hundred feet below we could see the lodge. Small eroded dips in the rock were natural rock pools for rainwater and condensation. Other larger bowls, smooth and perfectly round, were where women would have ground the grain – the result of many years of hard work. More pottery fragments were carefully stacked together, and each of us went off in different directions to see if we could find any to add to the collection.

Before long I found several shards that looked like the remains of a large cup or basin. I sat down, holding in my hands these old fragments of a civilisation long gone and wondered what tales these pieces of pottery could tell – who had used them, what was their fate? I gently replaced them, trying to envisage the last person who might have placed them there. I looked up to see a Black Eagle soaring above me in the brilliant blue winter sky and imagined the sound of the attack signal of the Ndebele warriors and the beating of assegai on shield. The atmosphere of this site was truly haunting.

All too soon, we had to leave and begin our descent. If ascending

Grain Bin Hill had been difficult, the return journey was nigh on impossible. At least gravity helped, but I soon found I was clutching at twigs and grass in an attempt to steady myself. Eventually, I decided that sliding down on my backside was the best option, hoping that any snakes or scorpions would keep well clear. On reaching level ground, I found that my knees were trembling with the effort of the last three hours. I looked back to where Jo and Neil were, some way behind me. Suddenly, Jo disappeared in the long grass. Thinking that she was answering a call of nature, I went on to the Land Rover with Gordon. A good ten minutes later Jo and Neil arrived – Jo hobbling along, having fallen down a hole. Thankfully, she was only bruised, but she informed us all with her customary good humour that this was the last time she would go for a walk this holiday!

After several drinks and a well-earned lunch, a siesta was called for. I had just got out of a shower and was looking forward to an afternoon of relaxation on my bed, when there was a knock on the door. It was Pieter who had come to inform us that a ranger had found a black rhino in the reserve, and he was leaving in ten minutes to take us to see it. I groaned, but decided that this might be the only opportunity to see one of these very rare and endangered animals, so dressed, shoved my sunhat over my wet hair, and clambered into the Land Rover with Gordon. Jo and Neil arrived a few minutes later, having also decided that this was something not to be missed.

Pieter drove us into the reserve and began talking to the ranger on his crackling two-way radio. He parked the vehicle and told us that we were to walk behind him in single file, in silence. So much for Jo's resolution of no more walks! He reminded us that black rhino are much more aggressive, unpredictable and bad-tempered than the white variety, but he would try to get us as close as possible. If we were charged, the only option was to climb up the nearest tree or failing that, hide behind a termite mound. Their eyesight was notoriously bad, but their sense of smell and hearing was extremely good. Another option was to stand still and hope that the rhino wouldn't see, smell or hear us! Pieter was carrying a gun, but warned us that he would never shoot a black rhino – they were much too valuable. It was up to us to obey his orders at all times.

Suitably disciplined, we set off in single file, adrenalin surging and all our senses once again on full alert. After ten minutes, Pieter whistled gently and signalled us to halt. Out of the thick bushes came the tracker. He too was carrying a rifle together with a two-way radio and a pair of handcuffs in case he came across poachers. Apparently, a black rhino was about five minutes away. Off we tracked in thick bush. I looked around for any convenient trees to climb up, or termite mounds to hide behind, but all around were thickets of young trees. We stopped for the tracker to show us where the rhino had recently browsed – the branches of a bush neatly trimmed as though a hedge cutter had been at work. A few yards further on we came across a fresh puddle of urine, and around it, we examined the three-toed rhino print. We were close.

Suddenly, a signal came for us to crouch down. All I could see was thick bush and faded grass up to my knees. Ahead of us, there was a rustle and peering through the bush, I saw four large legs of a black rhino. We stayed rooted to the spot while the tracker and Pieter assessed the situation. The four legs moved away from us and we were motioned to stand up. There in a thicket no more than ten yards away was our black rhino. We were much too close to even think about taking photographs – the noise of a camera shutter would have been enough to disturb this magnificent creature. I gazed at its leathery hide and caught a glimpse of its twitching ears, working like revolving antennae. It turned towards us, its hooked-lipped mouth full of some twigs of a bush, and then it tossed its head and headed off away from us. We walked quietly back to the Land Rover, realising how privileged we were to have seen such a magnificent, endangered animal so close.

All too soon, it was time to fly back to Harare where we would spend our final night at Thetford House before returning to England. Jacqui and her father greeted us like old friends and we sat down to a delicious celebration supper. A charming French family were also staying with them – they were at the beginning of their safari, which hadn't started too well for them as none of their luggage had arrived. They were a bit dubious when we assured them that they wouldn't need much in the way of clothing, and even more apprehensive when we regaled them of our experiences. However much we tried to reassure them that they would have an experience of a lifetime, the more they looked as though they might well take the next plane back to Paris! Jacqui and her father were once again the perfect hosts and we were determined to stay in touch and hopefully stay with them again in the not too distant future. Little did we know that their beautiful home overlooking the Mazoe valley would become the blueprint for the much scaled down home we would build in South Africa – six years and many adventures later.

For a magical two days, we stayed at Fugitives' Drift, the home of David and Nicki Rattrey. David was our guide and took us around the battle sites of Isandlwana and Rorke's Drift. His skill as a raconteur, coupled with his empathy for the Zulu nation was an inspiration to everyone who was fortunate enough to go on one of his lecture tours. I feel tremendously privileged to have had this experience. David was a very special person.

Chapter 7

Buffalo, Battle Tours and Bush

The following autumn Gordon and I decided to return to South Africa and began planning our next trip soon after our return to Derbyshire. Sadly, Jo and Neil were unable to join us as Neil had been diagnosed with prostate cancer six months after our last safari together, and was fighting this cruel disease with his usual grace and fortitude, supported lovingly by Jo. We would miss them greatly, having shared so many happy times together.

We decided on a totally different type of holiday, driving ourselves around KwaZulu Natal and visiting the battle fields. I was not certain they would hold much interest for me, and felt I would miss the wildlife safaris, so we tacked on a brief visit to the Hluhluwe Game Reserve together with a couple of nights in a private game reserve bordering the Kruger National Park. We then planned to have a few nights relaxing at a lodge in the Lowveld, to recover from the whole trip. To break our journey up north, we arranged to spend two days in Swaziland, which we felt would be interesting.

Everything was booked and paid for when our elder son Shaun and his partner Caraline announced that they were going to get married in October – ten days after our arrival back home from our trip! Our delight was tempered with concern that we would not be there to help with any last minute plans, but they reassured us that they would organise everything and all we would have to do would be to organise our side of the family's seating plan. The wedding venue and reception were booked, invitations sent out, and as parents of the groom, it only remained for us to relax and go off to South Africa!

When discussing their honeymoon, Caraline mentioned that she would like to go to South Africa and spend some time with her sister and family who lived there, as they would not be coming over to the UK for the wedding. As a wedding present, we offered to pay for a few nights at the beautiful lodge in the Lowveld where we were to stay. We spent a very happy couple of nights there on our first visit to South Africa, and remarked at the time what a wonderful place it would be for a honeymoon. Little did we know what the future had in store for our family, as many years later, we would host our younger son Michael's wedding in our own home in South Africa! Determined that Caraline and Shaun should experience the joys of spending some time in the bush, we added three nights at the camp we were going to visit in the Kruger Park. They could then go on to spend the rest of their honeymoon with Caraline's sister and family.

Several telephone calls later to our wonderful safari planner, and Shaun and Caraline's honeymoon was booked. I thanked my lucky stars that we had such a good firm who specialised in travel to Africa. Nothing was too much trouble for them and over the years, we came to regard them as good friends. The firm floated ideas past us, planned itineraries, altered and re-adjusted things to suit us, and we were never disappointed with the safaris they organised for us over seven years and many thousands of kilometres of travel.

We left England in late September, and arrived at Johannesburg Airport after an overnight flight. Somehow, whilst rushing to make the connecting flight to Durban we managed to miss the representative who was to meet us with our accommodation and car hire vouchers. As we arrived at the departure gate, the public address system asked us to contact the information desk. Our flight was about to leave, and as we had no time to get back to the information desk without missing our flight and thus complicating matters even further, we decided the only thing to do was to go ahead and board the aircraft. We were sitting in our seats hot and flustered, but hopeful that our travel agents would fax the relevant information to us at our hotel in Durban, when a stewardess came up to us with a large envelope. It contained all the information and reservation dockets we needed for the next two weeks. Sometimes things really do work in Africa!

The high temperatures and humidity, which greeted us at Durban, took a bit of getting used to after the chilly autumnal weather in Derbyshire, but off we went undeterred to the lodge where we were to spend the next couple of nights. It was an hour's drive outside Durban and we spent the rest of the day relaxing in the tropical gardens by a sparkling pool, recovering from the flight. The following day, a lovely woman, Fay, who organised tours around local gardens, picked us up as arranged. We spent the whole day wandering around the most beautiful gardens, learning the names and medicinal uses of many indigenous plants and trees, and only broke off to have a delicious lunch at Fay's home. It was a gentle way of acclimatising ourselves to spring in the southern hemisphere.

The next day we set off for Hluhluwe Game Reserve, the oldest and third largest game reserve in South Africa. We took the coastal toll road, paid our dues and set off. After just a few kilometres, we discovered to our horror that Gordon's signet ring was missing from his hand. We hurriedly debated what to do and decided that we had to return to the lodge in case it had turned up there. As he never removes the ring, it was a mystery as to how it had disappeared. The ring held great sentimental value for Gordon; it was handed down to him on his father's death, so we had to do everything we could to try to find it. We drove off the next exit and then back onto the road we had come down, much to the amusement of the man on the toll gate where we had to pay another toll.

On arrival at the lodge, the manager greeted us. He looked very relieved to see us. He disappeared into his office, and came out moments later proudly holding Gordon's ring. Apparently, a maid had found the ring in a towel in our bathroom. Thanks to her honesty, Gordon still has his highly valued ring to hand down to the next generation in our family. The manager accepted our profuse thanks graciously and we left an extra tip for the maid. I only hope she got to hear how much it meant to Gordon.

Off we set again, causing even more amusement to the man in the toll booth. We were starting to become friends, and the South African road system was becoming quite a bit more profitable! A few hours later, we arrived at the entry to Hluhluwe National Park and, for the first time, experienced driving in the bush by ourselves. On our previous safaris, we were used to plains interspersed with umbrella acacia and termite mounds but not here. Vast rolling hills spread as far as the eye could see, with wide rivers flowing in the deep valleys. Rounding a corner we came across three rhino with the most magnificent, long horns – we had read that Hluhluwe was famous for its rhino and here were some in all their glory. A few minutes later, we came across yet more rhino, a large bull elephant followed by several giraffe and a herd of buffalo. We were back in 'Africa Proper'!

We could not believe the size of the chalet allocated to us and learnt that Nelson Mandela had slept in it during a visit to the reserve. We had no idea whether this was merely a spiel given to all tourists or whether it was true, although I could well believe it when I explored the multi-bedroomed chalet, situated at the very end of the campsite, and overlooking the most spectacular view of the reserve. What had we done to deserve such fantastic accommodation? Hilltop Camp and the views from our balcony confirmed its name. Hills, rivers, plains and pans spread before us, and looking carefully through our binoculars, the black dots we saw were unmistakably elephant and rhino. Some birds flew below us and raptors soared above, making use of the thermals to aid their seemingly effortless flight.

We had been car-bound for several hours that day and decided to book ourselves on a game walk, which was setting off in the afternoon. We got into our walking gear and joined a group of six, escorted by an armed ranger and tracker. Maybe it was the change in altitude from sea level up to the hills of KwaZulu Natal, but I found the going quite tough and was glad of the frequent stops to examine spoor. We walked downhill for several kilometres and came across three rhino, all peacefully grazing in the thin shade of some trees. I decided to stand by a tree that I could climb up if needed, but Gordon went closer with the ranger to get some spectacular video footage. Our guide insisted that these prehistoric animals were, on the whole, very docile, unlike the more aggressive and unpredictable black rhino, but I was not taking any chances! I just enjoyed being close enough to hear their rhythmic chomping of grass and having Africa 'under my feet' once more.

Reluctantly, we left the rhino for the long walk back to the vehicle. Unfortunately, it was all uphill. I struggled immensely with the gradient, heat and altitude, and saw that Gordon and the rest of the group were not doing much better, which was reassuring. However, after an hour of hiking uphill in temperatures that must have been up in the high 20s, I could endure no more, and the ranger decided he would stay with me and we would go more slowly. The rest of the group would continue to walk up the hill and round a corner of the gravel road with the tracker, to where, apparently, our vehicle was parked. This sounded like a good idea to me. I didn't like feeling this feeble and somewhat of a wimp, but I knew my own limits.

Slowly, I climbed up the last hill, the others having disappeared, and eventually arrived at the dirt track road, which was carved into the hillside. With the ranger by my side, and sweat pouring down my face, I paused for a moment and looked up. What I saw filled me with dread – a lone buffalo bull was just emerging from thick bush. I knew from previous safaris that no one trifles with a lone buffalo bull, and potentially, we were in a lot of trouble. I froze with shock. I am not certain who was more surprised – the buffalo, the ranger or me. 'Get behind me and stand still, Mam!' he ordered as his rifle came up to shoulder height. Suddenly, I heard the sound of an engine revving in the distance, and round the corner raced our vehicle, with Gordon hanging on, peering over the side looking very concerned. The tracker stopped the vehicle in between the buffalo, me and the ranger, and I clambered up onto a seat, rapidly followed by the ranger. Looking back, I saw a herd of buffalo ambling along the track towards us. 'And there you were, worried about me getting too close to some docile rhino, when you were face to face with an enormous buffalo bull!' exclaimed Gordon. 'You have no idea how quickly we drove to collect you when we realised that you would soon be in the middle of a herd of buffalo!' I grabbed a drink of water, gulping it down quickly, whilst wishing it was something stronger, and slowly recovered on the journey back to camp.

That evening we booked ourselves on an evening game drive, and were somewhat disappointed to find ourselves packed in the middle of a full vehicle of about twenty people. We were not used to this sort of experience, being huddled together with other tourists who seemed to expect to be entertained by the Big Five round every corner. However, we made the most of it, despite a fine drizzle setting in to make it cold and miserable. The game we saw looked equally unhappy, trying to shelter in the bush from the early spring rains.

Returning to camp wet and bedraggled, we stood on the restaurant balcony having a very welcome gin and tonic to recover, whilst watching a thunderstorm brewing around us. This was our first experience of a full-blown African storm. Suddenly, the wind rose to gale force, thunder claps resounded all around us, followed by a flash of lightning, which nearly took us off our feet. Fortunately, a tree a hundred yards away bore the brunt of the strike. We could feel the hairs on the back of our necks stand on end with the static, and rushed to the safety of our table inside the restaurant. Never again during all our time in Africa would we underestimate the violence of its spectacular storms. It was yet one more lesson learnt, thankfully with no serious consequences.

We wondered if we had made a mistake booking ourselves onto an early morning game drive the following morning, as we didn't want to be packed into a vehicle with twenty other tourists. Our previous safari experiences must have made us very spoilt; nevertheless, we set our alarm to wake us at 5.00. As we drew back the curtains the following morning, we saw that a fine mist lay in the valley below. We grabbed a cup of coffee and made our way to where the vehicle was waiting. Our ranger and guide were already there and by six o'clock, no one else had arrived, so we set off in solitary state, having the whole of the vehicle to ourselves!

Our reward for getting up early was the dawning of a beautiful fresh morning. All the dust had been washed away by the previous night's storm and the bush was sparkling and pristine once the sun had burnt off the early morning mist. Three hours of glorious game viewing followed, and we were sorry for the people who had booked to go on the drive and had decided to have a lie-in. Our ranger told us that he had expected a full vehicle, as twenty people had paid for the drive.

Elephant, buffalo, giraffe, antelope, and more rhino than we could count appeared before us in rapid succession, the final highlight being a pair of magnificent male lions. We followed these majestic creatures for a mile or so, sometimes driving alongside them whilst they ambled through the bush, occasionally marking their territory with pungent sprays of urine. Not once did they cast their eyes in our direction, so intent were they on preserving their kingdom from the potential threats of other intruding male lions. Their thick black manes stood out in the bush and it would be a brave lion indeed to challenge this coalition of lions in the prime of their lives.

Truly satisfied with our drive, we ate a hurried breakfast and quickly packed before setting off on our drive to Fugitives' Drift for the beginning of what proved to be the most incredible and moving three days. The journey took us into the depths of KwaZulu Natal, going through remote hillside villages with thatched rondavels scattered everywhere. These round homes, their walls covered with dried cow dung, were the only signs of habitation, and so atmospheric was the scenery that we were soon imagining historic battles and warriors brought to life by the epic film, *Zulu*.

Eventually, we arrived at the gate of the land that marked the boundary of Fugitives' Drift. Occasional giraffe and zebra eyed us with curiosity as we drove for what seemed several kilometres on a rough gravel road before we reached the lodge. Several dogs greeted us noisily, followed by our hosts David and Nicky Rattray. We were not expected until teatime, but were soon sitting down in the dining room with the rest of the Rattray family for a substantial lunch. Over the meal, we learnt that they expected the Prince of Wales and Prince Harry in a few days' time. The Rattray sons and David's mother Gillian were all staying at the lodge as David was going to give his battle tour talks with his family there in preparation for the Royal visit. What an incredible stroke of luck that we were to witness the dress rehearsal! Apparently, David had some problems with his voice and needed to conserve it carefully for the big day.

After lunch we were shown to our chalet, a beautiful room with a balcony overlooking the distant Isandlwana mountain, its infamous name synonymous with the greatest battle lost by the British army in the Anglo-Zulu War. It is a bitter irony that the mountain's brooding outline appeared to resemble a sphinx – the sphinx being the regimental crest of the 24th Foot Regiment, which fought so bravely there. Already we were immersed in the fascinating military history of the Zulu War and I was fascinated before I had even heard a single lecture.

Nicky tactfully ensured that we were not smokers, as our room was the one that the Prince of Wales would sleep in, and it was definitely not the done thing to have a smoke-tainted room, which had been newly decorated for its Royal visitor. We assured her that we would be ultra-careful and leave the room in the same pristine condition in which we found it! Never had I been more careful of doing anything to spoil the immaculate room and bathroom, nagging Gordon if he so much as left a fingerprint on a window! Whilst sitting on the loo, I chuckled to myself that in a few days' time a Royal bottom would be sitting there, hopefully enjoying the same spectacular view towards the mountain of Isandlwana.

Later that afternoon we were taken on a walk through the reserve to the Tugela River where we learnt how the fugitives fled from the battle at Isandlwana, and how Lieutenants Melville and Coghill carried the Queen's Colours belonging to the First Battalion of the 24th Regiment, rescuing it from the pursuing Zulu warriors. Mortally wounded, Melville and Coghill hauled themselves out of the swiftly flowing water, the strength of the current sweeping away the Colours from their grasp. The most important thing was that the enemy did not seize the Colours. They sat down, exhausted, on the bank of the river, their horses having been killed, and awaited their fate at the hands of the Zulus who were following them. Research shows that these two heroes would have died at about 3.30 p.m. on the afternoon of 22nd January 1897. At 2.29 p.m. a total eclipse of the sun plunged the battle scene into an eerie darkness. They were found several days later after the battle but their task had been completed and the precious Colours saved. The Colours had floated down-stream to come to rest on a rock named Coffin Rock. We gazed down at the large rock, its shape resembling a coffin. Melville and Coghill were buried near to the place where they died, and we walked to stand in front of their simple grave, honouring these two brave soldiers. Both were awarded the Victoria Cross posthumously. In thoughtful mode, we strolled back to the lodge, looking forward to the following day when we would visit the battle-field of Isandlwana.

David drove us to the site of the battle, and during the journey played us a recorded tape, which filled in so many gaps in our knowledge and prepared us for his lecture at the battle site. We passed many Zulus walking along the rough gravel track. David waved to each of them as we passed, and smiles and waves greeted us in return. Once there, we walked up the brooding, rocky hillside of Isandlwana, looking at cairns of small, white painted rocks scattered everywhere in the parched, dusty ground, marking the graves of the fallen. Under a bright blue African sky we sat down on rugs, thoughtfully supplied by David, and listened, entranced, to this incredible raconteur bringing to life the history of this famous battle.

We imagined the hoards of Zulu warriors sweeping across the hills towards the totally unprepared British army, encamped around the base of the mountain. We thought about the 1,200 British troops being attacked by 12,000 poorly armed Zulu, and heard the sound of Zulu war chants, together with the banging of their weapons against their shields. Perhaps what impressed me the most was how totally fair and unbiased David was in recounting the battle. He had learnt firsthand from grandfathers and great-grandfathers of the Zulu soldiers the Zulu side of the battle, and rightly honoured these brave warriors. I winced at the graphic descriptions of how once a Zulu had killed his enemy, he disembowelled him. This act, far from being savage, was a mark of respect for a brave soldier, as in Zulu custom this action honoured a brave adversary and allowed his spirit to rise free.

At the same time, David left no stone unturned in describing the many faults of some of the British officers. On and on, we lived through a day of the incredible bravery, both of the British and Zulu armies as well as the stupidity and arrogance of some of the officers in command of the British Army. We learnt we were sitting at the place where several brave British soldiers made a last stand before the survivors retreated to Fugitives' Drift. Men died fighting on the spot where we sat peacefully, listening to stories of their heroism.

This battle stunned the world – it was unthinkable how a so-called 'native' army could defeat the troops of a Western power. Of the 1,200 British soldiers, about 850 died. Two thousand Zulu warriors were killed from a total force of about 12,000. David told us that the battle of Isandlwana is still taught at army colleges, as an example of how not to fight a battle. The battle of Rorke's Drift, which was fought during the following 24 hours, and which we were to hear about the following day, is also taught to illustrate how to fight and win a battle.

At the end of his lecture, which lasted the whole morning, David suggested that we walked back down the slopes of Isandlwana by ourselves, taking as much time as we needed to look around the battle site. We walked around the many small white heaps of stones, marking the graves where soldiers had fallen. Silently, we left the mountain, full of our own thoughts, the ghosts of so many brave men, both Zulu and British never far away.

The following morning we relaxed at the lodge, looking at all the military memorabilia David had collected over the years whilst he and Nicky had been there. He had once been a manager of a famous game reserve adjoining the Kruger National Park, and it had been a leap of faith for him to buy Fugitives' Drift and set up their lodge there, running battlefield tours. Apparently, for some time it was very much a hand-to-mouth existence with few bookings, but by word of mouth the bookings started to come in until they were having to turn people away.

Now their visitors include Heads of State as well as curious tourists like us, and most importantly, relatives of soldiers who had fought there. Both David and Nicky could not really believe that in a few days the two princes were to stay with them.

As if on cue, one of their dogs came limping into the room with blood pouring from its paw, dripping all over the new carpet made immaculate for the royal visitors! The dog was shooed out rapidly and Nicky explained that it had cut its paw a couple of days ago and the cut, although not deep, kept opening up. She decided that if it didn't heal soon, she would have to take it to the vet – a round trip of over 50 kilometres on gravel roads. The paw was dressed and bandaged up, and Nicky and I got down on our hands and knees with bowls of water and cloths to try to rid the carpet of bloodstains. I attempted to reassure her that the Royal Family were well known for their love of dogs, and that I was sure the princes would understand, but for the rest of our stay we were all on dog duty, trying to ensure that one Labrador would not open up its paw and create domestic chaos again.

Soon after lunch we set off for Rorke's Drift, accompanied by the extended Rattray family. Once again, during the journey, David played one of his tapes to set the scene for the next few hours of spellbinding narrative. My initial impression of Rorke's Drift was one of surprise. I was expecting something very similar to that portrayed by the film *Zulu*.

However, there were none of the wide open spaces of the African plains; instead there was a small main building and several other additional outhouses in what seemed to be a very intimate setting, silhouetted by a small mountain and looking down to open countryside. The borders of the Mission, and the battle lines where the fortifications of mealie sacks were placed, were marked by painted white stones. The buildings had been accurately restored to their original condition, now housing a museum. Folding canvas chairs were unloaded from a trailer, and we arranged ourselves in a semi-circle, looking towards the Mission buildings, with David facing us.

Once again, David transported us into another world by the pure magic of his skill. He had hardly started when we noticed that three backpackers were edging closer to us, trying to listen to the unfolding narrative. David paused and beckoned them over. He learnt that they were Australian, and generously invited them to join us. Together we heard how the sole officer in charge of the Mission was a Lieutenant Gonville Bromhead. He learnt from a scout that the battle of Isandlwana had been lost and that another section of Zulu warriors, who had not fought at Isandlwana, was approaching the Mission. An order was given to dismantle the tents and fortify and link the buildings with mealie bags – the same command that unfortunately, was never made by officers at Isandlwana.

The battle for the Mission raged from late afternoon on the 22nd January to well into the night. We listened entranced to all the relentless stories of bravery, and occasionally laughed at amusing anecdotes, relieving the incredible tension created by this master storyteller. Finally, we learnt how at 7 a.m. a further body of Zulus appeared on the hill, but did not attack – they could see the Lord Chelmsford column approaching Rorke's Drift from the defeat at Isandlwana. David movingly described how the two retreating forces passed each other in silence, with only a few yards separating the two armies.

I wondered what must have been going through the minds of these weary warriors as they passed so close to each other. The Zulus believed their comrades had been defeated at Isandlwana; the British thought their army had been defeated at Rorke's Drift. Here, 139 British troops fought approximately 4,500 Zulus. Seventeen British soldiers were killed and ten wounded. There were around 500 Zulu casualties. Eleven men received the Victoria Cross, the most awarded in any one battle.

David was not only a superb raconteur; this gifted, slightly built man with his tweed cap, his rough wood stick, his arms waving to emphasise an important point was also a talented actor. During his narrative, he painted the scene with many anecdotes he had gathered firsthand from relatives of the survivors. He recounted movingly how one Welshman, a relation of a soldier who had fought there, was visiting Rorke's Drift when excavations were taking place. A regimental badge had just been found and David placed it gently in the old man's hand, telling him that the last time this badge had seen daylight had been during the battle.

Gradually, with the light fading, David came to the end of his lecture. As the sun set in front of the Mission he uttered the evocative words 'At the going down of the sun and in the morning, we will remember them.' He paused in silence and then walked slowly away from the group. Tears were streaming down my face and looking at Gordon, I saw tears on his face too. The three hardy Australian backpackers were also wiping away their tears. David's mother, Gillian, and Nicky had their arms around David. How privileged we were to spend the afternoon with them all. Gordon and I hugged each other and went off for a brief walk around the Mission before joining the family for the journey back to their home.

Over supper that night David told us how emotionally draining it was to bring these battles back to life for visitors from around the world. He had recorded all his lectures on tapes as he feared that one day his voice would fail him. These tapes are some of our most treasured possessions and every time we play them, we relive our three days in deepest Zululand.

We said our goodbyes to the family the following day, promising to meet up with David and Nicky the following year in London when he delivered his lectures at the Royal Geographical Society. This was a promise we kept, and continued to keep, for several years.

There was a tragic ending to our brief friendship with David. A few years ago, we were listening to the news in our newly-built home in South Africa when it was announced that David had been murdered in his home at Fugitives' Drift. We simply could not believe it, or understand why this wonderful 'White Zulu' who did so much to bring the Zulu history to life, and who loved and respected that nation, could have been murdered, apparently, for a small amount of money. The theme of his lectures was reconciliation, and how reconciliation can develop from conflict.

David, who did so much to inform, educate and reconcile, may you rest in peace.

During our journey from Fugitives' Drift to Swaziland, we talked continuously about the previous three days. Anything that followed was bound to be somewhat of an anticlimax. At the chaotic border post between South Africa and Swaziland, we queued for a long time in the scorching heat, and finally arrived at our lodge in time for an evening meal.

Unfortunately, we had a very disturbed night as Gordon went down with a tummy bug, and for the next couple of days it was impossible for him to move further than a few yards from our loo. What was to have been an opportunity to see a little of this tiny landlocked country, turned out to be pretty miserable for Gordon, and I was left to amuse myself by walking around the extensive grounds, bird watching and writing up my diary. Perhaps a couple of days of enforced rest was what we needed especially as our next part of the trip was a couple of nights at Mala Mala, a private game reserve situated on the borders of the Kruger National Park in South Africa. We would have to revisit Swaziland sometime in the future, as what little we saw was so very beautiful.

I drove to the border post to return into South Africa, and we entered the Kruger Park at the Malelane Gate. It was lovely being back in the bush again, and I was beginning to get the hang of driving and keeping a lookout for animals and birds. Gordon was still feeling under par, so I decided to call in at the medical centre at Skukuza, the Park's largest camp. After a thorough examination, Gordon was issued with some antibiotics which would hit for six any bugs left in his system, and we continued to the miniscule airport where we were to leave our hire car and meet up with a ranger from Mala Mala.

A tall young man who was the manager of our camp arrived at the airport, and greeted us with a knuckle-cracking handshake. Maybe it was to impress us with his manly strength, but for the rest of the holiday I nursed a very bruised hand – I was not impressed! We were staying at Harry's Camp, fondly known as Harry's Huts –

the least expensive, and less fanciful than the other Mala Mala camps. This suited us just fine as we did not need the 'his and hers' bathrooms and all the other luxurious goodies that some international visitors expect. We wanted a couple of days of good game viewing with a knowledgeable ranger and tracker and this is exactly what we got.

Andrew and his tracker Lux turned up trumps and the next 48 hours merged into a glorious kaleidoscope of the Big Five – lion, leopard, elephant, buffalo and rhino, together with all the plains' game and bird life we could wish for. This was being ultra lazy, just sitting back and waiting for the next fascinating scene to present itself to our cameras.

I looked back with nostalgia to our walking safari in Zimbabwe with Shane, and ruminated on what seemed to be missing. Maybe it was the sense of adventure and the satisfaction of walking for a long time tracking an animal. To be driven around by Andrew and see a National Geographic programme come to life was magical, but I yearned for something which was intangible at that time. All too soon our visit was over, and we arranged for a bottle of bubbly to be left, together with a card for Shaun and Caraline, who were to follow in our footsteps in less than a month. We asked if it was possible for them to have Andrew and Lux, as we had been very impressed by their skills, and this was arranged. We were certain that they would have a truly memorable first safari.

Off we drove through the Park and arrived at our final destination – Cybele Forest Lodge, in the depths of the beautiful Lowveld, where we had stayed before with Jo and Neil on our first ever visit to South Africa. Cybele was just as we remembered it, and as we drove down the magnificent tree-lined avenue, we were greeted by the same boxer dog, Bart, bouncing up and down at the side of our car. We could not believe our luck to learn that we had been upgraded to a superior chalet – one with its own swimming pool. Perhaps the fact that we had booked Shaun and Caraline into one of these luxurious chalets for the start of their honeymoon had helped! We spent the next three days in absolute luxury, recovering from the 5 a.m. dawn starts of our game drives, and preparing ourselves for the wedding. We left another bottle of bubbly and a card for the honeymoon couple, and drove off to the tiny airport outside Nelspruit for our shuttle back to Johannesburg and home once more.

In the tiny waiting room at the airport, I picked up a brochure for a newly opened golf estate. I thumbed through it until our flight was called, and then thought no more about it. Little was I to know that in four years' time and many safaris and adventures later, we were to buy a plot of land on that estate and build our South African home there!

At Mala Mala Game Reserve with our ranger and tracker.

One of the most perilous situations I have ever encountered. I am balancing precariously on a canoe, attempting to stay immobile, calm and upright as a large bull elephant decides whether he will come down the slope to get to the water. Thankfully, he was a gentleman and walked further along the bank before descending the steep slope to get a much needed drink in the Zambezi River.

Chapter 8

Mana Pools

Shaun and Caraline's October wedding was a beautiful, happy occasion, blessed with one of those golden autumnal days of blue skies and sunshine. Their South African honeymoon traced some of our footsteps as we had hoped. It was a great success, and they shared their safari experiences with us enthusiastically. After Christmas, Gordon and I settled down in the cold, dark evenings of an English winter and started to plan our next trip. We realised that anywhere other than somewhere in Africa was unthinkable – we were well and truly hooked on this amazing, complicated and fascinating continent.

We came to the decision that we definitely wanted to go back to Zimbabwe. Our previous safaris had offered us so many exciting options that we were spoilt for choice – the only limits were the time available to us and, of course, the perennial issue of having enough money! As usual, our travel agent came up with some wonderful ideas, and a simple trip rapidly took the shape of a marathon expedition. It was hard to say 'no' to so many suggestions, but over the next few weeks common sense prevailed; we refined our plans and eventually felt we had come up with a varied safari, which would not break the bank. We were very conscious of the fact that although we were both earning, once we were retired, we would no longer be able to afford such journeys, and we knew how fortunate we were to be able to grab the opportunity whilst we could.

It was inevitable that we would return to Thetford House to renew our friendship with Jacqui and her father, and to recover from the overnight flight there in their beautiful home overlooking the Mazoe valley. We had kept in touch with Jacqui and we were concerned to hear that she had developed breast cancer, but she was recovering well. On our arrival at her home, Jacqui greeted with big hugs, but we were shocked and saddened to hear that her father had died suddenly six weeks ago. We remembered him with great fondness – such an entertaining and generous host. We would miss his warmth and wit. Now Jacqui was facing a future without a man in the house – never an easy situation, but even more difficult in Zimbabwe we suspected. Once more, we strolled around the tropical garden and came across Mr Gulliver's grave. The deep red African soil was piled high over his final resting place, and we said our goodbyes to a lovely gentleman who had made Africa his home.

Some say that it is never a good idea to return to a place where you have been very happy, and the last time we were there was with Jo and Neil. Now Neil had also passed away, and an element of sadness tinged the couple of nights we spent with Jacqui. The beauty of the house and its setting worked its magic though, and we had some lovely meals with Jacqui before we left to start our safari, fully restored from our long journey.

Clambering aboard a miniscule aircraft, our carefully packed ten-kilogram bags were stuffed into the hold. I pondered how easy it had been for me to forget all about light aircraft flights in front of a roaring fire in the depths of an English winter. Somehow, I just wiped the thought of these bumpy, noisy, terrifying journeys from my mind when being swept along with the excitement of planning our travels. Once I set foot on the tarmac of an African airport, all my old terrors of flying came back with a vengeance. I clung on for dear life, cramped into a rickety seat, and endured the flight from Harare to a tiny, sandy airstrip bordering the Mana Pools National Park. Whilst we waited for our pick-up vehicle to take us to our camp, we started talking to a charming woman, Joan, and her daughter Sarah. Apparently, they were staying at the same camp, and we were all waiting for the same vehicle. Sarah was treating her mother to a few days in the bush to celebrate her 60th birthday and they were well used to Africa, as they had lived on the continent for many years before returning to Scotland. We could not have had more delightful safari companions for the next few days.

Our guide, Dave, and Joan and Sarah's guide, Iona, soon appeared to ferry us all to the camp. The dusty drive along an open rough track bordering the mighty Zambezi River transported us instantly to the magical world of the African bush. It was as though we had never been away. The sound of bird life, the dust up our noses and the jolting of the open Land Rover brought back poignant memories of our previous trips. We had returned home – or, at least, to what seemed our second home. Here at this home, however, there had been no rain for the preceding five months; everything was parched, the fallen dry, crisp leaves fluttering past us like large, alien butterflies.

Suddenly, we pulled to a rapid stop. Dave pointed out two lions, a male and a female, resting in the scant shade of a bush not ten yards away from us. How could we possibly have failed to see them? Their coats blended in perfectly with the sandy earth and dry vegetation. Dave turned off the engine, and slowly the lioness got up, walked around the dark-maned male lion several times, nuzzling him continuously. He rose to his full height and there in front of us the two mated. I cursed myself for having put my camera with the luggage at the back of the Landy. I had forgotten the first rule of any photographer – always have your camera available and ready. Never had I expected to come across such a scene so quickly into our short drive from the airstrip to our camp. We waited for about twenty minutes, and then the mating began all over again. I had read how lions mate virtually every twenty minutes for four days when the female is in season – no wonder they both looked a little tired! We decided to leave them in peace and set off for our camp to settle in and unpack.

Our camp was little short of idyllic. Perched on a shallow, sandy bank that sloped down to the Zambezi, our accommodation was a simple two-bedded tent, pitched under some trees. The front of the tent faced the wide, swift flowing river, whilst the back opened out to an open air shower, washbasin and loo, fenced in by a basic bamboo screen. Each tent was placed away from its neighbours, hidden out of sight by careful placing amongst the bush and trees. Two canvas chairs and a small table stood in front of our tent, and a short, dusty path led us to the mess area. Chairs were placed around an open log fire which would be lit in the evenings, and further down towards the river was a long, wooden dining table and chairs within six feet of the water. To complete the scene, a large, rustic chandelier swung gently in the breeze from a tall tree shading the dining table, adding a somewhat bizarre touch.

Gordon unpacked his bag whilst I sat outside the tent, content just to watch the water flow past. Previous camping trips had taught me that two people unpacking in one small tent is a recipe for marital disharmony at the very least. Once finished, he strolled off to explore and I was able to bring some order to the inside of the tent. I found him half an hour later chatting to Dave and devouring some of the most delicious looking scones, complete with strawberry jam and cream. Gordon is an expert on scones; we even returned to one specific tearoom in the Western Cape after an absence of several years to enjoy their scones, which Gordon had pronounced the best ever. Unfortunately, the restaurant had become a garage, so the round trip of over 50 miles was futile, much to his disappointment. There was not a trace of disappointment showing on his face when I looked at him here at Mana Pools – the expression 'happy as a pig in muck' comes to mind!

Again we were astonished by the skill of our cook, a large smiling man called Patterson, who every night would stand in front of us all and in halting English tell us what was on the menu. We soon discovered that applauding after his pronouncements would bring a broad grin to his face. Consequently, he would expand on the basic information in rapid broken English, before taking a deep bow and dashing off to his bush kitchen to add the finishing touches to his culinary delights.

We learnt that the camp only took two couples plus their guides. Doug, a lovely, quiet, unassuming man ran the camp like clockwork, assisted by a young man, Trust, the general helper around camp. Replete with scones, we all decided that we would just relax, enjoy being in this amazing place and get to know our new companions. Before we knew it, teatime turned to sundowner time; G and Ts were poured, the campfire lit, paraffin lanterns were placed to light the paths to our tents, and the brief African dusk slipped quickly into night.

We gathered round the dining table, now illuminated by paraffin lanterns slotted into the chandelier, and enjoyed a delicious casserole, washed down with a good red wine. Gordon's face spoke volumes of huge satisfaction at the sight of the sponge pudding and custard that followed. I pondered over the reason why grown men always swoon with delight over sponge puddings – these 'nursery' puddings must bring back contented memories of early childhood. Completely satisfied, we were happy to sit round the campfire with more drinks, and discuss our plans for the next day. As Joan and Sarah had a separate vehicle together with their own guide, Iona, we decided to go off for separate game drives in the morning. We also decided we all wanted to go canoeing down the Zambezi in the afternoon, and Doug would drive the Landy and trailer to pick up the canoes and us at a pre-arranged place.

Tired and happy, Gordon and I retired to our tent, deciding that showers could wait for the morning – I would rather see clearly what insect or animal life was in our shower, and the dim light of a paraffin lamp was not enough to ensure that I would have a relaxing one. I snuggled down on my camp bed, making sure that the whistle to summon help and a torch was within easy reach, and slowly drifted off to sleep to the sound of the Zambezi flowing past our tent and the gentle rustle of leaves. A couple of hours later Gordon nudged me and whispered, 'Did you hear that?' A few seconds later, the sound of lions roaring in the distance and the whoop of hyenas soon had me wide awake. We lay listening to the sounds of the bush until they faded away and finally, we went back to sleep.

The next thing we heard was a gentle 'knock knock' from Dave, signalling the break of dawn and time to get up. After a quick shower we were soon sipping cups of coffee and dunking our rusks in the restorative, hot drink, wishing Joan 'Many Happy Returns' for her 60th birthday and wishing them both good luck with their game viewing.

We set off with Dave, and drove for a short time before he parked the Landy. Off we hopped, ready for a walk in the bush. He asked us if we had heard the lions last night, and suggested that we might like to see if we could find them. Well, okay, that is what we were here for, but those lions in the night sounded somewhat loud and aggressive and Dave had yet to prove himself to us as a guide. I would have trusted Shane, our first guide, with my life, and we were well aware that the Zimbabwean training for guides was second to none, so we nodded silently. Perhaps it was a mistake to have told him that we had already been on a walking safari in Zimbabwe, but he obviously had faith in us, so we started our trek, having had the obligatory safety talk of the 'what to do' and 'what not to do' whilst walking amongst wild animals.

The temperature gradually rose and once the sun had risen, it became increasingly hotter, but thankfully the humidity levels were not too high. This was only the beginning of the Zimbabwean summer, and we had not expected it to be quite so hot. Dave stopped at regular intervals for us all to have refreshing drinks of water and we were thankful for the times when we paused to examine spoor. How anything could survive in this parched but beautiful landscape seemed amazing. We walked to the banks of the Zambezi and its sandy flood plain, the distant hills of Zambia faintly visible through the heat haze on the far bank of the river.

Suddenly, Dave ordered us to run. He had seen a lion in the distance facing away from us. Knowing that I had to obey our ranger at all times, however ludicrous the order seemed, I started running, rucksack bouncing on my back, and camera, binoculars, sunhat and sunglasses flying in all directions from their various straps around my neck. Gordon was also running as fast as he could with his video camera and tripod slung over his shoulder. After about two hundred yards, I decided that I had had enough. I was *not* going to run after a bloody lion in temperatures of nearly 30 degrees centigrade, and even if I was the first person on the whole of the African continent ever to disobey their guide, I was not going to run another foot! I did another forbidden thing and shouted to Dave. Rebelliously, I sat down to prove my point. Gordon came back to me, followed by Dave, who looked somewhat bemused.

As I was recovering my breath and waiting for Dave to read me the riot act, he turned round and pointed. 'Look! There are three more lions there in the reeds.' As if on cue, three sub-adult male lions sprung to their feet and rushed off in the opposite direction. I managed to get to my feet and take a photo of the backsides of these cats in the distance. I then decided that attack was the best form of defence, but being hot, tired and breathless was probably not the best time for me to read *my* riot act to Dave. I proceeded to tell him in no uncertain terms that I was not prepared to run in 30 degree heat, even if my life depended on it. That aside, he had told us never to run, as every animal in the bush was faster than we were, a fact clearly demonstrated by the speed at which the lions had taken off. Angrily, I wiped away the sweat that was dripping down my face and attempted to untangle the numerous straps around my neck that were in danger of strangling me. I added that I was never again going to run after a lion or any other animal for that matter, and what on earth did he think he was doing trying to kill both of us with heart attacks?

Gordon watched this scene unfurl, attempting, not very successfully, to hide the wry grin on his face. His sympathies seemed to be with Dave. He knew me only too well; he had witnessed many such outbursts when our sons were growing up, and I was trying to instil a bit of common sense into them. He knew that when I was worked up about something, the only thing to do was to retire gracefully from the scene and let me get on with it. I wish I had been a bit more tactful, but Dave took it all with a grin on his face, especially when I reminded him that we were both middle-aged tourists from England, and this was supposed to be a holiday, not an endurance test of our stamina. From then onwards we got along together very well and developed a mutual trust – both parties aware of our boundaries and limits. At least

Dave found out, like the rest of our family, that my outbursts were soon over and forgotten.

We walked to where the three lions had been, and found the remains of a buffalo carcass they had been eating. I began to understand that all Dave wanted was for us to end up with good photos and video footage of the lions. He had proved to us how most animals were more afraid of us than we were of them. Gradually, I recovered my sense of humour and began to chuckle to myself at the ludicrous scene of Gordon and I running after a pride of lions – no one would ever believe it back home! We got back to camp and with much hilarity, related our morning's activities to Joan, Sarah and Iona, who had enjoyed a rewarding but peaceful morning motoring around in their Landy. This confirmed to me how women are much more sensible than men, and I rather wished I could join these three women and let Gordon and Dave indulge in their macho male fantasies and go galloping around the bush after anything that took their fancy!

After lunch, we went back to our tents and I had another shower, which was blissfully cooling. The staff offered us hot water, but the water was already lukewarm, coming through some pipework straight from the Zambezi. We lay on our beds and chatted about the different styles of guiding. Overall, Shane had appeared to have been more cautious, whereas Dave seemed to like to get closer to the action. It was only after we got back home and looked at all of Gordon's video footage that we realised how much care Dave had taken when guiding us. In every single encounter with wildlife, there was Dave, in between us and the animals, alert and aware of what was happening all around us, his rifle always to hand. There we were, believing that we were face to face with the wildlife in the bush and nobody in front of us.

It takes a talented guide to give his clients such an experience. It was just as well that the lion chase incident occurred early on in our safari. Dave now knew we were there for the total experience, not just to get close-up photos. We all knew that injured or dead tourists were not a good thing to have on any guide's CV and that our safety was paramount to him. He also knew that he had a potentially rebellious woman on his hands, and Gordon laughed until he cried over the sight of me sitting down like a toddler in the middle of a 'terrible twos' tantrum, and refusing to run after a lion. Dave had met his match and Gordon could only empathise with him!

It soon became apparent that a restorative siesta was impossible in this stifling heat. I tossed and turned on top of my camp bed and finally decided that the only thing to do was to have a shower in my cotton dressing gown and sit dripping on one of the camp chairs outside our tent. For twenty minutes, I felt blissfully cool, but then the dressing gown dried out, so I had to repeat the exercise. Gordon soon decided that this was the only way to keep cool, so for a couple of hours we dripped and dried and dripped again, until the familiar 'knock knock' summoned us for a cup of iced tea or coffee and some delicious carrot cake.

Doug, our camp host, organised two canoes for us all, and soon we were floating down the mighty Zambezi, Gordon and I with Dave, and Joan and Sarah with Iona. The gentle breeze brought welcome relief after the overpowering midday heat. We were offered life jackets, but as we were all strong swimmers, we refused them. If I was to fall out of the canoe then I felt I would be more agile without a cumbersome life jacket. I then thought about the prospect of a hippo attack and how some extra padding might give me a little more protection from those massive lower canine teeth. These develop into tusks that grow up to twenty inches and are sharpened and honed against the shorter upper pair.

As if to emphasise my fears, I could hear resonant grunts and wheezes from a large pod of hippos near the banks of an island in the middle of the river. Then, twitching ears broke the surface of the water and many pairs of curious, bulbous eyes peered at us. Dave reassured us that they would not bother us if we stayed well clear of them. What we had to look out for were submerged hippos. For that reason he tended to keep to the shallow water, frequently testing its depths with his paddle. If he could touch the bed of the river, he knew there were no hippos ready to upturn our canoe. 'There might be the odd crocodile though,' he said with a broad grin, and added,

'Remember to keep your hands out of the water at all times.' I decided to concentrate on taking some photos.

Soon it was time to leave the safety of the shallow water and cross over to the middle of the river where there were strings of islands. We were not allowed to go any further across the Zambezi as the border between Zimbabwe and Zambia was an imaginary line drawn along the centre of the river. Dave paddled rapidly, asking us all to keep an eagle eye open for any telltale ripples or bubbles, which might indicate that we were canoeing over some hippos.

As we approached an island, around thirty hippos that were peacefully sleeping on the sandy banks started to rush into the water behind us. The resulting waves rocked our canoes violently, but Dave reassured us that the hippos would remain behind us and that they were only rushing into the water because they felt safe there. Water was their preferred, natural habitat; however, a few brave hippos stayed where they were and eyed us suspiciously as we glided swiftly past them. The suspicion was mutual as far as I was concerned and I breathed a sigh of relief when we had left them behind.

The current was fast and it only needed an occasional paddle from Dave to keep us on course. In the distance, we saw a large bull elephant quietly grazing on some reeds on an island. Silently we floated nearer and nearer. Dave whispered to me, 'Now you're not going to abandon ship, Maggie, are you?' I smiled back somewhat ruefully, and concentrated on taking yet more photos. Once again, I was in awe of these gentle giants, one of which was towering above us on a bank only a few yards away. He continued to munch contentedly, and we drifted past, leaving him to enjoy the only bit of green vegetation to be seen.

On we floated until it was time to cross back to the shallow water. A few tense minutes later and we were safe, able to see the bottom of the river bed again, and soon Dave was paddling up a small creek with Iona following with Joan and Sarah. We rounded a bend in the narrow waterway and there grazing peacefully on the bank was a herd of around thirty buffalo. Dave stopped paddling and gently we floated closer. The ones nearest to us lifted their heads, stopped munching, and peered around curiously. Eventually, we floated to within ten feet of them, and first one and then the whole herd snorted, tossed their heads, and headed off away from us.

We knew that buffalo have very bad sight but acute hearing, and for several minutes, they had obviously realised that something was not quite right. It was only when we were close enough to see individual hairs growing around their mouths that they rushed away. Some years later, in the Kruger National Park, we were watching a herd of buffalo from the safety of our car, when something disturbed them, and one old bull collided with a road sign in the rush to escape from an unseen danger, so poor is their eyesight.

Dave called across to Iona and they manoeuvred the two canoes alongside each other. As if by magic they produced G and Ts for us all, and we sat contentedly in rather damp canoes, toasting Joan on her birthday and thinking that life couldn't get much better than this.

Soon the sun started to sink lower on the horizon, so empty glasses were packed away and off we paddled. In the distance we saw a figure wave to us from the bank. Doug was there waiting with the Landy, together with the trailer for the canoes. Dave paddled up to him and beached the canoe. We clambered out, trying to keep our centre of gravity low to avoid tipping the canoe over. Thank heavens I had a childhood full of sailing and rowing on the river Deben in Suffolk, but these childhood experiences did not include coping when under the influence of a stiff G and T! I actually felt more at home in a canoe on the Zambezi, despite the threats of hippos and crocodiles, than I did trekking after wildlife on dry land. We all helped load the two canoes onto the trailer, and set off for camp, smiling from ear to ear after a blissfully lazy afternoon.

Over supper and yet more toasts to Joan, we all decided that the day's format was perfect, and that we wanted to do the same thing the next day. We said goodnight and strolled off to our tents with the aid of the lanterns marking the pathway and our guides escorting us to make sure we were safely zipped up before they left us. I came to the conclusion that a camping safari is one of the best ways I know to ensure a good night's sleep. An exciting day full of new experiences followed by delicious food, ample wine, delightful company, and a chat around the open fire sipping a nightcap, ensured that we slept a good seven hours each night.

In the morning, we were amazed to hear that a couple of elephants had decided to visit our camp that night, and to prove it, Dave took us round the back of our tent to the shower, and there were the fresh footprints of some elephants. How could we possibly have slept through this visit? Dave had got up and shone his torch at the elephants until they decided to leave our tent!

After our early morning coffee and rusks, it was time for more African adventures. Doug decided to come with us this time and I wondered if it was to ensure that there was an extra man to cope with me if I threw any more wobblies! Dave assured me that Doug often came as he was training to be a guide and needed as much experience as possible. We were soon walking in the open bush. The grass underfoot was completely dry. We came across many dry mud pans, the earth hard and caked – these pans giving Mana Pools its name. Apparently, after a good wet season, wherever one looked these pans were full of water. The only colour now was the fresh green spring growth of leaves on the deciduous trees and the dark green leaves on some ancient mahogany and ebony trees which keep their leaf canopy throughout the year. Even though the rains were yet to come, it was amazing to see trees sprouting new growth in expectation of the rainy season.

Walking was easy in the mild dawn, but soon the sun started to burn off the faint mist, and we were stopping to have a much-needed drink of water. Dave spotted a group of three elephants in the distance. He decided that we would walk nearer to them, and warned us that if he told us to retreat we were to go behind the nearest termite mound. Thankfully, there were many of these tall structures – rock-hard, sand coloured beacons emerging from the parched earth. Over the next hour, we gradually got closer to the three elephants who were strolling along from tree to tree, feeding on whatever meagre nourishment they could find. Dave told us that they were well aware of us and that they were relaxed and behaving like true 'gentlemen'!

At one point, we got a bit too close for Dave's liking, and were told to go back a few yards to behind a convenient termite mound. Dave stood perfectly still, rifle stock resting on the ground, the three elephants no more than twenty feet away. They meandered off a short distance and Dave beckoned us forward. We walked slowly towards him, and he motioned Gordon to come forward with his video equipment. I stayed behind with Doug who asked me quietly if I would be happy to stay where I was if he went closer to join Gordon and Dave. I nodded silently, and propped myself up against the gnarled trunk of a nearby tree, enjoying the opportunity to rest in the shade.

I watched the three men – Gordon crouched low, filming and the other two standing alongside him, intently watching the three elephants browse on some tree branches less than fifteen feet away. I took some photos, hoping my hands were not shaking too much. The elephants meandered off to another tree further away and the four of us withdrew to the shade of an enormous ebony tree and sat down to have a drink of water. We watched these magnificent creatures pull down some high branches, which hit the ground with a resounding thump, sending clouds of dust up into the air.

Dave slowly stood up when the elephants started to stroll slowly towards us. The two younger ones paused to pick up some tasty morsel of greenery, but the old bull continued on his path towards us. Dave motioned us to stay absolutely still and silent. We watched in amazement as this, one of the world's largest land mammals, came right up to where we were and brushed his leathery, grey back beneath the canopy of leaves over us, sending leaves floating down onto our heads.

I could hardly bring myself to breathe. It was impossible to take a photo, as the click of the camera shutter would have sounded like a clap of thunder. Without moving my head, I raised my eyes to see the tail of the elephant swish in front of me, only to disappear from my line of vision. Dave adjusted his stance slightly and nodded towards the other two younger bulls. I slowly raised my head and saw that they too were approaching our tree. I wondered whether my nervous system could stand the stress and excitement of any more close encounters. We waited to see if these two younger bulls would follow in their mentor's footsteps, but when they got to within twelve feet, one of them tossed his head and veered off to avoid us. His companion followed him, flicking his head towards us, as if to say, 'I know you are there but I don't want to get any closer, thank you.'

Dave turned round to face us, grinning from ear to ear. I smiled weakly, and wiped away the tears flowing gently down my face – such an incredibly emotional experience. When the three elephants were well past us, we started to talk quietly about the encounter. Dave explained that he had been observing the elephants closely for the best part of two hours and knew that they were relaxed with us around. They showed no signs of nervousness or aggression whatsoever, and were well aware of us.

It was difficult not to project human emotions into the behaviour of these animals, but Dave surmised that the old bull was confident and relaxed enough to come to within six feet of us, just to tell us that he knew we were there, that he had no fear of us, and that he would not harm us. He could easily have brought down a branch of a tree onto us, or worse.

If ever there was a show of mutual trust and respect between humans and animals then this was it. The two younger bulls were a little bit more cautious of coming so close to humans. Undoubtedly, they would remember this encounter, and it would lodge in their incredible memory bank. I hoped fervently that they would never be let down by any human beings in the future, and that they would be able to continue to trust them.

We walked on and on at a slow pace. It was already late morning and we were baking in temperatures of over forty degrees. Dave took pity on us and sent Doug off to get the Landy. Off Doug ran whilst we struggled to put one foot in front of the other. These Zimbabwean guides are certainly a tough lot! After half an hour, we heard the welcome sound of a vehicle engine and Doug rounded a corner in a cloud of dust, drawing up beside us, and looking as cool as a proverbial cucumber. We clambered up and within twenty minutes we were back in camp, relaxing under a lukewarm shower to rinse off all the dust of our morning in the bush. I chuckled to myself, remembering the many times we had seen elephants dash down to the water to enjoy a long soak and splash, using their trunks as an effective shower- head to get rid of a day's dust, and thought how many similarities we shared with these remarkable animals.

That afternoon, Dave arranged an extra canoe for us. He had seen we were relaxed and confident on the river, and Trust the camp helper was a keen canoeist and would take me; Dave would take Gordon, and Joan and Sarah would go with Iona as usual. We all wanted to go a bit further down the Zambezi to where there were some high sand banks. Here we hoped see a colony of carmine bee-eaters, some of the most beautifully coloured birds to visit this area in summer. We floated down the river, now able to take photos of each other canoeing up to hippo pods resting on the banks, posing with elephants feeding on the islands behind us, and just relaxing in the afternoon heat, which we knew would slowly be losing its intensity as time passed.

We drew up close to the sand banks that Dave had mentioned, and through my binoculars, I could see hundreds of flashes of crimson and turquoise. The carmine bee-eaters had returned to nest. Trust paddled the canoe towards the bank, trying to steady it so that I could get some good photographs. In his eagerness, he caught his T-shirt on an overhanging branch; the canoe went forward, and I looked back to see Trust trying to disentangle himself, desperately attempting to stay in the canoe and balance it at the same time so that neither of us would topple into the water. I grabbed the nearest branch and pulled the canoe closer to the bank. Gradually, I was able to haul it against the current so that Trust could untangle himself.

Amidst gales of laughter from our supposed allies, we finally stabilised the canoe and reached the bank safely but not without enquiry as to why we intended to go for a swim in crocodile-infested waters. With as much dignity as was possible, given the situation, we jettisoned the prickly branches that stuck fast in our hair, T-shirts and in the bottom of the canoe, and launched ourselves off the bank to join the others who had some wonderful footage of a near disaster in the making. Trust decided that discretion was the better part of valour, and assuring him I was fine and that I could get good photos with the aid of a telephoto lens, he concentrated on keeping the canoe stable – a safe distance from any branches!

Over the next half hour, we watched enthralled as the colony of birds swooped over our heads, entering and emerging from the holes in the sandy bank where they were making their nests. The brilliant carmine feathers on their breasts and the iridescent flashes of turquoise and cinnamon flashed backwards and forwards; the flocks of birds made a soft twittering sound, interspersed with individual birds making a 'terk-terk' call. All around us there was a symphony of colour and noise, making it difficult to concentrate on photography. I decided just to sit back and relax to fully appreciate and enjoy this beautiful scene around us.

When our senses were totally satisfied, we continued down the river until we came to the place where Doug was to collect us. We paddled up to the shallow bank and Trust jumped out of the canoe ready to haul it up the steep bank so that I would not have to get my feet wet. The other two canoes were already beached and everyone was standing on the sandy shore a few yards from us. I started to clamber out of the canoe only for Dave to signal to everyone to stand still. He had climbed up the steep, sandy bank and had obviously seen something. He raised his rifle – I recognised the 'danger' signal.

There I was, standing upright and precariously balanced in the canoe ready to disembark, when over the bank appeared a large bull elephant. Dave signalled to Trust to hold the canoe steady and keep still. We all kept completely motionless, and waited to see where the bull would go. He stood stock-still and then started to sway gently on his enormous legs. His trunk pointed towards me, sniffing the air. He stared at me, and then at the bank. He wanted to go down into the water! I remembered the warning from Shane on our previous walking safari: 'Never get between an elephant and the water.' Here was I in just such a dangerous situation, unable to do anything about it.

It was impossible for me to go back onto the river in the canoe without disturbing the elephant even more than we were doing, although my initial instinct was to disembark from the wobbling canoe and step into the deep water, taking my chances with the crocodiles and hippos. My legs trembled, which did not help the balancing of the canoe, but suddenly the elephant tossed his head gently, his ears sending up clouds of dust and he turned back. I looked at Dave, who silently signalled to Trust that he should haul the canoe further in, and that I should get out of the canoe onto dry land. I crawled up the steep, sandy bank on all fours, and there was this magnificent animal with its trunk outstretched, balancing on its front two legs with its hind legs stretched out behind him, reaching up to feed from a nearby mahogany tree.

We gathered together, and I managed to get one of my most prized photographs of this scene. Dave then led us away from where the elephant had wanted to go down to the water, and a few minutes later he stopped feeding and lumbered ponderously down the bank, carefully avoided our canoes, and started wading out into the river, to enjoy a delayed and well earned drink.

We walked further along the top of the bank and watched the setting sun come down over the far hills – another perfect end to another perfect day, which in some way or another we not only survived but which also provided us with memories that would last a life time. The sound of the Landy driven by Doug brought me back to reality, and soon we were loading the canoes onto the trailer and quickly making it back to camp before dark set in.

There was more laughter over supper, and we chatted over our experiences, sad that this was going to be the last evening we would all be spending together. Joan and Sarah were going on to Kariba on the same flight as Gordon, Dave and me, and then back to Harare to stay with friends for a couple of days. Their host was a silversmith who made the most exquisite silver jewellery and ornaments. Joan gave us his telephone number and we mentally made a note to go and visit him if we had any spare time when we were back at Thetford House at the end of our safari.

Inevitably, our talk turned to the light aircraft flight in the morning. Sarah was as apprehensive as I was over these flights, and asked if she could sit in the back of the plane, so that she could cover her eyes with a coat and ignore what was going on around her. Gordon, in a tactless vein, remarked that the turbulence was much worse in the back of a small aircraft, but Sarah was adamant that she wanted to sit there, as she felt safer. Here was a plucky young woman who had grown up in the bush, and who had shot a buffalo when hunting with her father, admitting to being terrified of flying. I felt a wave of sympathy for her, knowing how much she was going through to get to these isolated places. I gave her a big hug, and off we went to spend our last night in our tiny tents on the banks of the Zambezi.

Years later, and with many safaris under our belts, I still remember Mana Pools as the ultimate, most beautiful and exciting place to visit and enjoy. Here is unspoilt Africa at its best. We were entirely isolated from the outside world, with no crowds of tourists in mini buses gathering around wildlife sightings. I fervently hope that this magical place remains so special and unspoilt, and count myself unbelievably fortunate to have been able to experience some of this vast wilderness.

Wherever I am in the world, if I have difficulty sleeping, I have only to recall those few precious nights we spent in our tent on the banks of the mighty Zambezi, and the memories of the sounds of the bush, and water flowing past, help me to drift off to sleep with a peaceful smile on my face.

Walking with elephants in Mana Pools, Zimbabwe.

Lake Kariba is a photographer's paradise. We walked either in the early morning or in the late afternoon when the heat of the day less intense. The stark dead tree trunks silhouetted against a setting sun were more than enough to keep me entranced until couple of elephants walked slowly across the shoreline and completed the scene.

Chapter 9

Lake Kariba

The following morning we got up quickly and packed our canvas bags. After a quick breakfast, it was time to say goodbye and offer our heartfelt thanks to Doug, Trust and Patterson, all of whom had worked tirelessly to ensure our safari was forever memorable. Over the years, it has become increasingly difficult for me to say farewell. I only hope that the wonderful, caring people we have met, scattered throughout the African continent, realise that they remain in our thoughts and will continue to do so for many years.

All too soon, we were at the airstrip, waiting for our plane to arrive. From out of the clear blue sky, a tiny speck emerged, and with a gentle roar, our light aircraft landed and came to a halt, sending up clouds of sandy dust all over us. Once aboard, the doors safely secured, we taxied for take-off. I glanced back at Sarah, hunched up at the tail of the aircraft, getting ready to pull a sweater over her head, and gave her what I hoped was a reassuring smile. The noise of the engine swelled as the single propeller whirled into action. The whole aircraft shuddered and we sped down the dirt strip, which served as the runway. We were just taking off when there was a noise that sounded like a machine gun scattering bullets all over the fuselage. I ducked low in my seat and covered my head with my hands.

Up we went into the sky for a few minutes, gaining height all the time, only to make a rapid, violent turn, after which the pilot calmly announced that he would have to turn back and land the plane quickly. I grabbed hold of Gordon's hand and held on tightly, feeling sick with apprehension. Sarah appeared from underneath her sweater and asked us what was happening as she could hear nothing at the back of the aircraft. Gordon gently told her that we needed to go back to land at the airstrip, and she replaced the sweater over her head. No one spoke – each of us immersed in our own thoughts. Wondering what was going to happen next, I willed this little aircraft to land safely. A couple of minutes later, which seemed like hours, we landed with a bump, safely back on terra firma, and once the engine was switched off we were instructed to get out of the aircraft quickly.

Without so much as a word, we all scrambled out of the tiny exit, and on the pilot's instructions, we ran to the shade of some trees bordering the take-off strip. Dave looked around us and murmured something about his rifle still being in the hold of the aircraft. I had completely forgotten that we were still in the middle of the bush – but wild animals seemed to be relatively easy to cope with after this latest experience. After a few minutes, the pilot approached us, apologising for the unexpected emergency landing. He had been busy inspecting the propeller.

Apparently, on take-off, a stone had been thrown up, which had caught the propeller and then ricocheted down the fuselage, causing the rapid firing noise we had heard. He showed us where the stone had chipped a piece out of the propeller, and we looked with amazement at the indentations along the fuselage. I briefly wondered what would have happened if the stone had hit the windows or fuel tanks, but quickly pushed such horrors from my mind. The pilot told us that the aircraft would have to stay grounded until a replacement propeller was flown out and the plane given a thorough overhaul. In all probability, the aircraft could fly but he was taking no chances in case the propeller suddenly became unstable in mid-flight. Sarah was looking white-faced – my face was probably the same ashen colour, and we all went to sit in the shade whilst the pilot radioed back to base. Gradually, speech returned to us, and I relished the thought that we might now spend an extra day or two back in camp.

A few minutes later the pilot re-appeared, informing us that another aircraft was on its way to fly us to Kariba, and would be with us within an hour. So much for an extra night in camp! I was very impressed by the organisation, and we filled the hour chatting with the pilot. He had been flying for many years and it was the first time this had happened. Seeing that Sarah and I were still very shaken, he told us how he loved flying these light aircraft, and how he would never fly in a large passenger jet if he could help it. These tiny workhorses of the bush were, in his opinion, infinitely safer than their larger relations. If an engine should fail, it was a relatively easy thing to glide it down to land in a very small area in the bush, whereas large jets need long smooth runways.

At the time, I was not totally convinced, but having survived this near disaster, ironically, instead of being even more scared of flying, this had given me the chance to see how I reacted in such a situation, and I felt re-assured that I had remained relatively calm and had not panicked. I was also impressed with the professionalism of these bush pilots, and the fact that they did not take any chances with their passengers' safety.

In exactly an hour, a replacement aircraft landed and for the second time we loaded ourselves into it, preparing for yet another take-off. This time our flight was uneventful, and soon we were circling over an immense stretch of water – Lake Kariba. After landing at the airport, thankfully on a tarmac runway this time, we said our goodbyes to Joan, Sarah and Iona, promising to keep in touch. We were very touched when Joan hugged us and told us we had been the perfect safari companions, making her birthday celebrations very special. We had grown so fond of this lovely woman and her daughter – having shared some incredible moments together, some exciting, some scary, and some hilarious, and were sorry to go our separate ways after this memorable time together.

Dave sorted out transport for us, and soon we were at a yacht club jetty where the motor cruiser, which was to be our home for the next three nights, was moored. Joseph, the captain, and the cook, Thambo, helped us aboard, greeted us warmly and showed us our cabin, which consisted of a large double bed taking up all the width of the cabin and most of its length, with an adjoining small shower and loo. I hastily unpacked a few vital things, leaving most of my clothes in the holdall, as there was little space for anything. It was also incredibly hot and humid, and I wondered how I would ever be able to sleep at night in these conditions. The engine started up and we went up on deck to watch our departure from the yacht club.

As soon as we were under way, we felt the beginning of a breeze, and went up to the bow where we sat down on deck, grateful to cool down. Once out of the harbour, the engine throbbed at full throttle, the wind strengthened and we bounced from wave to wave. Thankfully, neither Gordon nor I have ever suffered from sea-sickness, and simply enjoyed being back on a boat, albeit a somewhat noisy one – and what a complete contrast this was to the last few days of utter tranquillity, camping and canoeing at Mana Pools.

We caught the delicious aroma of cooking coming from the galley, so Dave sorted out some very welcome ice-cold beers for us, and we toasted our survival from near disaster and the next part of our safari. Over a late lunch Dave explained that we would cross Lake Kariba that afternoon, which would take us about two hours, and were going to what he thought was the most beautiful area on this great inland lake – the Matusadona National Park.

The flight's delay meant that we would not be arriving until nearly nightfall, so a brief walk in the afternoon was out of the question. This news certainly didn't worry me – I was quite content to relax and recover from the day's stresses. Replete and sleepy after an excellent lunch, the three of us retired to snooze on deck, liberally covering ourselves with sunscreen. The sound of the boat's engine reducing speed woke me, and peering sleepily to one side, the shoreline, bordered by the hills of Matusadona appeared in the distance. We had slowed down to negotiate the many dead trees, the 'drowned forests', still there nearly thirty years after the filling of the lake once the Kariba Dam had been built.

This was a photographer's paradise! I grabbed my camera and took a few shots, until Dave suggested that it might be better to wait until the following day when he would take us out on the boat's tender and I wouldn't be troubled by the vibration of the engine. We approached the shore slowly, the engine was turned off, and we were expertly anchored in a small isolated inlet just as dusk was falling. The silence after two hours of motoring was intense. G and Ts were poured and we watched contentedly as the sky became pink and then crimson, turning the bright blue of the horizon to gold. The reflections of the tree trunks in the water darkened, and the sun sank out of sight. Within half an hour, the stars were clearly visible and we lay out on deck, Dave pointing out all the major constellations of the Southern Hemisphere. What a perfect end to a day that at one point I thought I would never survive!

Another delicious meal appeared as if by magic, and I tried to do justice to Thambo's efforts. Perhaps it was the excessive heat, or it could have been the fact that we had not exercised all day, but all I wanted was to go to bed and have a good night's sleep. Dave suggested that we might like to sleep up on deck as it was so hot down below in our cabin. This sounded like a brilliant idea, so our mattress were brought up, our bed made, and after a quick shower and liberal applying of anti-mosquito lotion on all our exposed skin surfaces, we retired to our bed under the stars. A soft breeze rocked the boat backwards and forwards and from side to side. I fell asleep to this gentle cradling motion whilst gazing at the vast African sky studded with millions of glittering stars overhead, the Milky Way a haze of shimmering light.

I awoke just as dawn was approaching, feeling distinctly chilly with only a sheet covering me. Listening to the birds gradually begin their morning chorus, I watched as the darkness slipped gently away and grey shapes on the shoreline became shrubs and trees. I have always loved this time of day in the bush, when everything is starting to stir, and the chill of the night gives way to the heat of yet another day. Snuggling up to Gordon for a bit of warmth, we whispered together about the coming part of our safari. We heard the sound of something moving on the shoreline, and sitting up, saw a herd of buffalo in the distance coming down to drink at the water's edge. Dave's polite 'knock knock' followed by him bringing us an early morning cup of tea and rusks, sprang us into action. There he was, showered and dressed, ready for an early morning walk, when we had only just woken and were still in our pyjamas! Twenty minutes later, we were clambering into the tender, and after a couple of attempts to start the small outboard motor, Dave took us further along the shoreline away from the retreating herd of buffalo.

Dave secured the tender's painter under a large rock, and we set off on our bush walk. It was pleasantly cool, but it promised to be another scorcher of a day, so we were determined to get a fair amount of walking in before it became too hot. In between numerous stops to look at spoor, Dave explained that we would only see a fraction of the Park. Its area was immense – about 338,000 acres, and we learnt how Operation Noah rescued much of the wildlife before the flooding of the lake. Species that did not survive were gradually being re-introduced, including the very rare black rhino. However, he had yet to see one in the wild, despite many safaris here. He mentioned that there was a black rhino sanctuary not far away, and suggested that we might like to go and visit it the following day, to which we instantly agreed.

We came across a skeleton of a large bull elephant, which had presumably died of old age, and I closely examined the bones. What I hadn't known before was that the bone structure of an elephant's foot means that they actually walk on tiptoe. The tusks were missing, and Dave explained that the Park rangers would remove these rather than leave them to tempt any poachers. Whilst we were chatting, Dave lowered his voice and we could hear the very faint roaring of lions in the distance. I wondered if one of the buffalo was now breakfast for a pride of hungry lions, but apparently, it sounded more like the territorial roar of male lions. We sat down on the shoreline and spent the next hour looking at the prolific bird life. A solitary grey heron was standing in the shallow water, and we watched as it stood motionless for several minutes before it crept forward silently in a crouching position, rapidly immersing its long beak in the water in search of an elusive fish.

We sat quietly observing a blacksmith's plover settle on the ground with its mate walking purposely around the area. She could well be sitting on a nest. The haunting cry of a fish eagle broke into the silence and looking up, we saw this magnificent bird fly overhead before coming to rest on a nearby tree in the lake. This interruption caused the plover on the nest to get up and walk away, its distinctive, metallic 'klink, klink, klink' call signalling its agitation. I now realised why it was called a blacksmith's plover – the noise it made was just like a hammer hitting an anvil! We looked through our binoculars, attempting to see if there were any eggs in the small, scooped out scrape, and eventually, I saw three eggs – they were so camouflaged that when I looked away and then returned to focus on them again I found them impossible to find. The distraught bird stopped her frantic calling and resumed her position on the rudimentary nest. Peace was restored and I turned my camera lens onto the fish eagle, perched motionless on the tree, its image perfectly reflected in the lake.

I have often seen wonderful photographs of fish eagles diving into the water and rising with a fish in their beaks, and would love to add such a definitive image to my collection. We waited and waited, becoming hotter and hotter on the open shoreline. My arms ached from holding the camera steady on my knees, wishing I had taken Gordon's advice to bring a tripod. The fish eagle called to its mate, who somewhere in the distance faintly answered back, and I got photo after photo of him flinging back his head, his plaintive, haunting call breaking the silence of the bush. Half an hour later, we all decided that enough was enough, and started the long walk back to the tender in the stifling heat. The gentle motoring back to our boat cooled us down, and after several long glasses of refreshing fruit juice we sat down to a very welcome brunch.

Dave rigged up some shade for us on deck with the judicious use of some sheets and we all decided to take it easy under this makeshift awning until the heat of the day eased. Thankfully, a gentle breeze appeared around midday, making our enforced siesta much more bearable. I considered getting into my dressing gown and repeating my Mana Pools cooling operation, but as privacy was at a premium, I decided not to subject the men on the boat to such a spectacle. Unfortunately, going for a swim in the inviting cool water was not an option as hippos and crocodiles were a constant danger.

After we all had spent a couple of hours resting, Dave sorted out some fishing tackle, and he and Gordon spent the next hour trying to catch something for our evening meal. A fish eagle obligingly came to rest close to the boat on the branches of a tree, probably hoping for some fishy morsels to come his way. He waited in vain, and I also waited in vain, camera ready for a much wanted photo. We decided to venture forth on the tender again, and motored out of the inlet where we moored to explore more of the shoreline. A large herd of buffalo came down to drink; we estimated there must have been over 500, and I wondered where their predators were. Dave was certain we would come across lion during this part of our safari.

We motored on and eventually landed on an isolated stretch of shoreline. We walked for half an hour until the sun started to go down in front of us. The dead trees' reflections lengthened in the still water, and Dave pointed out five elephants walking slowly along the shore, their outlines silhouetted perfectly against the skyline and the enormous round orange sun. The colours of this perfect scene slowly deepened. The sky turned crimson and orange with touches of light purple and lavender melting into the deepening blue. The elephants continued their ponderous journey, providing me with some of the most beautiful photos I have ever taken, and reluctantly we turned back to get to the boat before darkness finally descended.

After another night spent sleeping under the stars, we motored in the tender to the black rhino sanctuary. The staff welcomed us and took us on a tour of the facilities. Apparently, all the rhinos here are orphans, often their mothers killed by poachers or by snares. De-horning rhinos had not worked, as unfortunately, poachers also killed de-horned rhinos. If they spent days tracking the animal, only to find that there was no horn to sell, they would kill it to ensure that they did not waste time tracking the animal in the future. Poachers were a constant danger, both to these endangered animals and the ranger patrols trying to preserve them. And all for a piece of horn ground up into powder which has no medicinal function at all, or else for some rich Middle Eastern or Asian men who like to display their daggers with ornately carved rhino horn handles.

To a certain degree, I could understand that if a family were starving, a poacher might risk life and limb to get a rhino horn, but the money he received would be minute, the profits being made far higher up the trafficking line. This sanctuary was actively educating the local population in the conservation of the black rhino, gradually getting them to see that there are more advantages to their community to preserve rather than kill these rare animals. We were introduced to a few of the rangers, discovering that many were poachers turned gamekeepers – a very positive sign.

We walked to meet some of the sanctuary's precious inhabitants – the rhino calves. Each one had its own keeper who fed it, took it out into the bush and generally acted as a surrogate parent. We entered the enclosure where four small rhinos were feeding, their meal placed in several rubber tyre rings. Large bowls of water were nearby. Through necessity, these little orphans were habituated to human beings; they posed no threat to us and we were able to get close to them, seeing clearly their hooked front lip, which, together with their smaller size, differentiated them from their white rhino cousins.

Gordon crouched down to do some filming at eye level. Suddenly, one of the calves caught sight of him, and rushed over to inspect this strange being. Gordon was so intent on getting some good footage that he was sent flying! Camera and tripod flew up in the air and Gordon rolled over in the dust. The rhino backed off in surprise, whereupon his minder took him away to continue with his feeding. Gordon dusted down both himself and his camera equipment. Thankfully, no damage was done to either, and we all were taken to another enclosure where the tiny rhinos were bottle-fed.

The rhinos were accustomed to being enclosed in a metal cage for feeding and weighing purposes. This made things easier for both the feeder and the calves who would queue to be put in this structure to get their twice-daily bottles of formula. Bottle is probably the wrong word – it was a four-litre plastic container with a long teat attached to the outlet. I was invited to feed one of the calves and whilst one of them was placed gently in its feeding frame, this heavy container was placed in my hands. The calf started to make mewing sounds, and I placed the teat in its mouth, only for the container to be dragged out of my hands and fall on the ground. I had not expected the force an infant rhino exerted when sucking. The mewing increased in its intensity, and I again placed the teat in its eager mouth. This time I hung on, and in a couple of minutes the four litres had disappeared into one hungry rhino's stomach. I stroked his rough, leathery side and then was told to tickle it behind his ears. The skin there was as soft as the finest leather gloves, and he nuzzled against me. I was not sure who enjoyed this more – him or me!

We ventured out into the bush to a large enclosed area where we could stroll around with several rhinos and their keepers. We were given a small stick, and told that if any of them got too boisterous, waving it in front of them would help restore the peace. For the next hour, we walked with these precious animals, observing their behaviour – how they browsed on branches rather than graze on grass, and how they interacted with each other like playful children in a crèche. The small mewing sound they made fascinated me. It was hardly louder than a domestic cat – an incongruous noise for such a large animal. What a privilege it was to be so close to some of the most endangered creatures on this planet. Reluctantly, I left them, breathing a silent prayer that they would be safe from men whose greed could extinguish them from the face of the earth.

After lunch and our customary siesta, Dave suggested that we take a further trip in the tender to explore another part of the shoreline and when it got cooler, maybe walk for an hour or so in the bush. Half an hour later, we were slowly chugging along a couple of hundred yards from the shore when Dave cut the engine and stood up in utter amazement, violently rocking the boat. We clung on to our cameras, wondering what on earth was going on. There in the distance coming down from the tree line towards us was a rhino. Not just any rhino, but an adult black rhino male with a large horn! I have never seen a guide so excited. This was the first black rhino Dave had ever seen in the wild. He sat down in the boat, mopping his brow and shaking his head from side to side in utter amazement. 'This is crazy!' he murmured, remembering to keep still and quiet in case the rhino disappeared into the bush. 'It's hot and the middle of the afternoon – it ought to be resting in the shade rather than being out in the open. This is the very last thing I thought we would see. You really don't know how lucky we are!'

We watched silently, willing the rhino to come closer to the water's edge. Slowly, he made his way towards us, sniffing at the air, and every so often lifting his head and snorting gently. The wind was carrying us towards the shore and soon we had no need of our binoculars to see his prehensile lip clearly. We just had to wait and see what would happen. If Dave started up the motor, the engine noise would mean that this would be the end of our sighting. The rhino almost reached the water and then became uncertain. The wind was carrying our scent towards him. In all probability, he could not see us as a rhino's sight is very poor. He snorted in our direction, tossed his head and with an incredible spurt of speed set off at full gallop, only to turn round and come to a violent stop, thick dust flying everywhere. He then galloped back to where we were, turned in a tight circle, and set off again at an impressive speed. Gradually, he slowed down and then rushed off into the thick bush, his tail curled over his back.

Such an amazing sight left us breathless. We had just observed how agile and fast a black rhino can be. I was grateful we were not on foot, as avoiding this 1,360 kilogram animal, which can run up to speeds of 30 miles per hour, and turn in its own length at full gallop was certainly not a close encounter I would relish. Its volatile temperament, great speed and agility, coupled with a lethal looking horn make it an animal to be avoided at all costs when out walking.

Catching our breaths from all the excitement, we relaxed and had a drink of water, wondering if the rhino would make another appearance. Gone were any thoughts of a walk, and we chatted softly to each other, watching some buffalo come down to drink, followed by a couple of old elephant bulls, their speed increasing the closer they got to the water. They stood in the water, trunks extended, satiating their thirst. That satisfied, they continued to wade in further and we watched them roll over and submerge. What bliss it must be for them to be weightless in water, and cool off after a hot day of foraging for food. Eventually, they returned to dry land and finished off their ablutions with liberal clouds of dust – the perfect talcum powder, which would protect their skin from the sun and from ticks and parasites.

We gently cruised back to our motor boat after a day full of black rhinos, sad that this was our last evening with Dave who had proved himself such an excellent guide and entertaining companion. We talked through our experiences with him, and thought about what we would be doing next. This holiday was full of contrasts, and once again, we were impressed by the organisation and care taken in planning such a varied safari.

I woke up just before dawn, and savoured this quiet time when the stars were fading overhead, before the sun rose to bring the inevitable and relentless heat of the day. In the distance, I heard a faint sound of what might have been a buffalo snorting, and then possibly a lion snarling, but I decided not to get up and have a look. I would rather enjoy the peace of another dawn breaking. It was going to be a busy day with a flight to Victoria Falls, and a snooze before we had to get up was just what I needed. Dave woke us up with a start – none of the gentle 'knock knocking' and a cup of tea. He ordered us to get up quickly as there had been a lion kill on the foreshore. I looked up blearily and there in the distance on an inlet were some blobs on the sand, which I assumed were the lions feeding off a carcass. We had just about time to walk to it before departing for Kariba.

We dressed hurriedly with no time for any niceties such as brushing our teeth, and set off at what seemed like a trot. Dave led the way, rifle slung over his shoulder. He turned to look back at his two middle-aged clients and slowed down. It was probably the recollection of my tantrum and refusal to run that prompted this action. He waited for us to catch our breath and grinned apologetically. In between gasps, I told him that I had heard what might have been the sound of a buffalo and even a lion in the distance, but had dozed off to sleep. 'What! You didn't even get up to have a look?' he exclaimed in utter amazement. Obviously, he would remember me as the client from hell!

On we walked towards the lions and the kill. When we were about 30 feet away, one of the lionesses looked towards us. We halted behind Dave who slowly stooped to pick up a largish stone – rather a stone than a bullet was his motto. Standing motionless, we watched as first one lioness and then the other three stood up, four pairs of amber eyes fixed intently on us, their muzzles red with fresh blood. As if in slow motion, they turned away and slowly ambled off into the bush, their full bellies as taut as drums. These four animals were not going to need any more food for some time. Slowly we approached their kill, Dave keeping an ever vigilant watch for any re-appearance of the lionesses, who could still want to protect the remains of their kill.

I wondered if there was a male lion lurking somewhere that had yet to feed, but Dave seemed confident that if there were a male around in this coalition of females he would have soon arrived at the kill to take the so-called lion's share. Usually, lionesses had the hard work of bringing down the kill, with their lord and master appearing to eat his fill before the females were allowed to feed. I hoped Dave was right, but I was also surprised at my lack of fear when virtually face-to-face with four lionesses, blood dripping from their jaws. It was possibly the fact that I remembered the previous lions running away from us when they also had been on a kill.

We went up to the kill – a buffalo as we had expected. The blood was still fresh and had yet to dry, and there was enough meat for further meals, although a large amount had been devoured. As there were only four lionesses on the kill, there was enough meat to go round, preventing the often vicious fighting when space is at a premium. This explained the lack of noise, and the fact that we managed to sleep through the whole episode. I took a couple of photos, and realised I had not even bothered to take any photos of the lionesses; neither had Gordon turned on his video camera. We were now enjoying the total experience of the bush rather than shielding ourselves behind the lenses of photographic equipment.

Many years later, I can remember this encounter as clearly as if it had happened yesterday, without the help of any hastily shot photos. I still adore wildlife photography, but over time, I have learnt that to sit back and allow the scene to unfurl is often infinitely more satisfying to the senses.

As soon as we were back on board, the engine started up and we left the perfect mooring place that had been home for three magical days and nights. I went down below and had a very rudimentary shower, trying to avoid being thrown from side to side when the boat picked up speed and started to bounce from wave to wave. Gordon decided to remain unwashed and wait until we arrived at our next destination.

Over a filling brunch cooked with much dexterity by Thambo, we had to face the task of packing our holdalls. Two people trying to pack in one small, stifling hot cabin on a tossing boat is not a wise move, so whilst Gordon relaxed and snoozed off the effects of Thambo's cooking, I earned some brownie points and did the wifely thing of packing, grabbing everything I could see and stuffing it all into our holdalls. Hopefully, that evening we would be able to sort out all our clothing, as it would be in desperate need of the attentions of an iron. I quickly returned on deck to get a breath of fresh air and enjoy what remained of our passage across Lake Kariba.

After yet more goodbyes and heartfelt thanks to our caring crew, we got into a taxi to the airport for our flight to Victoria Falls. Whilst waiting for our plane, we exchanged addresses with Dave and, with much laughter, recalled our many experiences together. From what he said I now really believe he had enjoyed his time with us, despite the hard times I occasionally gave him. He had given us some wonderful memories, which will last a lifetime, and once more, we were faced with saying goodbye to someone who had made a lasting impact on our lives.

Lake Kariba and our boat in the distance, behind a forest of dead tree trunks.

Miss Ellie and I enjoyed her daily bath time together. She liked to sneak a crafty drink from the hose, and then squirt the water over me. I used to talk to her gently and when I paused, she would give me a nudge as if to say, 'Well, go on, I'm still listening.' When walking with her in the bush I soon got to know the bushes and trees she preferred to eat. Her speed quickened to a swift amble so she could reach the tasty morsels before the other elephants. I was heartbroken to say goodbye to her after three very special days.

Chapter 10

Jock, Miss Ellie, Jumbo and Jack

Thankfully, our flight to Victoria Falls was uneventful and we soon arrived at the lodge, where we were to spend the next few days learning about, and interacting with, four of the most amazing pachyderms. Iced drinks in our hands, we sat overlooking a small pan filled with muddy water, and talked to our host about our first walking safari led by Shane, and his recommendation to visit here. As if by magic, Shane, followed by his father, appeared out of the bush, and we greeted each other with broad grins and big hugs. What a wonderful surprise – we were certainly not expecting to see them!

Shane was about to start another walking safari, and I felt a tinge of envy for those fortunate guests who would be embarking upon such a wonderful adventure with him. Over several more drinks, we caught up with each other's news, Shane roaring with laughter when we related some of our recent exploits. Suddenly, four elephants appeared out of nowhere and we sat watching them with their keeper as they dashed down to the pan and, after quenching their thirst, started to play in the water. They proceeded to amble up closer to us and began to play-fight as if showing off to strangers. Once this performance was over, they walked off into the dry bush to 'behave just like ellies', as Shane put it.

We would be allocated our own elephant, and would ride it out into the bush with a mahout seated in front of us. We would wash it down, give it food, and get to know and understand its behaviour and character during our time spent here. I had so many questions that needed answering. We discovered that all four elephants had been orphaned, abandoned or injured. Rather than let nature take its course, it was decided to see if they could be hand-reared and trained to obey simple commands. This was one of the first places in Africa to embark upon such a project, as it was always assumed that African elephants could not be domesticated, although for centuries, Indian elephants – a completely different species – had been trained for various tasks.

All four elephants had taken to this new life, and an added advantage was that they had forged close bonds with each other, forming their own new family structure. No form of cruelty is used in their training – if one of them 'misbehaves', it receives a swift verbal reprimand followed by a tap with a hooked stick. They regarded their trainers as the matriarch, who, in the wild would discipline the young using their trunks to deliver a sharp whack when needed, and trumpeting their displeasure should the younger members of the family get out of line. As a result of this humane training, Miss Ellie, Jack, Jock and Jumbo were considered safe and predictable enough to carry people on their backs on safari in the bush. A reward system worked very well – handfuls of nuts were their favourite, and the four elephants were allowed ample freedom in the bush with minimal human intervention, before being rounded up at night-time to rest in their enclosed shelters.

After lunch, reluctantly, we said goodbye to Shane, and retired to our room for a brief siesta, looking forward to our first close encounter with 'our' elephants. Gordon was allocated Jock, and Miss Elllie was going to be my companion for the next few days. We were taken to the stabling area, told to stand quietly with the trainer, and wait for the two elephants to approach us. This was to make sure that the elephants took a liking to us and no memories of their traumatic past would be triggered by our presence. Miss Ellie ambled up, her trunk extended towards me, sniffing the air, and she placed the tip of her trunk gently into my outstretched hands. I noticed that she was quite a bit smaller than Jock and had only rudimentary tusks, whereas Jock was a full-grown bull, and had a pair of impressive white tusks, chipped and scarred by years of foraging in the bush.

The trainer handed me a few nuts and with incredible dexterity, Miss Ellie picked up the nuts one by one with the two finger-like projections at the end of her trunk, transferring these treats delicately into her mouth with obvious relish. I was far too overwhelmed to even glance at Gordon with Jock, but apparently, Jock did the same, but without so much feminine grace and politeness – just a quick grab and in a trice, all the nuts offered were in his mouth. Already we were noticing differences in their behaviour.

Introductions over, we went to the area where we could wash them, and were soon holding a hosepipe in one hand and a brush in the other. On command, both of our elephants lay down on their sides, and Gordon and I were shown how to give an elephant a bath! Jock had tougher skin than Miss Ellie and enjoyed a vigorous scrub with the brush. Miss Ellie had delicate skin and I washed her with either a sponge or my hands. All the time I talked softly to this gentle giant, whispering sweet nothings as though she was my precious child, as indeed she was for the next few days. Miss Ellie and I had wonderful conversations about everything under the sun. When I stopped talking she would nudge me with her trunk, or a quiet rumble would issue forth from her throat, as though she wanted me to continue talking.

She was a typical female, and seemed to love catching up with all the gossip, hearing all about my family back in England, my experiences in her country, and my hopes and fears. On one level, I knew it was only the sound of my voice to which she responded, but for me it was a very therapeutic practice, well known to anyone who has experienced the pleasure of talking intimately to a much loved dog or cat. However, Miss Ellie was a wild animal weighing 3,500 kilograms, and it was purely the mutual trust and respect we had for each other that enabled me to remain safe with her.

I learnt from her keeper that they thought Miss Ellie might be pregnant, but it was too early to know with any certainty. We 'talked' together about being a mother – how her life would change completely once she had a little one to care for. I didn't envy Miss

Ellie her twenty-two month long pregnancy, but assured her it would be worth it in the end. She let out a long sigh and proceeded to draw up some water into her massive trunk from the hosepipe, which she promptly squirted over me. Perhaps that was her opinion about being pregnant! These bath-times were the most precious of all the times I spent with Miss Ellie – two females sharing intimate moments.

Gordon and Jock, however, were typical males – there was a job to be done and it was completed with the minimum of fuss and little chatter. Once Gordon finished all the scrubbing and hosing down, he would give Jock a light thump on his backside with a 'There you are, Jock, all nice and clean . . . off you go!' Jock lumbered up onto his feet, put his trunk around Gordon's shoulders, as if to say 'Thanks mate' and then proceeded to squirt muddy water all over himself and Gordon!

Bath-time over, Jock and Miss Ellie were led off into the bush to finish their ablutions with a shower of dust to dry themselves and to protect their skins from sun, ticks and parasites. Gordon and I looked at each other and burst out laughing. We were both soaked from head to toe; our feet, legs and arms were covered with gelatinous, red mud, and our clothes splattered with this sticky substance. The laundry service would be working overtime to keep us in clean clothes. Off we went to our own bathroom to make ourselves presentable for dinner.

Over a sun-downer we met our fellow guests – two delightful African Americans, both of whom were anaesthetists equipped with an emergency First Aid pack which would not have been out of place in any Western A and E department. It even included a full resuscitation kit, intravenous drips, fluids – the lot! It was their first visit to the African continent and they came fully prepared for any eventuality, although they were somewhat embarrassed by all this excess luggage. Thankfully, the equipment remained unused and as they were going back to America the following morning, they decided to donate it to the local clinic. I admitted that we too always brought two small First Aid kits, which included syringes, needles and sutures. Up to now, they remained unused, but a couple of years later on safari in Tanzania we were very relieved to have included these emergency packs in our luggage.

Not so delightful were our other companions at supper – a middle-aged maiden aunt and her twenty-year-old niece, also out from America on an extended safari. Nothing appeared right for them and they were the proverbial moan-a-minute minnies. The niece expounded on her various plans to 'save Africans from their appalling living conditions', once she had completed her degree, and her aunt smiled benignly at this arrogant young woman who was planning to haul the whole of the African continent into the twentieth century. I tried to make allowances for youth, but failed miserably, everyone at the table having to endure a meal dominated by this one–sided, grandiose conversation. I caught the eye of one of the anaesthetists, and we smiled wanly at each other. Over a nightcap, the aunt and niece having thankfully stalked off to their bedroom, they apologised profusely for the behaviour of their fellow Americans.

Unfortunately, our anaesthetist friends had suffered the misfortune to be with them for a couple of days, and were totally exasperated and ashamed by the behaviour of two of their fellow compatriots. The four of us spent the next half hour putting the world to rights with a bit of common sense and a lot of laughter, and then retired to bed. I sometimes wonder what became of this young woman, and hope that with time she mellowed and became less self-opinionated and arrogant, developing some humility and insight into the myriad difficulties Africa experiences. Our brief encounter with her reconfirmed all our beliefs about how to behave as guests in someone else's country. Empathy, compassion and good humour – yes. Arrogance, complaining, and wanting to change things to what one is used to back home – never!

We were up early the next day, excited at the thought of riding our elephants in the bush. Jock and Miss Ellie greeted us like old friends, jostling to nuzzle us with their trunks, probably in the hopes of a tasty morsel or two. They were taken to the platform where we would embark, and enormous leather saddles were strapped onto their backs. A difficult manoeuvre was about to follow! From the safety of the high platform, I was required to stretch over a gap between the platform and the body of the elephant, and land safely onto the back of Miss Ellie! The ground seemed a very long way down, but with the help of the trainer already sitting just behind the dome of her head, with her enormous grey, ears flapping gently behind him, I managed to grab his hand for support and landed on Miss Ellie's back. Gordon found this exercise much easier, having longer legs, and after securing our feet into some stirrups, we set off into the bush with a ranger walking alongside us.

It took some time to get used to the rolling motion of an elephant walking; it was not unlike sitting onboard a boat in a gentle swell. What surprised me were the continual rumblings of Miss Ellie's stomach – not only the sound but also the feeling of these gurgles vibrating against my legs. Then there was the flatulence! I had no idea so much methane gas was expelled so regularly by an elephant, often followed by the sound of dung being dropped, large dollops hitting the ground with a resounding thud. Every time this happened, we came to a gentle halt, generally by a bush or shrub where Miss Ellie could multitask and ingest more food for her enormous body to process into yet more dung. Once I was used to these natural sounds, I began to look around me and enjoy the bush from a completely new perspective. Being several feet higher, I could see for miles over the scrub and bushes, which would normally hide game if we were on foot or in a vehicle.

What was very special was the fact that other game completely ignored us, as long as we humans remained quiet. After all, these were just elephants as far as they were concerned, and there was nothing to alarm them. We could approach within a few feet of giraffe, and watch them feed on the tops of acacia trees. We were near enough to hear them chomping thorns and leaves, and see their enormous prehensile tongues wrap around these tasty morsels. Zebra, impala, wildebeest and waterbuck were totally unfazed by us, and it was magical to get so close to these animals, and to sit watching their natural behaviour.

Just as we had to keep a lookout for tree branches when we were driving in an open vehicle in the bush, we had to be very aware of overhanging vegetation, especially when the elephants stopped to browse. The only time the handlers had to raise their voices in command was when either Jock or Miss Ellie wanted to feed off branches that spread over our heads. The prospect of large, heavy branches coming down on us was to be avoided for obvious safety reasons; the elephants had ample time alone in the bush, without their passengers, to bring down enough heavy vegetation to satisfy their natural instincts.

Jock and Miss Ellie were allowed to eat from low bushes, but sometimes the temptation to stride off after a delicious snack from a tall tree proved too much. This prompted a quick but gentle slap with the stick, and when order was restored, a rewarding handful of nuts was all that was needed. I began to predict when this might happen as Miss Ellie increased her speed to a quicker rolling gait – a signal for me to hold on tightly until she resumed her more stately progress through the bush. I also became used to dodging the branches she had snapped off and held in her trunk. She waved these trophies with glee over her back before settling down to the task of neatly folding them up into more manageable mouthfuls.

I avoided looking down too much, as the ground was hard and littered with rocks capable of causing serious injury or worse if we were unlucky enough to take a tumble. It is amazing how sure-footed these large animals are on the roughest terrain. They picked their way carefully over these sometimes, massive boulders, never once stumbling or losing their balance. After an hour or so, we reached a more open area where we were to stop for a drink. It was then I realised that I was expected to get off Miss Ellie's back without the aid of a mounting platform. I had not anticipated this, but decided I had no option but to get down, as the two cups of tea and a fruit juice before we set off were beginning to make me feel in urgent need of a comfort break. The streams of urine descending like waterfalls from the elephants did nothing to alleviate the situation either!

I watched Gordon hang on whilst Jock slowly lowered his rear legs to a sitting position. He held onto the saddle with both hands, swung his legs over Jock's back and placed his feet onto the elephant's carefully folded front legs, before sliding down onto terra firma. I repeated the same exercise with the help of Gordon who had waddled over to me. I wondered why he was walking so awkwardly but soon found out. After over an hour of sitting astride an elephant's very wide back, our legs seemed to have fused at right angles to our pelvic girdles. I too waddled like a duck, attempting to get my lower limbs into their correct position, wondering if I would ever be able to walk normally again. Gordon was in even more discomfort – at least I had the advantage of being female, having wider, more flexible childbearing hips!

Once our guide had made certain there was nothing untoward behind the nearest bush, Gordon and I staggered off behind it, like sailors reaching dry land after months at sea, to answer the calls of nature, only to return to have a refreshing drink whilst Jock and Miss Ellie quietly got on with yet more browsing. I knew that elephants fed for some sixteen hours a day, but this was seeing it in action for the first time. Their life was a continual mealtime, with only a few minutes between each mouthful.

Refreshments over, my task now was to get onto Miss Ellie's back again. The guide instructed me to grab one of her ears to help me haul myself up, and after questioning whether it would hurt her and being assured that it would not, I clambered up onto her obligingly bent leg, holding one of her massive ears to support me. I learnt yet another lesson – when holding her ear I registered that it was, in fact, several degrees cooler than the rest of her body and my own hot, sweaty hands. I remember being told that elephants flap their ears in order to cool the blood flowing through the vast system of blood vessels in their ears. Now I had actually experienced this! Their ears are very efficient air conditioning units. With a toss of her head, her ears wafting a fine, red dust over me, Miss Ellie ambled off into the bush again, searching for yet more nourishment.

Towards the end of this first ride, the insides of my thighs became increasingly more uncomfortable – hundreds of prickles were stabbing my skin and I wondered if I had inadvertently picked up some ants when answering the call of nature behind the bush. After scratching my trousers for some relief, I felt Miss Ellie's grey, leathery hide and realised how tough the hairs of an elephant really are. These short hairs were actually working their way through my trousers and pricking my skin like fine needles. I attempted to raise my legs off her back for some relief, but this made the ride more uncomfortable and distinctly unstable as my feet were then out of the stirrups. Gordon was apparently suffering the same fate, and of course, according to him, Jock's bristles were infinitely more irritating than Miss Ellie's! At the end of the morning when we had safely dismounted, we arranged for some additional thick blankets to be draped over the elephants' backs for future rides. Problem solved!

The days with our two elephants sped by much too quickly. At the end of a morning ride, we would sometimes arrive at a picturesque picnic spot where lunch had been laid out for us on a table, complete with white table napery, silver and glasses, under the shade of a tree. Jock and Miss Ellie were tethered a short distance away under the watchful eyes of their mahouts whilst we wined and dined in splendour. In such circumstances, experience dictated that it was wise to tether the elephants at a distance from human food, as they have a preconceived idea that their monotonous menu of grass, leaves and tree bark deserves to be supplemented by a more varied human diet. Apparently, oranges are totally irresistible!

Gordon decided early on that he would walk with Jock for most of the rides rather than suffer bristles and the risk of his hips becoming permanently fused into an impossible angle! Off we would set, Miss Ellie leading, with Jock, Gordon and the trainer following, together with an armed ranger. This worked very well, but on one occasion, Miss Ellie spotted a bush, which obviously offered up a favourite delicious morsel and she was determined to reach it before Jock. Jock was having none of this and in an attempt to win the race, he ambled smartly up to Miss Ellie, nudged her and forgot that Gordon was in between. A sharp reprimand and a swish of a stick brought order to the situation, and Jock was clearly told that this behaviour was unacceptable. He put his trunk over Gordon's back as if to apologise. Thankfully, no damage was done and Gordon lives to tell the tale of what it is like to become squashed between two elephants!

All too soon, it was time to leave and say goodbye to our elephants. I was dreading this moment. Miss Ellie had gently and generously shared these few precious days with me and taught me so much about her species. I had washed her every day, fed her, held her enormous ears, scrubbed her toenails – four on her front feet, three on her rear feet, and examined her lined and wrinkled footpads, memorising her individual footprint so that I would know instantly where she had been in the bush. I had grown to know which was her favourite vegetation, and could recognise her unique rumblings when I drifted off to sleep. She had treated me with infinite gentleness and was now part of my life.

I went up to her, tears streaming down my face and we said our goodbyes to each other, her long trunk nuzzling over my body and sniffing me. I inhaled her moist, sweet breath for the last time, caressing her grey, floppy ears and gazing into those fathomless, dark eyes. Slowly, I turned away from this gentle giant and with Gordon's arm around my shoulders we went towards our car, both of us too overcome to say anything. Sobbing, I turned back for one last glimpse. I saw Miss Ellie toss her head, and flap her large ears – shaped like the map of Africa. She swung her trunk backward and forwards, and slowly ambled off into the bush where she belonged.

Jacqui greeted us warmly on our arrival back at Thetford House. We sat down to dinner with her, and recounted some of our recent experiences on safari. Whilst talking about our stay at Mana Pools, we remembered Joan suggesting that we should try to visit her friend the silversmith, Patrick Mavros, when we were in Harare. Jacqui immediately phoned him, confirming that he would be delighted to see us the following morning. As Jacqui was going into Harare to do some shopping, she would take us there and collect us later on when she had finished getting food and groceries. She was very concerned that the Zimbabwean dollar was starting to go into free fall, and wanted to stock up on essential supplies. We were astonished that in the couple of weeks we had been in the country, the amount we were getting to one pound sterling had risen from twenty to the pound to over fifty.

We were witnessing first-hand the collapse of a vibrant country's economy, and were horrified to learn that even the price of bread had doubled in the last week! How were these friendly, proud people ever going to manage to survive? Three years ago, we were told how Zimbabwe was the breadbasket for much of Africa, exporting their food surpluses to neighbouring countries. Now it seemed there was not going to be enough food to feed its own people. We felt very chastened about even considering buying luxury items such as silver, but Jacqui generously re-assured us that by spending some foreign currency and supporting the local work force, we could help this rapidly ailing country.

Jacqui dropped off at the Mavros' home the following morning, and a jovial giant of a man greeted us, and told us that we had only just missed Joan and Sarah. He felt he knew us already from all the stories they had shared of our stay at Mana Pools together. Patrick took us into his show room and there in front of us were displays of the most exquisite silver. There were elaborate candelabra of giraffe feeding off acacia trees. Jewellery, ranging from bracelets and necklaces to cufflinks and earrings incorporating the heads of hippos and elephants vied with salt cellars, pepper pots and other table ware. His work was breathtaking!

Gordon, being a metallurgist, was fascinated by the intricate detail of the work, so Patrick took us off to see the casting facility where it was all made before we were shown around the workrooms where local labour finished off the silver castings by hand, and polished each piece with infinite care. When we returned to the showroom, I had the impossible task of choosing some gifts to take back home for our family. Our sons each received a pair of hippo and elephant cufflinks, our daughter-in-law a bracelet with links of elephants' heads, and Gordon and I together chose presents for ourselves – salt and pepper pots shaped like hippos, and a pair of tiny elephants to remind us of Miss Ellie and Jock. I could easily have bought the whole showroom but common sense and limited funds prevailed.

Purchases made and carefully placed in elegant black boxes embossed with the now famous Mavros logo, Patrick invited us into his home where he served drinks on the stoep overlooking the rolling hills of his stunning property. Although we were on the outskirts of Zimbabwe's capital city, here we sat enjoying a magnificent panorama where zebra and giraffe grazed peacefully. He told us of his plans to start selling his beautiful pieces to shops in the UK, and was just negotiating a deal with a famous London store.

The sound of dogs barking announced the arrival of Jacqui and we said goodbye to this talented man, asking him to keep in touch with us, as we would love to buy some more of his work sometime in the future. A couple of years later we commissioned a small pair of African Wild Dogs as a wedding anniversary present to each other and a celebration of coming across a pack of these fascinating, endangered animals in Tanzania.

Many years on our family are now the proud owners of some of the first pieces Patrick made. We have met up with him in his showroom in London several times over the last few years, and, amazingly on a flight out to South Africa – one of those surprise chance meetings where we caught up with his news. He exports his work around the world where it adorns the tables and bodies of the rich and famous as collectors' items. I only wish we had had the foresight to buy many more presents for our family during that memorable visit to his studio when the Zimbabwean dollar bought so much because now the price of most of his pieces are beyond our means!

Again, it was time to say a further goodbye to Jacqui and Thetford House. As I got into the car waiting to take us to the airport, I had a premonition – we would never return to this very special place. As the car wound down the twisting road, I looked up the hill to where the house stood, and saw Jacqui waving in the distance. I said my own private farewells, wondering what the future might bring to Zimbabwe. I hoped it would somehow weather the seemingly inevitable storms, which, tragically, would eventually bring this incredibly beautiful and hospitable country to its knees.

In the grounds of Thetford House, Zimbabwe.

We drove half the length of Namibia to visit Fish River Canyon and were not disappointed. It is breathtaking in its grandeur, and we spent a morning walking along part of its rim, gazing into its depths in awe. It was well worth a very early start as the shadows and colours are at their best soon after sunrise. The intense silence and beauty of the canyon is spellbinding.

Chapter 11

Fish River Canyon, Namibia

In Zimbabwe, the tragic monetary collapse continued relentlessly and brought consequent unrest. Under the circumstances, we decided that we would be unwise to return to what had become our favourite country in Africa. What we were certain about was that we still needed to get our yearly African 'fix'. Gordon and I were typical examples of the well-known saying that once Africa gets into your blood it never leaves you, so once again we consulted John, our travel expert, and an invaluable source of suggestions and planning in the past. Our children were beginning to think that we alone were keeping John's travel firm in business!

Together we decided on something entirely different. Namibia sounded fascinating and beautiful, and John submitted a detailed itinerary for us to think over and modify if needed. When we saw how much it was going to cost we certainly needed to make some serious modifications!

John had planned an exciting three-week tour of the whole country with our own guide, camping in remote places, and the occasional overnight stay in a lodge to give us a bit of a break from bush showers and cooking over a campfire. This was going to be outside our budget, so we needed to do some creative thinking. We could obviously cut the time we would spend exploring this vast country, but as this was probably a 'one off' visit, we wanted to see as much as possible. Unfortunately, at this stage very few of our English friends shared our deep passion for Africa. They were fascinated and sometimes horrified by our various exploits, but preferred a more conventional holiday. However, when we had built our own home in South Africa they decided that perhaps Africa was not quite as scary as they had first thought, and visited us frequently!

The option of sharing this adventure with much loved friends was unfortunately, a non-starter. Just when it seemed impossible for us to go on this amazing trip, I phoned John and enquired whether he had other clients who wanted to visit Namibia and who might be prepared to share the cost of the trip with us. Initially, he was very doubtful about my suggestion, as the thought of two sets of valuable clients not getting on with each other and being forced to spend three weeks in close proximity seemed to him like a recipe for disaster.

A week after my phone call, John was back on the phone to me, saying that a couple had contacted him about arranging a visit to Namibia and were prepared to share with another couple to help keep their costs down! As I whooped with delight, John, ever the professional, suggested that we got in touch with the couple and come back to him if we all felt it could work. Several long phone calls later with Ann and Conrad, resulted in mutual agreement that we should contact John and start to organise our Namibian safari together.

It was a great leap of faith for us, but instinctively we felt that we could get on with each other and make the safari work for us all. Over the next few days, John worked tirelessly to adapt the trip to suit everyone. The only alteration to the schedule was that we wanted to go to the south of Namibia to visit the world's second largest canyon, the Fish River Canyon, whereas Ann and Conrad would miss this part and meet up with us in Windhoek to begin our safari together.

One sunny day in September, we landed at Windhoek's airport where we were met by the owner of the local safari firm, which would be looking after us for the next three weeks. Amazingly, he came originally from an area of Derbyshire only a few miles away from where we lived. We went to his home for a welcome breakfast and the all-important safety briefing on driving on Namibia's gravel roads. Afterwards, he took us to collect our hire car, and waved us off, saying he would collect us in four days' time here in Windhoek, and was looking forward to hearing all about our journey down south.

Nothing could have prepared us for the wide open spaces and the long straight roads as we drove to our first overnight stop at a lodge bordering the Kalahari Desert. Our maps were helpful on the main road south – we could hardly go wrong as this was the only road south. However, as soon as we turned off onto gravel our directions were somewhat rudimentary, with instructions measured in kilometres from one landmark to the next and it took a great leap of faith to believe we were even on the right road.

After half a day of driving, with each of us taking it in turns and Gordon's dire warnings about adverse road cambers and gravel surfaces when I was driving, we saw the signpost to our long-awaited destination. We continued down a narrow track of deep red Kalahari sand, Gordon concerned that we might get stuck in sand miles from nowhere, and questioning why we ever agreed to drive ourselves into the back of beyond. We were both tired, hot and worried after the overnight flight – hardly surprising none of our English friends wanted to come to Africa with us! We counted off the kilometres on the trip meter, anxious to discover whether we were still on the right track.

Eventually, in the distance, we saw some signs of habitation and Gordon drove triumphantly to the front of the lodge, only to stall the car just before he reached the sun awnings under which other cars were parked. Observing our predicament, some obliging gardeners pushed the car through the sand to a shaded parking space. The receptionist greeted us warmly, and organised a very welcome iced beer for us before showing us to our room.

We collapsed exhausted onto the large double bed after twenty-four hours of travelling. It was a miracle that we had made it to our first stop without mishap or getting lost! Driving around Namibia by ourselves in the next four days was certainly going to be different. In a sleepy haze, I gazed out of the large picture window in front of us, and watched some weavers dart in and out of an enormous nest in an acacia tree. In the distance, some deep red sand dunes formed a dramatic backdrop to miles and miles of desert wilderness. I saw a shape emerge at the base of one of the sand dunes and ignoring my tiredness and snoring husband, found my binoculars and focussed on my first sighting of an oryx, otherwise known as a gemsbok. *This* was Africa!

We were invited to go on a game drive later in the afternoon, so after a brief snooze, and a partial unpack in order to get into some more suitable clothing, we were soon perched up high in an open Land Rover, speeding across the arid, deserted landscape. Within a few minutes we came across a herd of gemsbok and were able to watch these striking antelope, which embody the spirit of the desert. Their vivid pale brownish-grey coats with black side stripes, long, black, flowing tails, the black and white masks on their faces, and their long straight horns distinguish them from all other antelope. We learnt that they can adapt to the extreme desert temperatures by allowing their body temperature to rise to 45 degrees centigrade. Although they drink regularly in the wet season when water is more freely available, they can exist in the dry season and in droughts by eating melons, bulbs and tubers as their only source of moisture. I was in a photographer's paradise! The background of red sand dunes and these elegant antelope silhouetted against a rapidly darkening sky provided me with some perfect shots.

We crawled up the dunes in the labouring vehicle until at last we were at the summit, and there spread before us was a vast panorama of the Kalahari and . . . a small table with an array of drinks and snacks! Yet again, John had organised a perfect lodge for the beginning of our Namibian adventure. We toasted each other, and settled down to watch the sun finally set. The brilliant stars of the Southern Hemisphere appeared in the clear, dark blue sky with not a hint of any light pollution anywhere. The silence was profound, and my weary body soaked in the healing powers of the vast African wilderness. So quiet was the silence that the stars seemed to buzz their own message from across the ages. If only we could bottle this magic and take it back to England with us as a soothing balm for the noise and bustle of the small island we call home.

We were up early the next morning, ready to go on a walk with some Khoisan Bushmen. After breakfast, we were taken out into the desert to meet three small men who were to be our guides for the next few hours. These people were tiny compared to me, barely reaching up to my shoulders – their skin, a vibrant yellow-red ochre, resembling the red of the Kalahari sand. Their faces bear no resemblance to the more usual African facial structure; their eyes slant in an almost oriental manner and their facial bones are finely sculptured. They were clad in loincloths made out of animal skins, and each carried a bow, with a quiver full of arrows, together with a small leather pouch attached to their loincloths. Two spoke no English, the third acting as an interpreter in very rudimentary English, explaining that the so-called Western culture was gradually eroding their ancient way of life. They were proud of their heritage and spoke with dignity about how their ancestors were the original hunter-gatherers going back many thousands of years.

No longer were they able to roam freely wherever they wanted; they and their families were confined mainly to reserves where they eked out a meagre existence by taking visitors out into the Kalahari and doing manual work for the land owners. Gradually, their way of life was disappearing, their children now receiving basic education with all the other perceived advantages of the twentieth century. I was saddened and depressed by the gradual loss of a culture – a self-sufficient one, able to teach us an infinite amount about sustainability in our wasteful modern world. But, who am I to deny them the benefits of modern day medicine and education? Surely, somehow each culture could co-exist and give each other something of real value?

Uncomfortable conflicting thoughts stayed in my mind during the next few hours. We learnt about the medicinal uses of plants and tubers. Whenever the Khoisan picked a plant for their own use they made sure that enough of the plant remained, thus ensuring future supplies. We watched them make animal snares with a piece of twine made from the meagre grass, the snares anchored by small stones until an unsuspecting bird or small animal ventured into the snare and was trapped. These three men mimed the actions of the bird walking into the trap, and squealed with delight at the imagined capture.

The Khoisan store water in blown-out ostrich eggs, and seal the hole with a plug made out of leaves from a plant that has anti-bacterial qualities. This ensures that the water remains fresh and sweet for over six months until it is needed in the dry season. The men came across one such water supply, guarded by branches of acacia thorns, and dug into the hard, unyielding earth until they uncovered the eggs to show us one of their precious water reserves. Their language is fascinating – a symphony of glottal and musical clicks. I tried in vain to imitate the sounds, much to their amusement. However hard I tried to speak a few words, and however hard they tried to show me where to place my tongue to make these sounds, I failed miserably!

We walked on into the desert, stopping occasionally to examine tracks of animals. The Khoisan would imitate the animal's behaviour – what it had been doing, where it had settled down to sleep, where it had walked off to, and how many hours ago it had been there. We were witnessing a map of the desert gradually come to life before our very eyes. The men demonstrated the expertise with which they used their arrows to bring down an animal, and the poison they used to tip the arrows to ensure that the animal died and did not suffer if they had not wounded it fatally and it had run off into the bush. They would track the wounded animal until they found it, however long it took. Everything of the killed animal was utilised – skin, sinews, bone, and, of course, the flesh for the pot. Eventually, we reached the Khoisan settlement where their families lived. The women greeted us shyly, and the children hid behind their mothers' legs, peering at us with their dark, enquiring eyes. Gradually, these children emerged from the protection of their mothers, fascinated by Gordon's video camera.

Making sure that it would not offend anyone, Gordon started to film some of their antics and then replayed it back to them. Like children the world over, they laughed and pointed and jumped up and down at their images on the tiny screen. I walked over to a small girl who was huddled by the open fire, clutching a bundle of cloth. Tenderly, she unwrapped the cloth, and there was a newborn baby fast asleep on her lap. The girl looked no older than ten and I wondered whose baby it was until the interpreter informed us that it was this young girl's first child, born a couple of days ago. With difficulty, I hid my feelings of utter surprise, and admired this peacefully sleeping infant, surrounded by its extended family of sisters and aunts.

I watched these women making necklaces from ostrich eggshells, and realised just how simple their lives are. They made use of everything the desert provided, and the desert provided everything. I sat down and watched as they chipped the tough eggshells into squares, which were painstakingly rounded off into circles before a hole was drilled through the middle. The women strung hundreds of these tiny beads onto grass strings to make necklaces to adorn themselves and any visitor who wanted to buy one. I am the proud owner of such a necklace, which is just as treasured as any piece of Patrick Mavros' jewellery.

We said our goodbyes and shook hands with everyone before we walked back to where our vehicle was waiting to transport us back into the twentieth century. I wondered how I would cope living the Khoisan way of life. Our time with them certainly put another slant on sustainable living, and our efforts at recycling and trying to be more 'green' seemed pathetic compared with the lives of these families.

After a good night's sleep, we set off early to complete our journey down to the south of Namibia to explore the Fish River Canyon. The long straight road with desert on either side stretched as far as the eye could see, and the heat haze produced shimmering mirages, until a cloud of dust appeared, signalling another vehicle coming in the opposite direction from the South African border. We greeted this novelty of a passing car with waves and smiles. We kept up our water intake with frequent sips from the ample supplies we had bought from a wayside petrol station, where we filled up the car and bought a snack lunch.

We stopped for a break and changed driving seats. The car thermometer registered 37 degrees inside but it was only when stepped out of the car that we felt the scorching effect of the overhead sun bearing down on us. In the searing temperature, we quickly circled the car to check the tyres, and gave our legs a welcome stretch. We set off again, gradually cooling off under the full blast of cold air from the vital and thankfully, very efficient air-conditioning unit.

Eventually, we turned off onto a gravel road where we had another hundred or so kilometres until we reached our next destination. We drove on endlessly, no other car in sight, but at least we had left the long, featureless straight road and we were now negotiating sudden bends, which took some getting used to. We recalled our safety briefing in Windhoek and the fact that all vehicles drive in the middle of the road. To negotiate a blind bend meant that you always pulled over into the rough, ungraded side of the road. Should you have the misfortune to come head to head with a vehicle, the only thing to do was to brake gently to avoid making the car skid, so that the potential collision speed is minimised!

After nearly two hours of nothing but gravel, dust, heat and desert, we were getting seriously concerned that we might have missed a turning which should have appeared by now. We stopped on a relatively straight bit of track and re-calculated how far we had travelled since leaving the tarmac road, debating whether we should turn back, when the welcome sight of a cloud of dust coming towards us heralded the arrival of a car. We didn't need to wave him down as he came to a stop and got out to see if he could help. We were indeed on the right track and our maths were correct! If we had continued another couple of kilometres, we would have seen our destination in the distance! With heartfelt thanks, we continued on our way, finally reaching the lodge after a day's hard driving.

As we were sitting down to a well-earned meal washed down with a bottle of wine, the manager of the lodge called us to the phone. Only our sons, immediate family and next-door neighbours in the UK had our contact details, so we hurried to the phone imagining some terrible disaster. Our relief was immense when we heard the tour organiser's voice calling from Windhoek to check that we had arrived safely! We returned to our meal and started to plan the next day's trip to the Fish River Canyon, before retiring to our chalet, which was perched on some rocks in a beautiful position overlooking the desert.

I woke suddenly in the middle of the night to the sound of rustling somewhere near our luggage. I switched on my torch, and looked in the direction of the sound, which promptly stopped. Was it a snake? I decided I had better wake Gordon, although I was less afraid of snakes than he was. At the mention of a possible snake in our room, Gordon left nothing to chance. Armed with my hiking stick, he examined every possible place it might be hiding.

Finding nothing, we turned off the light and tried to go back to sleep, only to hear the same rustling a couple of minutes later. We turned slowly and quietly in the direction of the sound and switched on the torch to see a small mouse scampering off. I suddenly realised it was after a bag of crisps in our emergency food supplies. The tasty morsels deposited on the veranda, we returned to our slumbers.

We set off at dawn the following day; we wanted to see the canyon in as many different lights as possible. Within a quarter of an hour we had parked the car and were standing on the rim of the second largest canyon in the world – the Grand Canyon in America being the biggest. It was impossible to take in the vast scene spread out before us. We gazed down to the bottom, 1,800 feet below, seeing the Fish River meander its way round massive bends. Most of the river was a grey green colour, as it was coming to the end of the dry season, and often the river disappeared completely into a series of pools.

The different layers of strata were clearly defined – black, red, orange and sandstone colours. Occasionally, the layers ran horizontally, then rose up vertically, the result of some cataclysmic event over 600 million years ago. We started to walk along the rim, meeting very few people that early in the morning. Slowly, the soft morning light grew stronger, and the shadows of the rocks became less intense and dramatic.

The going was tough over rocks and loose gravel, but the magnificent views were more than worth the effort in the ever-increasing heat. The river began to shimmer as the rising sun reached the bottom of the canyon. After an hour, we decided that we would have to turn back, as the heat radiating off the rocks was becoming too intense. Although the air was dry and we had no humidity to cope with, we did not want to risk sun or heatstroke.

We arrived back at our car and attempted to sit down on a rock, only to immediately jump up. It was like sitting on a hotplate! We sipped from our bottles of water and watched some tiny specks at the bottom of the canyon materialise into human beings. Slowly, these minute figures climbed up the winding path towards us. Finally, they hauled themselves up the last bit of path, and triumphantly celebrated their herculean achievement. We clapped and cheered their efforts, and learnt that they had spent the last five days walking the length of the canyon.

Full of admiration for them, we drove off in air-conditioned luxury, wishing we were several decades younger and infinitely fitter so that we could have made the same journey by foot. What an incredible experience to trek along the base of this deep canyon! We stopped off at numerous view points, and I took more photos, but soon realised the best of the dramatic light was fading; the rock strata was becoming flat and the colours washed out. Our pre-dawn start had certainly been worth the effort, and with one last glimpse of this incredibly beautiful scene, we set off back to the lodge for a late lunch and yet another siesta.

Gin and tonics in hand we watched another sunset over the desert, before having an early supper and retiring to bed. We had to be up at the crack of dawn the following day in order to complete the return journey to Windhoek before dark. This was going to be a tiring day's drive, but we both agreed that it had been well worth the long return trip to experience such dramatic scenery.

It was still dark when we had a snack breakfast, and as dawn was breaking, we set off towards Windhoek. Every hour or so, we took turns in the driving seat, and soon we were off the gravel track on the main road north and had no more navigational problems. It was just a question of keeping our speed down to the legal limit and remaining alert to oncoming traffic and the occasional goat or cow straying onto the road, not to mention the local population journeying with what seemed like all their worldly possessions stacked precariously in battered-looking bakkies.

Whilst Gordon was snoozing in the passenger seat, I saw a large sign marking the Tropic of Capricorn, which we had somehow previously missed. I came to a screeching halt to take a photo of this milestone, and we now have a picture of a half asleep husband propping up this rather dilapidated sign, pock-marked with the signs of target practice. Frequent stops for fuel and water broke the monotony and by late afternoon, we reached the outskirts of Windhoek and followed the directions to the car-hire garage where we came to a welcome stop. Before long, the tour organiser arrived and took us to our overnight lodge on the other side of Windhoek where we shared a welcome ice cold beer on the stoep with him and were de-briefed on our experiences.

We were on our second beer when his mobile rang. Apparently, a young English couple he had waved goodbye to the day before had come to grief and overturned their car on a gravel road. Apart from injured pride and a few bruises, they were not seriously hurt, and he arranged for another hire car to pick them up. This was a salutary lesson for us. I was relieved that we had no more driving to do during the next couple of weeks, and looked forward to relaxing and enjoying the scenery with someone else being responsible for our safety and finding the way around this vast and beautiful country.

We arranged a time to be picked up the following morning, and retired to our room overlooking the surrounding countryside of Windhoek. We re-organised our luggage, sent some clothes to be laundered overnight, and had a welcome shower in an effort to look presentable, as we were meeting our travelling companions and wanted their first impressions to be favourable! We need not have been concerned, as the rest of our holiday with Ann and Conrad was to be a fantastic shared marathon, travelling vast distances up to the north where Namibia meets Angola. Within a few of days, we were laughing together, hanging out our undies to dry on tent strings, and showering in the bush with a miniscule amount of water.

Sossusvlei is another photographer's paradise. Although the larger dunes are spectacular, I preferred the smaller ones with the occasional trees to provide an added interest. Again, this was well worth an early start to capture the intense shadows and early morning light. I was surprised how chilly the mornings were in the desert, and hot drinks were very welcome when we stopped for a picnic breakfast.

Chapter 12

Scorpions and Sand Dunes

We met up with Ann and Conrad in the garden of the tour operator's home, where we were introduced to them, together with Ian who was to be our guide and driver, and Petrus, a young Namibian youth who was Ian's helper. As we chatted over coffee, the remains of the camping gear were stowed away, together with our canvas bags, all carefully wrapped in tarpaulin to prevent the relentless red dust seeping into our clothes.

We were all excited, greatly looking forward to the trip, and set off full of expectation, having sorted out the seating arrangements. Conrad and Gordon decided to alternate sitting beside Ian in the front, and next to Petrus who sat behind Ian, with Ann and I relegated to the back seats of this long wheelbase Land Rover.

A massive trailer carried our luggage and all the camping equipment needed for the next two weeks, with basic food and drink supplies, which Ian would replenish en route as and when he could. The seating arrangements worked so well that throughout the whole of the trip we all stuck to our original arrangement, and when the men offered to change seats with Ann and me, we declined with no hesitation. We were set in our ways, knowing exactly where we each had our cameras, bags, binoculars and all the other paraphernalia women the world over seem to collect, and were quite happy chatting in the back. Petrus was often re-charging his batteries and more often than not fast asleep!

Ian drove us up to the highest vantage point overlooking Windhoek and placed a map on the bonnet of the Landy, showing us our route and where we would be stopping for our first night. He also showed us the invaluable shortwave radio, instructing us how to operate it if we ever had to use it in an emergency, together with the strictest warning never to tread on it when clambering around the Landy as our lives could well depend on this vital piece of equipment being in full working order.

We set off, chatting nineteen to the dozen, getting to know each other. Ian was a stocky, dark haired young man, totally occupied in giving us the experience of a life-time. His knowledge of flora and fauna was immense and the love he so obviously had for his country was infectious. Petrus was training to be a qualified guide, but his command of English was rudimentary, and so Ann and I took it upon ourselves to teach him some basic English during some of the long journeys – when he was awake! Ian joked about how Petrus could sleep standing up, and we became used to the friendly banter that went on between the two of them.

We were soon swapping life histories, which were gradually enlarged upon as the days went by, and we settled down to a relaxed first day together, stopping for a picnic lunch overlooking the vast vista of the rolling hills of the arid, desert landscape dotted with the occasional shrub and tree. The colours of this almost lunar landscape fascinated me. I never imagined such bleak scenery could be so beautiful. Red earth and boulders mixed with grey shale, and sandstone stretched as far as the eye could see, the relentless sun beating down on this vast, inhospitable area.

There is nothing like having an essential loo stop in the middle of nowhere to bring down any remaining barriers between strangers. With nothing but the Landy to provide any privacy, Ian instructed the men to one side and Ann and I to the other, having first ascertained that there were no cars, bakkies or lorries in sight for miles. Being the perfect host, he tactfully reminded us that he could provide a shovel and loo paper if required! We would have ample warning of any approaching traffic as plumes of grey dust in the far distance heralded anything on the gravel road.

We soon got used to rapidly winding up our windows to prevent being covered with dust when a vehicle passed. Just the warning 'Windows!' was enough to galvanise into action anyone who was sitting next to a window, and many a forty winks were interrupted by this one word of warning. This manoeuvre was soon refined to take place at the last possible moment, as there was no air-conditioning, and the only way we could get a much-needed cooling breeze was to have all the windows open. Within half an hour, any claims Ann and I had to a specific hairstyle disappeared. This was remarkably liberating, although by the end of each day we all looked forward to having some sort of shower to get rid of the fine dust, which settled into every nook and cranny.

Our first overnight stop was at a small guest farm about sixty kilometres outside the Namid-Naukluft National Park – the largest conservation area in the whole of Africa. Our hosts who were also a consultant cardiologist and a dental surgeon, made us feel at home instantly. Our rooms were in comfortable tin roofed chalets, and as we sat down to afternoon cups of tea and the now obligatory scones, jam and cream, Ian briefed us on the next couple of days.

Early next morning Gordon and I were to go on a light aircraft flight over the famous Sossusvlei sand dunes and part of the Skeleton Coast. Ann and Conrad decided to forego this excitement, and more than once, I wondered if they were being very prudent. Thoughts of forced landings in the desert or on the Skeleton Coast were uppermost in my mind! Once our dawn flight was over, Ian would pick us up and return us to the farm, where we would all spend the rest of the day exploring the area together. Now, however, we had been in the Landy for most of the day, and we all decided to go for a walk, as we needed some exercise.

Accompanied by the owners' dogs, we set off in the refreshingly cool late afternoon breeze and took some photos of the setting sun before returning to our rooms. I was delighted that Ann was a keen photographer, and Gordon was equally delighted that she also was more technically able than I was, so they spent hours discussing the minutiae of lenses, filters and settings. Conrad and I tended to be the 'point and shoot' type, much to the disappointment of our respective spouses. Despite this handicap, over the years I have managed to take the occasional wildlife photo that has been published, even though I was never as proficient as Ann.

After supper and the most delicious bottle of Pinotage we had ever tasted, Ann and Conrad decided on an early night to recover from their overnight flight. Gordon and I had a nightcap with our host who told us he was in the process of developing medication for heart patients from the venom of scorpions. He invited us to have a look at his laboratory, and then suggested we went out into the desert surrounding his lodge, where we could watch him catching scorpions for his research. Nothing daunted, Gordon and I set off with him, together with his two small children, who were clearly used to going out with their father on such expeditions. Armed only with an ultra-violet light and a couple of jam jars with screw tops, we ventured into the star-lit desert on a scorpion hunt!

As soon as the ultra-violet light was switched on, we watched in amazement as scorpions, small and large, fluoresced in the dark, and before long the jam jars were full of these poisonous creatures. I had absolutely no idea that the desert was so full of these potentially lethal invertebrates – everywhere we looked there were the illuminated purple-blue shells of crawling scorpions! I stood rooted to the spot, looking down at my feet, clad only in open sandals. At that moment, our host looked at his two visitors' sandal-clad feet and burst out laughing. 'I ought to have told you to put proper shoes on!' was his only comment.

I looked down at his feet and saw that both he and his children were wearing gumboots! Murmuring to myself that at least if we got stung we had instant medical care on hand, we cautiously made our way back to the lodge to watch how the scorpions were milked for their venom and then returned to the wild. Apparently, this was an ideal evening for such an operation as the wind was getting up and scorpions are at their most active in the wind.

We chuckled together as Gordon made certain that there were no such creatures anywhere in our room, and reminded ourselves that from now on we would carefully shake out our shoes and clothing before getting dressed each morning. Somehow, we had managed to forget to do this, erroneously believing that as we were not in the more familiar bush, neither were the creepy crawlies!

Our sleep was fitful, as a howling gale developed and the tin roof sounded as though it was going to take off. Gust after gust seemed to lift the roof, slamming it back down onto the rafters with a metallic crash. Sand blasted viciously against the windows, reminiscent of a hailstorm, and when I wasn't worrying about scorpions I spent the rest of the night worrying about our early morning flight. Surely, we wouldn't be able to fly in such conditions? Dawn broke and a knock on our door woke me when I had at last sunk into a deep sleep. Ian told us that he was going to telephone the local pilot to see if he was able to fly us. He returned a few minutes later to inform us that it was still too windy to take off and our flight was cancelled, so we could go back to sleep for another hour or so.

Exhausted from lack of sleep we gathered for breakfast, Ann and Conrad looking as though they had experienced another sleepless overnight flight. We all decided that we would take it easy and have a gentle day, driving minimal distances locally on a photographic safari in the desert. We certainly had a relaxing time, learning about the desert flora from Ian, recharging our batteries and taking reel after reel of photos of this most incredible landscape.

Ian drove the Landy up a mountain to the perfect place for sundowners, and a further opportunity to photograph another vivid sunset, made all the more spectacular by the dust in the atmosphere. We were so fortunate that Ian was a keen photographer; he took endless care getting us to the right spot at the right time for the ultimate photo. This evening was to prove something of a trial though, as the wind got up yet again, and blew so strongly that our tripods had to be anchored. Gordon and Conrad hung on to them for dear life to prevent them from taking off.

It was to be an early night, as we had to be up by 4.30 a.m. for the journey to Sossusvlei and the world famous sand dunes. We all prayed that the wind would abate, otherwise our day would be ruined by sandstorms and zero visibility. Thankfully, our prayers were answered, and we set off before dawn so that we could be there in time for the magical moment of sunrise. We were not disappointed. We watched in awe as gradually, the sun lit up the top of one of the highest dunes and over the next hour, we gazed entranced as the deep red sand changed colour, the emerging daylight eventually lighting up these incredible, ever-moving natural structures.

In the far distance, tiny trees at the base of one of them started to produce shadows, and the sand changed from pink to orange, the oldest dunes being the most intense red. Ian told us how these had developed over millions of years, the sand being swept from the Orange River into the Atlantic Ocean, only to be transported by the Benguela current back onto land, thus forming these mighty structures. The highest of these rolling hills of sand is apparently over 656 feet high, and each has its own name, the most famous being Dune 45 – the most photographed one in the world. We certainly added to the number of photographs taken, wondering if our ample supply of film would be sufficient to see us through the next couple of weeks.

Slowly Ian drove us deeper into the Namid-Naukluft Park, the Landy coping admirably on the rutted surface and the drifting sand. I was spellbound at the ever changing views, and both Ann and I had to stop ourselves from yelling 'Stop!' whenever a new angle appeared before us. Ian knew his sand dunes though, and without fail managed to find us the right spot at the right time for yet more photographs.

Eventually we reached the end of the track, where more dunes surrounded us. We stopped at the edge of a large pan, which every ten years or so filled up with water from the underground rivers. Now it was rock hard and grey, devoid of water for a couple of years, but Ian showed us a picture that he had taken then – the massive pyramids of sand reflected in the crystal clear water and the desert blooming into an oasis of green.

I noticed how vegetation partially covered the more stable dunes even after several years of drought, getting just enough moisture from the deep underground rivers and the moisture from the daily morning fogs that drifted in from the Atlantic Ocean. We got out of the Landy, and Petrus and Ian set to work preparing brunch for us, whilst the four of us walked around gazing in awe at the scenery.

Conrad decided to climb to the top of a nearby dune, whilst the rest of us scrambled up a less steep slope, rapidly realising that walking up a shifting bank of sand was hard work – often one step forward and two backwards. Soon I was on all fours, hauling myself up by grabbing what meagre vegetation there was in an effort to reach the top where Gordon was standing. He hauled me up the last few feet and when I saw Ann struggling, I reached out to give her a helping hand, whilst Petrus broke off from his culinary duties and dashed to give her a shove from behind.

We collapsed, laughing hysterically, in a sandy heap at the summit before shaking off the sand, and making sure our cameras were still safely packed in their protective bags. Once we had recovered, we set about taking more photos of the rolling panorama stretching far into the distance, including the sight of the athletic Conrad waving triumphantly from the high summit of another dune. After slipping and sliding our way down, we tucked into the brunch as though we had never had a square meals in our lives, before slowly making our way to our next stop – the Sesriem Canyon.

This canyon is the much smaller cousin of the Fish River Canyon, little over a mile long, a hundred feet deep and only six feet wide in some places. Nonetheless, it was well worth the detour, and Gordon, Conrad and Ian clambered down the path to the base of the canyon, while Ann and I decided to take a leisurely stroll along the rim, peering down into the canyon's depths. It was hot and we were content to let the men struggle in the overhead midday sun. However, curiosity soon got the better of me, and leaving Ann with Petrus, I started to descend into the canyon, gazing up in awe at the colourful layers of sedimentary rock, laid down some 20 million years ago.

I got some idea of what it must be like to be at the bottom of the Fish River Canyon, and was glad I had decided to make the effort, meeting up with the men when they appeared from around a corner. Hot and red-faced, their water flasks exhausted, and gasping for some liquid, they told me that there were some rock pools still filled with water from the last rains but had decided not to quench their thirst with this murky water.

We struggled up the rocky path to reach the Landy, and the large containers of water in the enormous cool box. Ian always topped up the water at each stop we made, in case of an emergency in the desert when our very lives would depend on having enough liquid to survive. I realised the importance of this place for the early traders in the desert because after many years of drought, there was still some life-giving water available here.

The following day we made our way to Walvis Bay, Ian's hometown, where he was going to stop off to stock up with all the food and drink we needed for the following week. After a day's hard motoring along gravel roads with the desert on either side of us, we arrived at this great sea port, the fresh, salty tang of the sea reaching our nostrils long before we could see the Atlantic Ocean.

Ian left us to walk along the long seafront where flocks of flamingos were feeding off the rich pickings on the shoreline, providing great photo opportunities when they took off and landed in their hundreds, their vivid pink and white feathers an intense splash of colour against the grey seascape. We had arranged to meet Ian at a fish restaurant, whilst Petrus was going to spend the night with some of his numerous relations.

Over drinks, Ian instructed us to make the most of what he described as our last civilised meal for some time. From now on, we were at the mercy of his cooking and whatever fresh supplies he could buy en route. After a delicious and satisfying meal of freshly caught fish, we walked back to our overnight lodge.

It seemed strange to be back in the middle of a town and I looked forward to the next part of our trip where we would be out of touch with all the so-called amenities of television, hairdryers and air-conditioning. We were about to explore the vast open areas of Namibia, and travel right up to the border with Angola.

Gordon taking a walk down the track to our guest house near to Sossusvlei.

Driving up the Skeleton Coast was one of the many highlights during three wonderful weeks in Namibia. The swirling sea fogs that sometimes made driving difficult only enhanced the absolute desolation. Aside from the mists, we had to contend with the drifting sands. We drove for twelve hours and during that time only came across one vehicle! Our vehicle and trailer with all the camping gear behaved impeccably – it is not the place to have a breakdown! Shipwrecks, seals and a hyena provided added interest to our journey.

Chapter 13

The Skeleton Coast and Damaraland

I recalled Ian's latest warning about the potential quality of food to come and decided on a hearty breakfast the following morning! We were soon leaving civilisation behind, motoring along the first bit of the infamous Skeleton Coast. In front of us was a straight, rough gravel road with mile after mile of desert on the right and the grey, rolling Atlantic Ocean on the left. An hour later, we stopped at the seal colony at Cape Cross, and walked down to the edge of the ocean. The noise of honking seals, the stench of ammonia and fish remains overwhelmed our senses.

Ian re-assured us that after twenty minutes or so the stench would hardly be noticeable, so I set to the task of taking some photos of this vast panorama of hundreds of seals, their bodies packed together – mothers, fathers, youngsters and pups, all vying for the best position on a piece of narrowing shore as the tide came in. The noise was deafening as mothers called for their pups and the old bulls asserted their authority to anyone who attempted to usurp their piece of shoreline. Soulful eyes looked up at me, whilst my eyes streamed from the assault of ammonia, and looking round, I saw that Ann, overcome by the stench, had returned to the Landy.

I decided that enough was enough, and went to join Conrad and Gordon who were looking at a large cross, a replica of the original one the Portuguese explorer Diego Cao placed there when he landed in 1486. I wondered what his thoughts were when he arrived on this desolate coast, and strolled off for a short walk along the shore, the noise of the seals blending with the massive Atlantic rollers crashing onto the sand. Back at the Landy, Ian told us that he was going to drive for another half hour or so and then we would stop for a coffee break, well away from the malodorous seals.

We stopped at the remains of a shipwreck, seeing first-hand why the Skeleton Coast earned its title. During the next couple of days, we witnessed many such shipwrecks littering the coast together with the bleached bones of whales, which formed surreal, architectural sculptures in the stony beachscape. Occasionally, we came across derelict rigs used for mining minerals. Sea birds perched on precariously built nests around these massive wooden and rusted metal structures, which moaned and rattled in the wind.

I grabbed a fleece to protect me from the vicious onshore wind, and sat down, dipping a rusk into a steaming hot mug of coffee. The sun had disappeared under a low, incoming mist and I realised for the first time since arriving in Namibia that I was feeling distinctly chilly. As Petrus packed up the mugs, I walked a little distance from the Landy, and was amazed to see some animal tracks. Ian came over to examine them, and declared they were the tracks of a hyena. We followed the spoor for a short while when Ian suddenly pointed into the distance to a lone hyena, skulking off towards a dilapidated rig. How an animal could survive in such an inhospitable terrain beggars belief. Ian told us that very occasionally, desert lions are spotted on the shoreline but he had never been lucky enough to see any.

Our journey took us inland where we escaped the mist and the temperatures rose to their more usual scorching heat. Ian pulled off the track and took us for a short walk, certain that we would find some garnets. Sure enough, on careful inspection, there, in the gravelly sand were tiny red garnets littered all over the desert. Ian re-assured us that they were of no use to anyone, so I picked up a few of these tiny gemstones, no bigger than a pinhead, and slipped a couple into my trouser pocket.

I was used to the old adage that we were to 'take only photos and leave only footprints', but seeing the vast amount of these minute red stones, scattered everywhere, I decided not to feel too guilty. Later, Ian showed us a strange looking plant, which we were not to touch under any circumstances, as this was protected. It was the unique Welwitschia Mirabilis, a plant which grows nowhere else on earth. Its two, strap-shaped leaves, shredded by many decades of thrashing by the desert winds, spread horizontally across the dry earth, producing the weirdest, ugliest plant imaginable.

The Welwitschia Mirabilis grows 8–15 centimetres a year, depending on the moisture it receives; some are estimated to be over 1,000 years old. Gordon made a rough estimate of the length of one of these strange plants, to give us some idea of how old it was, and after a complicated calculation, we reckoned that it was about 700 years old.

Further along the coastline we stopped for a picnic lunch. Petrus surprised us by producing large, individual cardboard cartons each containing a veritable feast of chicken legs, rolls, hard-boiled eggs, salad, fruit and cake. We teased him about his wonderful cooking whereupon his now familiar grin spread from ear to ear, lighting up his handsome, black face. He told us in broken English how Ian had sent him to an hotel in Windhoek to collect these pre-packed meals.

All memories of a hearty breakfast put aside, we tucked into this feast, as Ian told us that we would not be eating again until we reached Terrace Bay, our overnight stop at the furthest most point along the Skeleton Coast. Driving a vehicle beyond this point was not permitted. This was going to be a long haul, and we would not be stopping unless we had to, as the Skeleton National Park regulations stipulated that we had to reach our accommodation before dark.

We arrived at the park entrance an hour later and Ian disappeared into a cabin by the gate with our passports and the essential entry permit. Whilst he was completing the formalities, we strolled off to examine the gate that barred our way. Skulls and cross bones were painted over the entrance and two enormous whalebones were arched over the rough gravel road – a salutary warning to anyone entering this deserted coast.

Formalities over, we passed under the whalebones to continue our journey along the Skeleton Coast. Stories of shipwrecks and failed heroic rescue attempts rang in our ears as Ian told us about the numerous disasters and explorations, evidence of which littered this beautiful but deadly area. To add to the atmosphere, the sun disappeared behind a swirling, thick mist, and we saw life-giving moisture collect on the windscreen. All around us, the colour of the desert faded into grey, mimicking the grey gravel along which we were travelling.

After a couple of hours of driving, meeting no other vehicles at all, we were startled to see a car coming towards us flashing its headlights. We stopped and drew alongside, only to find two pretty, but very worried, French women who thought they were lost. How exactly they came to be in this situation was a mystery, as there were very few turn-offs and all of these were marked clearly with the exact number of kilometres to the exit in large lettering. Ian patiently showed them on his map where they were, and how they had better get a move on to reach the entrance gates by nightfall, otherwise they would be heavily fined. We checked that they also had an adequate supply of water, said our adieus and went our respective ways.

We drove for hours, counting off the kilometres at each signpost, and seeing no other vehicles. Occasionally, the sun would re-appear only to be hidden by the incoming mists, which sometimes were so dense that Ian had to switch on the headlights. The sound of the Landy's tyres against the rough gravel track, the moaning of the wind, occasionally strong enough to sway the vehicle, and the ever-present background noise of the waves crashing against the shore were hypnotic enough to lull me to sleep. Ann and I were woken by the announcement that we were within twenty kilometres of Terrace Bay, and looking out of the window, I saw faint gleams of sunlight breaking through the mist.

Terrace Bay loomed into view. It was originally an old mining settlement but now featured a small collection of buildings erected mainly for fishermen, with the vital petrol and water filling pumps, a bar and a restaurant. Ian informed us that he had been able to book the President of Namibia's fishing lodge for us all! Suitably impressed, we stretched our legs and looked around at this desolate place, an overall colour of grey, which matched the ocean and shoreline.

Gannets, cormorants and gulls flocked overhead, their calls mingling with the sound of the huge waves relentlessly pulling the stony beach back and forth. We entered the fishing lodge, and I was taken aback by the large conference room with a huge boardroom table – an incongruous reminder of who normally stayed here for his annual fishing trip in January. Our rooms were simple and functional, and after a quick wash and brush up, we gathered on one of the small terraces facing the ocean.

As soon as the sun had set we went indoors to warm up, and after a couple of sundowners, we decided to treat Ian and Petrus to a meal at the restaurant where we had a delicious, nourishing hot stew together, joking that Ian had warned us often enough about his cooking. We suggested that a good meal was in order before we set off into the camping part of our journey the following day!

On the wall behind the bar, I noticed an incredible photograph of a couple of desert lions strolling along the Skeleton Coast. They were seen several years ago, but not since, so I mentally crossed them off my 'hope to see' list. The one animal I was really hoping to see was the desert elephant, and Ian assured me that he would do everything he could to fulfil this wish. He had also organised a day with trackers to search for the rare and elusive black rhinos during the time we were to spend camping in Damaraland.

Strangely, I was not concerned about the lack of wildlife during this trip. The stunning scenery of the past week had been more than enough to fill my senses, and I was happy and relaxed to let wildlife take a back seat for once. I lay in bed that night, with the windows open, listening to the waves crashing onto the Skeleton Coast and fell asleep, thinking how very fortunate we were to experience this great wilderness – one of the least visited places on earth.

Gordon and I were up at dawn the following morning, and quietly brewed a cup of tea, grabbing a rusk before going out onto our terrace. The wind had dropped overnight and the sky was clear, the rising sun lighting up the ocean and its massive waves that rolled in relentlessly onto the shore. In the distance, we saw Conrad doing a bit of beachcombing, so we joined him, and together we strolled along the shoreline, taking care not to get in the way of any extra large rogue breakers. One slip could easily sweep anyone out to sea, and the vicious undertow would mean instant disaster.

I sat down higher up the shore and examined the beautiful pebbles – red, green, purple and orange stones worn smooth by the constant tumbling of the surf. The heat of the sun surprised me, as it was unusual for the mists to burn off so rapidly. A little sunlight transformed the grey, fog-covered scenery of yesterday to a sparkling, blue-green seascape, flecked with the white spume of the breaking waves. I was thankful that I had seen both the menacing, cold atmospheric scenery as well as the colourful, sun-baked Skeleton Coast, both equally as beautiful and deadly.

We checked out of the park, and once more, we were on our way, leaving the Atlantic Ocean and its icy Benguela current behind us. We were soon roasting in the heat of a relentless sun, thankfully relieved by the breeze coming through the Landy's windows. Along the gravel road, the familiar red sand dunes stretched far into the distance on either side. After a couple of hours, Ian swung off to the right, and almost immediately, we found we were driving along a dried-up river bed, much to our amazement. He explained that this was the easiest way to get to where we were camping for the next few nights. Thank heavens we were not driving by ourselves, and we were equally relieved that we were with someone who knew his way in the desert.

Occasionally, we saw a few tracks of vehicles, but overall we were travelling on virgin sand. As we reached a group of trees, we slowed down and stopped. Ian announced that we would have a picnic lunch under the shade of these tall, impressive trees – anaboom or ana trees. Folding chairs and a table, complete with a tablecloth appeared from the trailer, and soon we were sitting down to our picnic in the middle of a river bed, surrounded by sand dunes and mountains.

Appetites more than satisfied, Petrus packed up the picnic, refusing gracefully but firmly all our offers of help, and on we drove, the four-wheel drive coming into its own in the loose sand. We climbed out of the river bed and reached the top of a high sand dune, stopping for a view of the rolling desert several hundred feet below. Ian turned round, smiling at us, and without any warning started to drive down the steep sand dune. The men were speechless, whilst Ann and I screamed in horror, clutching onto the window frames as the bonnet of the Landy disappeared from view and all we could see was the deep valley below us.

Very slowly, we reached the bottom of the dune. A smiling Ian informed us that had he told us what he was going to do, no doubt all of us would have got out and walked back to the Skeleton Coast. Petrus just shrugged his shoulders, rolled his eyes upwards and smiled – he was obviously used to Ian's exploits.

I got my breath back, dared to open my eyes, and saw we were now travelling across a wide-open valley. Suddenly, Ian gave a whoop of delight, pointing to a group of desert elephants – mere specks in the far distance. He was concerned not to get too close immediately, as the trailer in tow would make it difficult to take evasive action should these desert giants take a dislike to us.

Slowly, we approached these incredible animals who were peacefully feeding from the leaves of some acacia trees, resting every so often in the scant shade. We counted five adult females, a teenager and a calf of no more than four months, making us all the more aware that we should not approach them too closely, as the mother would be very protective of her calf. We stopped a couple of hundred yards away and then moved a little closer – still they were relaxed, so moving even closer, I took photo after photo of these rare desert animals.

Somehow, Ian had to drive past them although there was more than enough space for us. Just as we were drawing alongside them, the mother trumpeted her displeasure; the teenager then decided to be a delinquent show-off, and trumpeting along with his mother, started to chase us. Ian stopped the Landy, and the teenager came to an abrupt halt. He shook his big ears at us and promptly returned to the rest of the herd. We were enthralled at this special sighting. So rare are desert elephants that there had been several trips when Ian had never even caught a glimpse of them.

Once on our way again, Ian told us about these special creatures and how over thousands of years their bodies have adapted to desert living, having several notable differences to the more familiar African elephant. Their feet are flatter and larger to make walking on the desert sand easier, and their trunks longer to enable them to reach water below the course of dried-up river beds. They have longer legs to help with the vast distances they have to cover in the desert, and so that they can reach the higher branches of trees for much needed nourishment.

Food is never plentiful for these elephants. Therefore, their bodies are smaller, resulting not only in them needing less food, but also their smaller bodies will absorb less heat, which is a great advantage in the punishing temperatures they have to endure. Finally, their tusks are shorter and more brittle than the ordinary African elephant, possibly due to the lack of minerals in their diet. I pondered the marvel of nature, how it can adapt, and hoped I would get another glimpse of these extraordinary animals sometime in the next few days.

Eventually, in the middle of Damaraland we came to the entrance of the campsite, which was soon to be our temporary home. We signed in, and drove past the few tents that were pitched close together next to a couple of huts. A further ten minutes' driving and we came to the perfect site – cleared of any vegetation that might have harboured snakes. We overlooked a dry river bed and there were trees around us to provide a little welcome shade.

Petrus leapt out of the Landy, and produced the folding chairs and table, whilst Ian miraculously produced some cold drinks for us, instructing us to sit down and relax whilst they got on with the task of setting up camp. We instantly ignored these instructions, wanting to help, but soon saw that we were getting in their way, and retired chastened, to sit down and watch as chaos reverted into order. Ian and Petrus put up two small tents with the minimum of fuss – they preferred sleeping out in the open, Petrus on top of the trailer and Ian underneath it! They erected a communal shower tent and long-drop loo tent a little way off at the back of our tents. Without further ado, Petrus invited us to inspect our sleeping quarters. Our luggage was placed neatly on the floor between two full-sized camp beds, made up with pillows, sleeping bags and sheets that were already turned down ready for us.

A rug between the two beds added the finishing touch. My smiles and profuse thanks to Petrus produced the usual broad grin of delight, and off he went, whistling a cheerful tune, to finish sorting out the kitchen area with Ian, only to come back with a very woebegone look on his face. Ian helped explain that somehow between the two of them they had forgotten to pack the canvas washbasins to enable us to wash our hands and faces.

The look on Petrus' face suggested that he had forgotten something far more serious – such as food or drink. It was a relief to know it was the mere absence of a washing bowl! Petrus appeared with a couple of small plastic containers, still apologising with numerous 'sorry, sorry, sorry mams' and an expression of absolute desolation and incredulity that we could manage to wash our faces and hands each morning in a small Tupperware bowl placed on the ground. No amount of reassurance could convince him, until the following morning when we performed our ablutions perfectly satisfactorily, and he continued his duties with the usual cheery grin on his face.

I watched as the kitchen and food storage area was finally sorted out, the pièce de résistance being a screen, which we immediately named the 'green baize door', explaining to Ian that in England this demarked the area behind which staff worked so hard to keep a household running smoothly. As dusk approached, a campfire was lit and soon the aroma of our dinner was wafting through on the gentle breeze. We relaxed and chatted softly to each other, not wanting to break the spell of perfect sunset. Sipping another gin and tonic, I was musing to myself that life really couldn't get much better than this, when out of nowhere three desert elephants silently drifted into sight. The setting sun silhouetted their huge, grey bodies as they walked past our camp along the river bed, their shapes dissolving into the night like ghostly apparitions.

Gordon and I slept like the proverbial logs that night, but, apparently, poor Conrad had to make several trips to the loo by torchlight. As we tucked into a full English breakfast, he wisely made do with tea and dry toast to settle his stomach. He decided to stay in camp with Petrus, to catch up on some much needed sleep, whilst the rest of us would go and explore the surrounding area where there was some rock art we all wanted to see.

We made certain that Conrad had everything he needed, and set off for Twyfelfontein, where a young Namibian woman guided us around the most incredible site of ancient rock engravings. Keeping to the rough paths, we clambered after her, up the slopes of a sandstone table mountain, which flanked a large open valley, and soon I was gazing in awe at engravings made by Stone Age hunter-gatherers some 6,000 years ago.

We trekked from site to site, trying to ignore the stifling heat, which radiated from the rocks. Each site was different, and we were shown engravings of giraffe, ostrich, elephant and rhino. To me, the most evocative of all the engravings were the human handprints, and the animal and human footprints – I wondered who had created such masterpieces so many thousands of years ago. What sort of people were they, and what kind of lives did they live in this arid, beautiful but desolate area of the world? As I took photo after photo, Gordon tried to create some meagre shade to enhance the engravings as the faint shadows produced some added shading and shape.

We climbed down steep slopes, over huge boulders, which our guide sprung over like the proverbial goat, but which we had to negotiate with extreme caution. Ann and I found the best way down was on our backsides, much to our guide's amusement, and eventually, even Gordon was reduced to this method. We staggered back to find Ian, looking as cool as the proverbial cucumber, waiting in the shade of a makeshift piece of canvas where the guides rested.

I looked at my watch and was amazed that we had been on the go for a couple of hours, and after a drink of much needed cool water, we set off to see the so-called Organ Pipes. We walked down the narrow valley, its sides of lined with vertical lines of dolerite columns, not unlike the Giant's Causeway in Northern Ireland. Here, these structures were in much better condition as they were not subject to the continual erosion from the sea. Slender towers of greyish black dolerite, packed together as the result of violent volcanic activity, reached high above our heads, creating a surreal landscape against the clear brilliant blue sky. Although we were equipped with sunhats and glasses, the intense sun and lack of cloud cover made us feel as if were being baked in a pizza over. We decided to call it a day and return to camp to see how Conrad was, and take a well-earned siesta after lunch.

Thankfully, Conrad was well on the way to recovery, and was able to join us for lunch in the shade of the trees, which surrounded our little enclave. After copious drinks of water, I decided I had catch up with a bit of laundry. For a small charge, local women would wash and press shirts and trousers for us. It was good to be able to help these people earn some extra money. However, our 'smalls' were our own responsibility. Petrus brought Ann and me a large bucket of hot water, and we crouched over our two plastic basins washing out socks, knickers and pants, chatting like two old washerwomen, whilst Gordon decided to have a bush shower.

Petrus was now in his element, as one of his main tasks was to make certain there was enough hot water whenever we needed it. He was continually making sure that the campfire had enough wood, strolling around the camp surrounds collecting dead wood, so that he could keep a huge bucket of water on the boil, ready for hot drinks, showers and washing-up whenever needed.

Once our womanly tasks were completed and our washing was decorating the guy ropes of our tents, I decided to follow Gordon's example and have a shower before my siesta. Wrapped in a large towel I made my way to the shower, Petrus following faithfully behind with a bucket of water with which he then filled the shower bucket, before hauling it up the tree branch overhanging the shower area. I turned on the tap, first making certain that the tap would always remain within my reach, as fond recollections of my first bush shower in Zimbabwe sprang to mind. I stood under the shower only to let out a shriek. The water was virtually scalding! I rapidly turned it off, and summoned my long-suffering husband, who was fast asleep in the tent.

A bleary-eyed Gordon appeared at the same time as Ian and Petrus, each of them thinking that I had, at the very least, been bitten by a snake. As politely as possible from behind the shower tent, I asked for a bucket of cold water, as I had no wish to be boiled alive. Petrus ran off to get another bucket of water, insisting that he should sort out the temperature for me. This did not seem a very practical idea, as I was naked, so Gordon did the necessary, and soon I was soaping and shampooing myself, removing the ingrained red sand and dust of the previous twenty-four hours. I even managed to save enough water for a good minute of blissfully cool water trickling down over me. Heaven! I was now ready for a welcome afternoon nap.

By this time, Gordon was fully awake and somewhat grumpy by the interruption to his siesta. He strolled off to the loo tent and I settled down with a book. A few minutes later, he appeared at the back of our tent, roaring with laughter. 'What is the most awful thing that can possibly happen when you go to the loo here? he asked.' My imagination ran riot, but I decided to play this one carefully so professed total ignorance. By now, he was totally beside himself with laughter and everyone gathered round wondering what on earth was going on. At last, between gasps, he apologized to Ian for destroying the carefully dug long-drop, which was now no longer a long-drop. When he sat on the seat frame, the walls of the log-drop had collapsed and he had landed feet first in the bottom of the drop!

At this point, everyone's gaze centred on Gordon's feet, and we withdrew from my husband as though he had some deadly disease. Eventually, once the lavatory-humour laughter had subsided, Ian sent Petrus to fill in the remains of the old loo and dig another one some distance away, whilst he organised another shower for Gordon. Ian was very pragmatic, saying at least he hadn't had to haul him out of the pit, whilst I instructed my husband not only to wash his feet thoroughly, but also scrub his sandals and leave them to dry outside before coming anywhere near me in the tent! We gathered for a cup of tea a couple of hours later, everyone still chuckling over Gordon's disaster.

An hour before darkness set in, we went off in the Landy, leaving Petrus to hold the fort and prepare supper. We drove along the river bed for twenty minutes or so, before coming across an isolated tent pitched there. Ian recognized that it belonged to some German tourists he had seen earlier, and as he was concerned that more desert elephants might well come along in the night, he left a note 'Achtung! Elephanten!', hoping that might prepare them for any visit.

When we got back, we saw an open Landy parked a few metres from our camp. Its owner, Samson, our guide from Save the Rhino Trust together with his two scouts introduced themselves. They would be spending the night with us so we could set off at dawn with them for a day's trek in the hope of spotting spot one of the rare black rhinos. During supper, all conversation was about these animals and the work the Trust was doing to ensure that they are protected here, the only place on earth where they able to roam freely.

We all decided to have an early night, so we retired to our tents, with Petrus and Ian in their usual sleeping positions under and on the trailer, and Samson and the two scouts sleeping out in the open next to their Landy. I felt very pampered and spoilt in our tiny tents with beds, but envied them being able to sleep under the clear starlit skies. Gordon and I decided to open all the flaps of our tent, as it was hot and we needed as much ventilation as possible, and we drifted off to sleep with the sound of a Scops owl, its burbling, soft 'prrrrp' lulling us into oblivion.

I woke suddenly when it was still dark, and shining my torch on my watch, I saw it was only 2 a.m. As I wondered to myself what had woken me I heard a slight sound of whispering and then some movement in the camp. Peering out of the window flap, I watched in total amazement as two desert elephants walked slowly and ponderously into our camp. Petrus, despite his fear of snakes, had decided that being under the Landy with Ian was preferable to being accosted by an inquisitive trunk. Samson and the two scouts also had moved under their vehicle.

I nudged Gordon awake, putting my hand over his mouth to prevent him from making a noise, and together we watched as these enormous animals wandered around our camp, sniffing out any tasty morsels of fruit to be found. Finding nothing, they rolled silently towards our tent, and we watched spellbound as the silvery, grey moonlight lit up their ivory tusks.

I switched off my torch to avoid disturbing these nocturnal visitors, and Gordon and I huddled together as first one, and then the other elephant picked their way delicately over the guy ropes of our tent before moving slightly to one side where they proceeded to feed off the branches of a nearby tree. Ten minutes later, they disappeared into the night and we could breathe freely again.

Ian came up to our tent, asking us if we were okay, commenting that we had done just the right thing in turning off the torch. He had been ready to get up and make a noise if they had started to feed off the tree over our tent, but had decided to see what happened before intervening. Hearing no noise from Ann and Conrad's tent, we settled down to try to get another couple of hours' sleep.

As the adrenaline surging around my body gradually subsided, and I dozed off to sleep, I mused on how half an hour ago, I was within touching distance of the world's largest land mammal with only thin canvas between us. I recalled just how gently and precisely they had negotiated the fine ropes, which held up our tent, and marvelled that somehow they had decided to avoid them and leave us in peace. 'Ours is not to wonder why,' I murmured and fell into a deep, dreamless sleep.

In the early morning mist we gathered round the campfire, amazed that Ann and Conrad had slept through the nocturnal visit of the desert elephants, and as we told them how close they had been to their tent, they could not believe that they had been oblivious to our visitors. Ian told us that he had never seen elephants walk so closely to tents before, and joked that these rare pachyderms must have sensed that I had wished for a close encounter. Stranger things than that have happened, I thought, and felt I was starting to get some rare insight into the animal world.

Perhaps both animals and humans can instinctively be aware of each other's thoughts, behaviours and even hopes. Who knows? However strange this may seem, all my contact with wild animals over many years has only reinforced this belief. In my experience, going out into the bush, yearning to see something special has frequently produced nothing. When relaxed, and accepting that I might or might not see anything, invariably this is the occasion when the bush presents me with unbelievable sightings – a wonderful gift from nature I have always treasured.

We all set off in the open Landy shortly after dawn, and were soon travelling deep into desert, the rough ground jolting us without mercy. Large, deep red rocks littered the rough tracks, and euphorbia bushes, the black rhino's favourite nourishment relieved the desert landscape with splashes of green. The relentless sun was beginning to scorch us despite the Landy's awning, and I watched in awe as the two trackers set off every so often on foot to examine tracks and bushes where rhino might have fed.

After a couple of hours, we stopped for a comfort break, and the trackers then spread out, using their two-way radios whenever they had information to share. As we motored along in the relative comfort of a shaded vehicle, these two dedicated men walked, then trotted, then stopped, only to begin all over again. They sometimes became mere specks in the distance and it was like watching bloodhounds search out their quarry. The terrain got rougher and steeper, and looking down the side of the Landy, all I could see was a drop of a hundred feet or so below me.

I clung onto the side of the vehicle, quietly praying that the four-wheel drive would get us safely up the next incline, when, in the valley below, we saw the trackers increase their speed. The radio crackled into life; they had come across some rhino spoor, but it was about twelve hours old. On and on we followed the trackers until, in the heat of the day, Samson called them in and they arrived back at the Landy, sweat pouring from their dusky black faces.

Apparently, they did this day after day, as it was essential to track the rhinos' movements continually.

After some much needed water and a snack, off they went again, whilst we watched from a distance. After another hour, it became obvious that the black rhino were going to remain elusive, and we had to return to camp before it got dark. Samson was very apologetic that they had been unable to find even one rhino, but we realised that it was like hunting for the proverbial needle in a haystack, and the trackers had given it their all, walking for mile after mile in the searing desert heat. I was more than content with the two desert elephants finding me last night, and accepted that a black rhino sighting was just not for us this time. Back at camp, Samson and the trackers bid us goodbye, and went off into the desert, only to begin the same gruelling exercise the following day.

In England, we have occasionally seen documentaries on television where Samson has been interviewed about his work with the Save the Rhino Trust of Namibia, and we relive that hot, tiring day we spent with those three dedicated men who are still working so tirelessly for the preservation of such an endangered animal.

Our tents in Damaraland, where the desert elephants walked over our guy-ropes in the middle of the night.

The Epupa Falls was the furthest north we travelled in Namibia, Angola being on the other side of the Kuene River. After many days of desert camping, we reached this swiftly flowing river and were nearly blinded by the dense green foliage of trees lining the banks. It is a true oasis and we camped here for a couple of days, enjoying the contrast of scenery, including the many baobab trees which grow like sentinels on either side of the Falls.

Chapter 14

The Epupa Falls

The following day we were woken at dawn by the sound of Ian and Petrus packing up camp. We had a long drive to our next overnight stop, further up north, en route to the Kunene River at the border of Namibia and Angola. I was sad to leave this very special place in the depths of Damaraland, but looked forward to the next part of our journey. Ian jokingly told us that if we thought the previous days had been tough travelling we had better prepare for the toughest part yet! Whilst packing our bags, I ruminated on how much tougher it could get, but soon found out when we set off for Ongongo. The roads got progressively worse, with tracks of rocks and boulders for mile after mile. Occasionally, the tracks turned into rough gravel roads, and for a few miles, we could relax our tight grips on the Landy's window frames.

In the middle of nowhere, we came across a Herero woman driving a donkey and cart with a small child sitting next to her. We stopped and Petrus negotiated the exchange of a couple of apples for some photographs of this beautiful woman, her ebony skin and headdress of brilliant cerise framed against an azure sky. This was the only splash of colour we had seen for days, and our first glimpse of the Herero people.

Fascinated by her attire, Ian explained this was derived from a Victorian lady's dress. She wore an enormous crinoline, under which there were layers of petticoats, and her horn-shaped headdress was supposed to resemble the horns of a cow, symbolising wealth.

How she remained looking so cool in this bizarre Victorian costume in the overpowering heat of the desert was totally beyond me. It was only when I had my photos developed that I noticed a badge securing the brightly coloured cloak tightly round her shoulders. It stated 'My future is my choice'. I wish she could know that my portrait of her now proudly adorns a wall in our home and is frequently admired.

Along a sandy track, with desert on either side of us as far as the eye could see, we spotted some feral horses feeding off scraps of scant vegetation. How anything could exist, let alone survive in this unforgiving landscape was incredible, but these animals looked fit. Apparently, they have descended from the horses left by the South African and German armies and have adapted to the desert conditions over many years of interbreeding to become known as the Namid horses. Most of them are found further south, but a few have made their way up north and have survived with minimal human intervention, apart from the occasional water trough to provide a bare minimum of water through the years of drought.

The miles sped by slowly, but there was always something to look at to break the grey bleakness of the desert scenery. The Herero people are proud cattle farmers, their cattle being their primary source of survival, and cattle kraals fenced off with long wooden sticks to prevent nocturnal predators, frequently appeared on either side of the road. We stopped only to fill up with fuel and water at a remote village, where we saw yet more Herero women dressed in their Victorian-style finery. On we journeyed, snacking on fruit, nuts and biscuits en route until we eventually reached a turn-off, marked 'For 4x4s only'.

This sign seemed a bit unnecessary to me, as a four-wheel drive vehicle is essential on this terrain, but, as Ian had warned, we now realised we were at the beginning of the roughest part of our journey so far. As we approached our overnight campsite, we were all hoping that we would be the only people there, as it was only a small site and Ian knew exactly where he wanted to pitch our tents. We drove down a narrow, steep track to a small stream where water flowed slowly over large rocks. We had to disembark at this point;

somehow, Ian had to get the Landy and the trailer across the stream.

We watched in amazement as, inch by inch, Ian carefully drove the vehicle forward, lurching precariously at impossible angles as he steered it over the water and rocks, the trailer following at equally improbable angles, until with a revving of the engine, he drove up the slope and arrived at our overnight stop. We carefully negotiated crossing the stream on foot and walked up to where the Landy was parked, not surprised to see that the small campsite was deserted – given the access road!

With their usual efficiency, Ian and Petrus began to unload the trailer, and half an hour later, our now familiar tents were ready for us, with our bags placed on the rug between our two beds. There would be no long-drop for Gordon to fall into this time! Ian pointed to the top of a nearby hill where a wooden shack stood – our loo for the overnight stop.

I estimated that it would take a good ten minutes to reach, and prayed that I would not need to use it overnight. As long as my digestive system behaved, hopefully, the now normal squatting behind a bit of vegetation for a wee would be adequate until morning. Over a cool beer we became slightly hysterical over the possibility of a queue wending its way up the hill, each mountaineer desperate to get to the one and only loo first, and Ian's reassurance that it was, in fact, a communal loo for two, did nothing to reassure us and only highlighted our lavatorial sense of humour!

Thirst slated with some cans of beer, Ian suggested that if we wanted a shower, the best thing he could offer was a dip in a pool, which, was described by locals as 'the clearest little rock pool in the Namid'. As this was going to be our only chance to rinse off the desert dust, we quickly changed into our swimwear and walked down a track to the head of a narrow valley where a small waterfall, fed by a natural spring, dropped from a high cliff into the most beautiful pool.

I clambered over slippery rocks, and launched myself into the crystal clear water, gasping as the cold water covered my body. It was absolute bliss to float in this reviving water, and looking around

I saw that everyone was grinning from ear to ear. After nearly a week in the baking desert, the luxury of bathing in unlimited cool water was indescribable – I vowed to myself that I would never again take water for granted.

To escape from the relentless sun beating down on our heads, there was a small overhang formed from the cliff, creating a perfect grotto and much needed shade. The four of us spent the next hour luxuriating in our natural swimming pool, occasionally going out into the sun to warm up, before swimming back into the shade. A call from Ian announced that sundowners were ready and the aroma of his braai drifted towards us in the gentle breeze. Reluctantly I hauled myself out of the water over the smooth rocks, Gordon giving a running commentary into his video-cam about a wife who resembled a beached whale!

The sun was going down, and I sat with a G and T in my hand, quietly chatting to our good friends. I pondered over how special this time was, and how privileged we were. I have always loved camping, enjoying living close to nature, and we all agreed that we would much rather holiday like this than join a tour with many people, not that many tours would be able to take us to the places we had been lucky enough to experience and enjoy.

Darkness came swiftly, and we ate a simple but delicious meal, illuminated by the flames of our campfire, and listened as Ian outlined the following day's plans. Tomorrow was going to be another early start as we had to reach the Kunene River before dark, and the going would be even tougher than today, as the tracks up to the Angolan border were rough and strewn with rocks all the way. Ian would give us a wake-up call just before dawn and after a snack breakfast, we would set off at first light.

I settled down on my camp bed, and through the open slats of our tent peered up at the sky, ablaze with stars, until I drifted off to sleep. Gordon and I woke just before daylight, and sneakily decided that we would trek up to the loo before anyone else was awake. Armed with our torches and still in our pyjamas, we climbed up the rocky incline like a couple of moonlit spectres until we reached our destination. There in solitary regal splendour we sat side by side, looking down into the valley to where our little camp was pitched. We decided that this was the ultimate loo with a view as we watched dawn break.

We clambered down the hill, slipping and sliding on the loose rocks. We could hear sounds of Ian and Petrus packing up the trailer once again, but this time the atmosphere was a bit frenetic as apparently, we had all overslept and we ought to have been on our way by now. We met Ann and Conrad scrambling up the hill, desperate to get to the loo before we set off. We flung our overnight clothes into our bags, and hurriedly grabbed some tea, rusks and fruit.

An hour later than planned, we set off on the next leg of our journey north. The track was indeed rough, and our average speed was less than 30 kilometres an hour. The further we travelled the more admiration I felt for Ian, the sole driver of these vast distances we were covering. I wondered how he managed to remain continually cheerful whilst driving, and at the end of each journey then have to pitch camp with the help of Petrus, and cook our evening meal. He always remained the relaxed host, continually entertaining us with anecdotes and information.

Sparse, grey bush covered with thick dust lined our narrow track, and the red dust seeped into every nook and cranny. There was nothing we could do to avoid being coated with it, as closing the Landy's windows meant that the temperature would rise to an impossible high, the outside temperature already over 35 degrees by mid morning. It was preferable to have the blast of hot air wafting around us, although sometimes it felt like being in a fan-assisted oven. As we sipped water from our bottles, the frequent jolts continually interrupted any conversation when we went over an especially large boulder, resulting in either groans or laughs dependent upon which part of our anatomy was being bruised.

We continued northwards to the Angolan border. As we were going round a corner, we were amazed to see three men on motor bikes driving towards us. We stopped for the inevitable chat, as they were the first human beings we had seen for a couple of hours, and learnt that they were motorcycling the whole of the length of Africa, from the Mediterranean to the Cape of Good Hope.

These three adventurers were sensibly clad in protective leathers, but I wondered just how they were able to survive in the heat. However, they were remarkably cheerful and told us to watch out for the book and film they were making of their epic journey. We gave them some water to drink, as they were limited as to how much they could carry, and Ian had filled up all our water containers before leaving camp.

Unless we met with some unforeseen disaster en route, we had supplies for a couple of days, more than enough to last us until we reached our destination, even if we had a breakdown. Their thirst slated, they waved goodbye and with much revving of their engines, they disappeared in a cloud of dust, leaving me questioning if they were adventurous or just barking mad – it certainly made our journey look rather inconsequential in comparison.

Gradually, as the hours passed, the scenery changed to open vast plains on either side of the track. We were now well into the Kaokoveld region, and it was still the parched, hauntingly beautiful desert I had started to love – the sparse vegetation grey with little hint of colour. It would need a good rainy season to bring life back into these scant trees and bushes.

Vast mountain ranges loomed around us in the distance, signalling our approach to the Angolan border, the northernmost point of our journey. We came across some Himba people herding their cattle into a kraal, seeing for the first time their homes – cone-shaped structures made with saplings, covered with mud and cow dung. Their red ochre coloured skins, Ian told us, was the result of them smearing cattle fat, ash and the ochre coloured sand onto their bodies as protection against the harsh desert climate.

We learnt that they are a proud hunter-gatherer race, largely unaffected by modern civilisation, and we would have an opportunity to meet some of these tall, proud people during our stay at the Epupa Falls. Thankfully, the Namibian Government was taking a great deal of care to ensure that their way of life remained intact. External visitors were limited, allowing them to be disturbed as little as possible by tourists. Petrus was looking forward to acting as our guide and interpreter as he spoke their language.

In the distance, we glimpsed the rare sight of green vegetation, and then heard the sound of water gushing over rocks – the Kunene River! The sight of fast flowing water with lush makalani palms and wild fig trees lining this perennial river was a shock to the senses, after so many days of gravel and desert. Ian drove up to our campsite bordering on the riverbanks, and we were thankful that the camp had only a few other intrepid travellers.

Each site was carefully screened from the adjacent one, being large enough to ensure ample privacy, and I was relieved to see that a basic shower and loo were provided for each site, screened off by wooden slats. Thankfully, no more trekking up a mountainside! Ian suggested that we went off for a walk whilst he and Petrus got on with the task of sorting out our camp, warning us not to go too near the river's edge, as the occasional crocodile had been known to grab both humans and wildlife! Off we went, amazed at the prolific bird life all around, and the haunting cry of a fish eagle reinforced the fact that we were indeed in an oasis of plenty. This was the first time we had seen a strongly flowing river during the whole of the time we had been in Namibia.

We strolled along the peaceful banks, and came across the occasional goat risking its life going down to the water for a much needed drink. Soon we reached the source of the sound of rushing water – the edge of the Epupa Falls. Numerous baobab trees were growing on the rocky surfaces bordering the Falls, these ancient trees with huge branches ending in thick stumps, giving the appearance of growing upside down – hence their nickname of the 'upside down tree'.

I watched mesmerised as the smoothly flowing river suddenly disappeared over a series of drops, and we decided to leave further exploring to when Ian was able to guide us, as we needed expert local knowledge to ensure we were safe. We wended our way back to camp, only to be startled as a soldier armed with an AK 47 rifle walked past us, greeting us with a friendly smile before he continued on his way.

It was then that the unwelcome reality of the outside world hit home. The river formed the frontier between Namibia and Angola, and the Angolan Civil War, which had started in 1975, was still raging in some areas of the country despite several intervening periods of uneasy peace.

In a state of slight unease, we arrived back at camp to be reassured by Ian that he had never known any trouble at this seemingly idyllic place. 'Just don't think of crossing the river though, as you might find yourself being arrested. I don't want to spend the rest of your holiday trying to organise your removal from an Angolan prison!' He laughed, before changing the topic of conversation, getting down to the essentials of life by suggesting that we might like to have a shower before sundowners.

I decided to let the others shower first, as I seemed to be fated to have problems with showers wherever I travelled on the African continent. Let Gordon, Ann and Conrad sort out any teething problems was my mantra from now on. Each appeared clean and refreshed after their ablutions, so off I went to the rustic shower cubicle, confident that there was an ample water supply as it came straight from the river.

I turned on the rusty tap and let streams of fresh, cool water flow over me. Turning off this abundant flow, I proceeded to shampoo my dusty hair, thankful that at last I could use shampoo, as the swim the previous day in the rock pool had been just a rinse rather than a wash. Humming to myself, I turned on the tap. Nothing happened! I tried to turn the tap the other way, thinking I had made some fundamental error. Still no water. I hit the pipes gently, wondering if there was an airlock somewhere that I could dislodge. Nothing. Not even a drop.

Quietly, I tried to attract Gordon's attention, not wanting to make a spectacle of myself yet again. I peered round the wooden slats and saw that he was sitting peacefully with the others, beer in hand, gazing at the setting sun slipping behind the Angolan mountains.

'Gordon!' I yelled after several quieter calls brought no result. He put down his drink, and I could just imagine his murmurings to the others about Maggie, showers and trouble, as he strolled over to me. He repeated my futile attempts to get the water flowing. At last, admitting defeat and staring at me, covered with shampoo bubbles from head to foot, he exclaimed he really didn't know what to suggest. 'Well I can't stay like this for ever. Get Ian!' I hissed, grabbing my towel for decency's sake. 'At least he, hopefully, will be more help than you!'

Ian appeared with a concerned look on his face, obviously well schooled by Gordon that it would be better if he took this feminine calamity seriously. He too tried all the obvious remedial tricks to no avail. He assured me that he would be back in a minute, and disappeared, only to return to tell me that somewhere down the line the pipe had become disconnected and was broken. There would be no more water flowing that evening! He had organised Petrus to bring a bucket of water so that at least I could rinse off.

I requested that he should bring me a cup too. 'What do you want, tea or coffee?' Ian was certainly following Gordon's instructions to the letter. With that, I collapsed into gales of laughter, eventually informing the bewildered man that I needed to scoop the water out of the bucket with something. Bucket and cup were duly delivered and I spent the next ten minutes attempting to rinse myself, cursing the amount of shampoo I had used, before I stalked off to our tent to make myself decent. Amid much hilarity, I sat down at the campfire accepting a stiff G and T from Ian as a peace offering, with assurances that he would get the pipe work fixed the following day.

We sat around the table, content to watch the stars appear, listening to the birds noisily coming home to roost until finally, the only sounds were the distant waterfalls, the crackling of the campfire, the rustling of the palm fronds, and the Kunene River flowing peacefully past. Over supper, we chatted quietly about our journey so far, and how we had now reached the northernmost point of Namibia. From here onwards we would be travelling south, but before that we were all looking forward to a couple of days here in this idyllic place, relishing the thought of being next to an ample supply of water in this verdant green oasis after the now familiar arid desert scenery.

After coffee and a nightcap or three, we retired to our tents. Ian reminded us that for once we could have a lie-in after all our early starts. I promised him we would not wake him if we got up before him, and volunteered to bring him an early morning cup of tea to make up for all the trouble I had caused him so far.

The gentle sound of flowing water lulled me into a dreamless sleep of eight hours. Dawn was just breaking when I peered out of our tent. I decided to get up and commune with nature on the banks of the river until everyone woke. I had a blissful hour to myself just sitting looking at the bird life.

A fish eagle called and was answered by its mate, and a malachite kingfisher perched on an overhanging branch, intent on the water below him. With a sudden dive into the river, it surfaced with a small, silver fish in its red beak, and positioning the fish to make swallowing easier, with a gulp it disappeared down its throat. This small, beautiful bird, its iridescent turquoise cap, and orange breast glistening with water, resumed its vigilant position, gazing into the clear water, alert for its next meal.

Slowly, one by one, Gordon, Conrad and Ann appeared from the tents, and we quietly put wood on the embers of last night's fire to brew our cups of tea. We sat in silence watching the bird life, mesmerised by the hypnotic flow of the river. This lazy start to the day seemed luxury personified after so many early starts. I crept behind the 'green baize door' to find tea and milk, careful not to disturb Ian and Petrus still sleeping peacefully on mats.

We quietly brewed up our early morning cups of tea, delivering two mugs to our comatose guide and helper, who quickly got up to sort out breakfast, despite our pleas to take it easy. Soon we were tucking into a South African breakfast – pancakes and maple syrup, together with the full monty of bacon, eggs, tomatoes and boerewors. We persuaded Ian not to think about any lunch, so he decided to cook a stew for our evening meal, leaving it to gently simmer all day whilst we went off exploring.

Ann decided to have a lazy day relaxing in camp, with Petrus staying behind to tidy up and do some laundry. The rest of us set off down the path we had taken the previous day, clambering over the rocky terrain along the banks of the river until we came to the Epupa Falls. I could only imagine what it must be like when there had been a good rainy season, as the sound of the rushing water made conversation difficult.

Down we went until we could see a small sandy strip of land bordering the river. To reach this tiny oasis we first had to climb down the side of some small cliffs and over large boulders, Ian reassuring us that it was safe and a relatively easy climb down. It might be easy for a young, long-legged, athletic guide and two six-foot men, but I soon needed help to negotiate the steep descent. Conrad went first, encouraging me that he was ready to steady me if I slipped, whilst Gordon held onto one of my hands, giving me a modicum of comfort that he would hold me when I had to stretch down over boulders that were double my height. I just hoped I wouldn't slip and bring Gordon tumbling down over us.

Eventually, we joined Ian on the sand, wary of not getting too close to the water's edge in case of crocodiles. Looking up, the Epupa Falls cascaded down towards us, the sparkling white spray foamed over the rocks, glistening in the sunlight and forming mini rainbows. The giant, ancient baobab trees stood sentinel on either side of the falls, and I could just make out some small figures stooping under trees, picking up fallen wood for their fires.

We sat in comfortable silence, the roaring water of the falls providing an hypnotic background to our thoughts as we watched the water swirl gently past us, almost as though it too was recovering from its recent turbulent descent. Eventually, the heat of the sun became too much, and reluctantly, we started the climb back to camp.

If it had been a struggle for me to descend to the bottom of the gorge, the ascent was to prove a mammoth test of my strength, at times, culminating with Gordon pushing my backside and Conrad hauling me up by his hands. Battered and breathless we all reached the summit of the cliff where Ian was standing, looking as cool as a cucumber, but generous in his praise for our efforts.

Hot and dripping with sweat I staggered along the narrow path towards our campsite and concentrated on the thought of recovering under a long cool shower. Petrus, having obviously completed the camp's domestic tasks, was sauntering along the riverbank, his sunny expression only to change instantly to one of desolation when he saw us approaching. I knew this look of old as it heralded copious 'sorries' before the bad news was announced. Apparently, the shower pipe would not be mended until the next day and the only water we had was a standpipe near the kitchen area.

As we neared the campsite we passed the lip of the Falls where there were several large rock pools. I gazed at them longingly and promptly decided that a bathe in the river was the only answer. I announced to Ian that the absence of a shower was really no problem. I would bathe in one of the rock pools.

I could see his imagination running riot at the thought of a naked, middle-aged English woman scandalising the sensibilities of the local population, but I assured him that I would keep my clothes on. 'I can kill two birds with one stone and my clothes will get a laundering at the same time!'

'Just mind that one bird isn't killed by a crocodile!' was his retort, and he went off to question some locals as to whether any crocs had been seen recently.

Given the all clear, I crawled on all fours over the slippery rocks, and reached the largest rock pool I could see. I slowly lowered myself into it. The gently flowing water slowly cooled my overheated body, and resting my neck on a smooth boulder, I sank into the shallow pool, a contented smile on my face.

Gordon busied himself with a few shots of his wife bathing on the very edge of the Epupa Falls, nominally keeping an eye out for any crocodiles, whilst Ian made his way back to camp, shaking his head in amazement at the antics his clients got up to. Gradually, I cooled down and relaxed in this perfect natural jacuzzi, the bubbles and ripples easing my aches and pains. I turned round carefully until I found I could lean over the edge of the pool and peer down over the very lip of the falls. The roar of the water was deafening as the gentle mist swirled upwards in surreal patterns. Closing my eyes, I drifted off into a trance-like state, only to be woken by a touch on my head.

I turned round and found myself face to face with a goat that had decided to investigate who had the temerity to use its watering place. I'm not certain who was more startled when I let out an involuntary yelp of surprise. The goat jumped over *my* pool with enviable agility, trotting off to rejoin its companions on the bank.

Deciding I had had enough of any wildlife encounters, I hauled myself out of the pool, and like a drowned rat made my way to our camp. The midday sun was so fierce, that in the ten minutes it took me to reach our tent, my clothes were almost dry. Showered, clean and with laundry done, I joined the others for a long cool beer, sporting a somewhat self-satisfied smile on my face!

We all decided that a siesta was called for, but after a few minutes in our tent, I found it was much too airless, so dragged my camp bed outside and spent a blissful couple of hours snoozing under a palm tree, its fronds rustling hypnotically in the cooling breeze.

Petrus woke us, announcing that a mug of tea was awaiting us, after which he would take us for a walk to visit some Himba people who had a small settlement not far away. He was dressed in smart trousers and a neatly pressed shirt. Ian explained that this was an important visit for Petrus and he wanted to look his best. I tidied myself up and changed into fresh clothes, not wanting to let the side down. Ian told us that we were to follow Petrus' instructions, and only take photos, if and when Petrus told us we had permission. As a thank you, Petrus had packed a carrier bag with fresh fruit. Sweets were not encouraged, however much they were appreciated, as dental care was non-existent.

We strolled slowly along in the late afternoon heat, pausing every so often under the scant shade of palm trees. I understood why this 'African Saunter', which can be mistaken for laziness, was in fact, a vital in-built characteristic of rural African people. Why walk quickly in furnace-like heat when you can walk slowly? Why walk in the sun when you can walk in the shade? And . . . why walk at all when you can sit in the shadow of a palm tree and watch the world go by?

Eventually, we came across signs of habitation, and were greeted by an old man who was obviously 'seven sheets to the wind'. He danced along beside us, brandishing a long, stout stick, shouting and gesticulating. Petrus advised us to ignore him as much as possible as he was asking for some more alcohol. It was difficult to ignore this wizened, sprightly old man when he was twirling around us in a drunken stupor, but eventually, he seemed to get the message that we carried no alcohol and that we were not going to take his photo for money.

He retired to sit in the shade, muttering to himself, and I thought to myself how easy it is to destroy an ancient way of life by the thoughtless acts of visitors to a country. How many times has he been given alcohol or the wherewithal to buy it by tourists who should know better? Maybe his tipple was just the home-brewed juice of the local makalani palm, but the way in which he approached us seemed to suggest that he was used to visitors' handouts.

We finally, reached the Himba settlement and stood back whilst Petrus introduced himself to the Elders. A complicated ritual of handshakes and gesturing continued for a good ten minutes before Petrus beckoned us forward and introduced us. Apparently, we were welcome to take a few photos of the women and children in the settlement, so proceeded to get our cameras out, Gordon setting up his tripod for his video-cam.

Yet again, this fascinated the small children, and soon they were swarming around Gordon who showed them a recording of yesterday's hike. He filmed them for a few minutes before rewinding the tape and showed the recording of them, producing incredulity initially and subsequently, like children the world over, fascination and peals of laughter. All barriers now lifted, we were tailed by a dozen youngsters watching us film and take photos of their mothers with their younger siblings.

Gracefully and patiently these Himba women sat in the shade by the banks of the river, smiling shyly, exposing their incisor teeth, filed to sharp points, which in their culture denotes great beauty. Their skin was covered in a protective coating of the red ochre dust mixed with animal fat, and their hair was also covered in this mixture, and braided in ornate patterns, which apparently signalled their marital status. Their bodies were adorned with multiple bead necklaces around their necks, wrists and ankles and the infants they carried, who were also wearing ornate necklaces, had shaved heads.

Not wanting to intrude into their lives any more than we had, we bade them goodbye, thanking them profusely for allowing us to meet them, Petrus gave them the bag of fruit and talked to them for a few minutes as we slowly made our way back to camp.

Over drinks, we discussed the Himba people and how much longer they and their culture could survive the encroaching technologies of the approaching twenty-first century. Who were we to say that they should remain in their primitive state, with lack of education and modern medical care? There were definitely no easy answers, and the deeper we went into these issues, the more unsolvable they seemed.

Hunger persuaded us to put the debate on hold, and we gathered round the table for the stew that had been gently simmering all day. In spite of the heat, this delicious meal disappeared in next to no time, washed down by a mature Pinotage, and we decided that modern day camping had its advantages. Replete, we had coffee and rooibos tea with the now obligatory Amarula – the African cream liqueur made from the fruits of the marula tree. The embers of the campfire died down and reluctantly we retired for our last night of camping under the star-studded sky.

Our first encounter with wildlife in Etosha was with an extremely bad-tempered black rhino. We were forced to make a rapid escape to the relative safety of an enclosed picnic area. The trailer attached to the Landy prevented us from taking much evasive action. Luckily, the rudimentary fences were enough to deter this irritable creature. After much snorting, huffing and puffing, he decided we were not too much of a threat and careered off at great speed to seek another source of amusement.

Chapter 15

Etosha

Packing up camp in the morning for our journey south and ultimately back to Windhoek and home was for me, a somewhat depressing experience. I had revelled in the camping, and the thought of the gradual return to civilisation and the Westernised world was a sad, sobering thought. I adored the vast wilderness areas, and would miss the remoteness, the peace and the space of northern Namibia.

We loaded ourselves in the Landy with the packed trailer behind us, and set off for a remote lodge in a concession area adjacent to the north western section of the Etosha National Park. Ian talked about the game we should see, and I soon cheered up, realising how absent this had been throughout most of our trip so far. Surprisingly, this had not concerned me, as the stunning scenery and our special encounters with the rare desert elephant more than made up for the absence of other big game.

We slowly journeyed south on the rough tracks of baked red earth, the dust streaming through the windows. On the odd occasion when we passed a vehicle coming in the opposite direction, the dust thrown up produced such a cloud that for a few minutes we were left in an impenetrable red fog, and Ian was reduced to grinding to a halt to allow the dust to settle. The risk of continuing driving blind was just too great.

We arrived at the lodge in the early afternoon and received a warm welcome, and an ice cold drink, together with a cold damp towel to refresh our dusty hands and faces. When I saw our immaculate chalet, with king-size bed and a double walk-in shower, I decided that civilisation was indeed quite welcome. Our luggage unpacked and laundry collected, I spent the next twenty minutes under the shower, which initially ran red with all the dust I had collected over the last few days. I emerged from our chalet feeling a new woman, with hair that was no longer sticky with dust. How fickle I was! In just a few hours, I had gone from not wanting to leave our camp to revelling in all the luxuries provided to satisfy the most demanding tourist.

I could see from Ann's expression that she too was just as content, more so probably, as she revealed to us that it was her sixtieth birthday, and Conrad had not forgotten, as she had feared, but was busy arranging a celebration meal for us all! Under the stars in the warmth of an African evening, we dined like kings and enthusiastically toasted Ann's health with copious amounts of bubbly.

I woke up as dawn was breaking, looking forward to a day of game viewing. We chatted as we dressed, only for the conversation to come to an abrupt halt when Gordon found a small scorpion in his shoe. Thankfully, he had remembered to shake his shoe before putting his foot into it. I went to the reception desk whilst Gordon kept an eye on the creature. There was no way we would let it run off to hide anywhere in the room!

The owner of the lodge responded immediately and removed the scorpion, telling Gordon he was very lucky not to have been bitten. A rather shaken Gordon replied that he was thankful it had not been in his trousers, and that from now on he would, without exception, shake all items of apparel. We had been lulled into a false sense of security in all this luxury, and should have remembered our previous encounters with fluorescing scorpions in the desert home of the cardiologist at the beginning of our trip.

We spent the morning in an open vehicle, exploring the concession area, and were soon seeing giraffe, kudu and gemsbok, together with an extraordinary selection of birds. Our ranger was an encyclopaedia of knowledge and he identified the many varied trees and shrubs; we gained yet more understanding of how they survived in these extreme desert conditions.

After a hearty brunch at the lodge, we all decided to spend the afternoon at a hide overlooking a waterhole. Our love of wildlife had been re-activated, and we wanted to see as much as possible during the last few days of our safari. The ranger organised a cool box full of ice and drinks for the four of us, which would be waiting for us in the hide, and we were shown how to get to the viewing platform. Apparently, it was safe to walk there, as the only large predators on the concession were the occasional leopard, and they would stay well clear of humans. At least we hoped they would! Although a herd of elephant had been sighted the previous day, they were far enough away not to cause any problems.

After a twenty-minute walk in the heat of the midday sun, we climbed up the rickety ladder into the hide. A sloping roof sheltered us from the relentless heat, and we settled down to an afternoon of game viewing. The large waterhole was a couple of hundred yards away, and surrounded on one side by some rocks. Every so often, the motor pumping up the water from the borehole would burst into action for a few minutes, harshly breaking the still silence.

It was as though we were in a lunar landscape; the white and grey rocks and boulders rising from the pale silver earth were the only colours as far as the eye could see. Gone was the vibrant red soil and lush green palms of the previous few days bordering the Kunene River to be replaced with the bleakest of all the desert scenery so far. Scant grey, skeleton-like trees and shrubs occasionally broke up the flat scenery, and the previous season's grass was reduced to some pathetic dried-out tufts. How any animal could survive in this hostile environment was a miracle.

Sunglasses were essential as the glare of the sun reflecting from the white rocky landscape was blinding. Quietly we waited, sipping iced water, and within a few minutes the first gemsbok arrived, cautiously approaching the waterhole and spending what seemed an inordinate amount of time before settling down to drink. Springbok then arrived, followed by a family of warthog. These were the comedians of the waterhole, scampering around and generally upsetting the peace, the young racing from adult to adult, their tails erect like radio antennae.

Within a few minutes, everything had disappeared into the distance and the waterhole was deserted. With the aid of our binoculars, we could see the next collection of game slowly approaching in the distance. The oven-like heat was almost unbearable in the shade of the hide, and I marvelled at how these animals had the strength to survive, let alone walk vast distances to reach the life-giving water.

As the afternoon wore on, the dropping of a bird book or, more seriously, a pair of binoculars slipping to the ground indicated that we were all sleepy, our eyes tired by the dazzling light and the effects of our brunch. We decided to take it in turns to grab a bit of shut-eye, as the slightest noise disturbed not only the occupants of the hide, but more importantly, any game at the waterhole.

An enormous eland, the largest of all the African antelope, had us all wide awake half an hour later. Its distinctive thick neck and large dewlap made it look like an ox in antelope's clothing, and as we watched it drink its full, more kudu and springbok arrived to join it. Suddenly, something made them stop drinking and each one turned to the right, staring intently into the distance.

We scoured the horizon with our binoculars, searching for anything that might have disturbed their peace, but could see nothing untoward. For several minutes they stood, immobile as statues, whilst we held our breaths, remaining as still and silent as possible, until first one and then the others returned to their drinking.

Several giraffe eventually joined them, and we watched them warily survey the surroundings for several minutes before spreading their front legs and inelegantly lowering their long necks towards the water. After a few gulps, they would jump up with water sprinkling around them, and then repeat the whole scenario several times before ambling off into the distance, thirst duly quenched. The wariness of all the animals around the waterhole emphasised to us just how vulnerable they were to predators when they came down to drink. Their survival depended on their vigilance and alertness.

Gradually, the blistering heat started to subside; the sun lost some of its intensity, and disappeared behind a thin layer of high dust, thus heralding a spectacular sunset. We reluctantly left the hide, as we had no wish to be caught walking back to the lodge in the rapidly descending dusk with the odd leopard and herd of elephant as walking companions!

At the lodge, we found the ranger busy packing up another cool box with sundowners for a short game drive before supper. We drove to the highest part of the reserve and sat on rocks, still warm from the heat of the day. Nothing more pleasant than to sip ice cold gin and tonics, whilst watching the sun set in a glow of orange and magenta red, the deep midnight blue of the now crystal clear sky providing the perfect backdrop.

The stars began to appear, heralded by Venus, the Evening Star, rising over the horizon, and soon the Milky Way arched over our heads in all its glory. The only way to appreciate the African sky is to lie down and gaze into the firmament, so ignoring the risk of scorpions and other creepy-crawlies, we lay down and in silence, watched nature in all its glory manifest over our heads. I have never really come to terms with the fact that the light we were seeing from these far distant stars and galaxies was emitted many thousands, if not billions of years ago, and if there is anything to put one's own life into perspective then an African sky is the perfect panacea.

It was hard to drag myself back to the fact that our supper was waiting, but Africa had one more gift for us that evening. In the glow of the spotlight, the ranger caught the brief sparkle of an animal's eye. He turned off the engine. Slowly and silently, a large male leopard strolled into view. This magnificent solitary cat approached us, its long whiskers twitching, its tail erect and swaying gently. I held my breath as it padded silently past us and disappeared into the night. What a sight to behold and what a wonderful end to our day.

The next morning, Ian and Petrus appeared, greeting us like long-lost friends after their couple of days off duty. The trailer was already packed with provisions for the next three days in the Etosha National Park, and once our luggage was loaded on board, we were on our way.

Entering Etosha, we soon realised how accurate its name was. Ian explained that it translates as 'Place of Dry Water' consisting of a huge flat pan of over 5,000 square metres, and we were seeing it at its absolute driest. Silver-white mirages stretched in front of us, the reflected glare painful to the eyes without a pair of good sunglasses, so intensely bright was the landscape. The rough gravel roads threw up white dust, and the only vegetation visible was arid savannah and grasslands, with thorn scrub, all of which were a colourless grey, coated with the dust.

Even when we came to a waterhole, the scrub around it was a monochrome tone, the scant life-giving water not enough to penetrate the surrounding vegetation's root systems; everything waited for the unpredictable summer rains. If we were looking forward to seeing the usual buffalo, hippo, crocodiles or monkeys, we were going to be disappointed – there was simply not enough rain to support them. Amazingly, we saw herds of zebra, wildebeest and springbok, all appearing in remarkably good condition despite several years of negligible rainfall.

As if to re-assure us that Etosha could and did support a variety of wildlife, in the distance we saw a plume of dust arising from the wilderness. This was far away from any man-made track so we ruled out a vehicle, and then Ian let out a whoop of excitement. There, coming towards us at a rapid speed was a rhino. With the aid of binoculars, we could then see that not only was it a rhino, but it was a black rhino! Its curved back and hooked upper lip left us in no doubt that this animal was the much rarer and more endangered species.

A week ago, we had spent the whole of one day with trackers trying to find one and now, here was one coming towards us! It paused for several minutes and then proceeded towards us in a seemingly effortless trot. Ian told us to hang on tightly as he was going to have to get to a fenced-off rest stop, thankfully not too far away.

Black rhinos are not to be taken lightly, and the last thing he wanted to happen was for one to charge us when he was towing a trailer. Not only was the rhino coming towards us, its trot was increasing to a gallop – it had spotted our movement and was hell-bent in seeing who or what was disturbing its peace. We had been told that black rhino were far more aggressive than their white cousins, and now we were experiencing it first-hand.

After several tense minutes of driving flat out and no doubt breaking the Park's speed limit, we reached the comparative safety of the fenced off rest-stop. We all breathed a sigh of relief. Ian told us that we could get out of the Landy and take some photos of this prehistoric animal just as long as we stayed close to the vehicle whilst he unhitched the trailer. This was a safety precaution in case the rhino decided that he was going to charge through the fencing, in which case we would have to drive off trailer-less to escape the attentions of this volatile, temperamental animal.

Cautiously peering from behind the Landy, I managed to take a few photos, attempting to steady my trembling hands. The rhino came to a shuddering halt a few yards from the fence. Ian motioned to us to remain absolutely still and silent. We listened to its puffing snorts whilst it decided what to do next.

After a few tense minutes, this massive creature decided that we were no longer a threat and with remarkable agility turned round, and still huffing and puffing, went off in the opposite direction in a cloud of dust. If ever we had a lesson in the behaviour of a black rhino this was it, its best way of defending itself being attack, totally unlike the white rhino, who by comparison is a gentle giant.

Excitement over, we gulped down some water and drove off to Okaukuejo, the camp that would be our home for the next two nights. Ian had been clever enough to book us into two chalets immediately in front of a large waterhole, fenced off by unobtrusive wire netting, and explained that the waterhole was lit all night, so that we could get up whenever we wanted and just wander the few yards to observe whatever happened to be drinking there during the night.

This oasis, although in a large camp, never seemed overcrowded with people, and thankfully, all our fellow game watchers had one thing in mind – to observe the wildlife in peace and quiet. Ann and Conrad shared one chalet with us, and Ian and Petrus had the second one, which doubled up as a mess area, where all the cooking was done. By the time we had re-appeared, there were drinks and a bucket of ice on the outside table, and we settled down to a late afternoon of game watching, drinks in hand, whilst a braai was lit for our evening meal.

As dusk came, swiftly followed by darkness, the waterhole spotlights were turned on, creating deep shadows and intense reflections of any animal drinking around the perimeter of the water. We sat on a bench watching giraffe, zebra, impala, gemsbok and kudu come down in large numbers to slake their thirst. As there was no threat to them of submerged crocodiles, they approached the water less cautiously, the only threat being lion or maybe an unruly herd of elephant or a bad tempered rhino. The plains game obviously depended on safety in numbers, and we saw this played out over the evening. Whenever there were large quantities of game, they headed straight for the water without hesitation and drank their fill, before going off into the darkness.

We tore ourselves away from this unending procession, and sat down to a hearty braai, occasionally standing up to see what wildlife was appearing a few yards away. We debated how we were going to spend the night. It seemed such a waste of time going to sleep when so much was happening right in front of us and we decided to bring out blankets and sit on the bench for as long as we could stay awake.

When we finally retired to bed, we would probably hear if anything exciting was happening through the open windows and could go out in our pyjamas with blankets. Sitting back, replete and satisfied, Ian motioned to us to be still, and pointed out a shadowy shape hovering by the side of our chalet. Slowly, a black-backed jackal approached into the light of the braai, its nose twitching at the smell of cooked meat. We watched as it continued sniffing around us before it ambled off towards other campers, hopeful of a tasty morsel.

Apparently, jackal were occasionally seen in the camp, slinking in unobserved at dusk. Whilst no real threat to adult humans, they were a nuisance and a potential threat to small children, plus they also carried the risk of rabies. Thoughtless campers in the past had no doubt, thrown scraps of meat to these opportunistic scavengers, and over time, they had become habituated to humans and easy meals. If only people realised that in feeding these wild animals they were ultimately signing their death warrant, as in the interests of human safety they would have to be destroyed when they became more demanding of food.

I questioned whether it was safe to sit outside alone in the dead of night with a predator inside the wire netting, and Ian suggested that we had better be safe rather than sorry and make sure that at least two of us were together at any one time.

A loud trumpeting sound heralded the arrival of elephant, so carrying our coffees and iced Amarula down to 'our' bench, we watched a breeding herd of elephant approach the waterhole. Amidst a lot of jostling and the scattering of zebra and impala, the matriarch led about twenty mothers, teenagers and babies to the water, increasing her speed to a near run the closer she got to the life-giving water.

In went their trunks, repeatedly transferring the water into their mouths, the sucking and gurgling clearly audible. Litre after litre disappeared down the throats of these parched animals – apparently an adult bull can drink up to 227 litres a day, 98 litres at a time. The smallest calves had yet to master the art of sucking up water via their trunks. They would put their mouths into the water initially to slake their thirst, before attempting to control their trunks by imitating their elders. Time after time, their unruly trunks would flap from side to side in valiant attempts to transfer water into their mouths, and we watched spellbound as they went into the water to cool off, always close to their vigilant mothers.

Once the adults had drunk enough, they started to squirt water over their backs. I could well imagine the relief this home-made shower brought to these dusty, hot giants. Occasionally, the matriarch would pause and then the rest of the herd would freeze, as though someone had suddenly turned off a switch. Immobile, they would remain like this for several minutes until, as one, their normal activities would resume.

We were watching one of the most fascinating displays of elephant communication. How wonderful it would be to hear the infrasound they emit over several kilometres. If we listened carefully, we could hear the occasional deep rumble, but we could only guess at the inaudible sound transference from elephant to elephant, herd to herd.

As if on cue, out of the darkness another herd approached the waterhole, their arrival signalling a flurry of greeting by trumpeting, growlings and rumblings, with the older members of the herd greeting each other by gentle trunk-twining and nuzzling. The youngsters stayed close to their mothers until the initial greeting display was over and peace restored as the new arrivals drank their fill. Then it was time for the calves to interact with the new arrivals, squealing and nudging each other until their behaviour got more boisterous, at which point, their mothers calmed things down with a gentle whack of their trunks and a warning trumpeting.

We watched as the first herd left the waterhole, following the large matriarch off into the dark, their grey shapes now patterned by the dark marks left by the rapidly drying water. Then the second herd went off in the opposite direction, leaving the waterhole to yet more zebra and buck.

Out of the darkness, we heard the sound of heavy hoofsteps scattering the small rocks and stones – quite unlike the silent tread of the elephants. In a flurry, a black rhino appeared, swiftly followed by another one. This was a black rhino day par excellence! We were treated to a display that can only be described as pure thuggery, as these two animals scattered the peacefully drinking animals in all directions, angrily snorting if anything should attempt to come within a few feet.

The rhino quenched their thirst quickly, clearly demonstrating who was in charge of the waterhole. A few more angry snorts and off they galloped into the dark, anything in their path fleeing rapidly in all directions. Twice in one day, I had seen the bad-tempered behaviour of these prehistoric animals, and was relieved that we had not found any when out with the rhino trackers. I imagined being on foot, not a tree in sight and the only protection being the spiky euphorbia bushes. They may provide vital nourishment for the rhino but would hardly be a lifesaver for me!

As the evening wore on we settled down, wrapped in blankets as the heat of the day gave way to a chilly evening. I lost count of the number of elephants that silently appeared out of the darkness like grey ghosts materialising in the African night. A couple of large bulls started to spar with each other after having drank their fill, but decided that a full-blown sparring match was not worth the effort and ambled off into the night. One herd appeared, followed closely by a bull in musth, the temporal glands streaming behind his eyes.

One small cow was the object of his attentions and it was soon obvious that she was not remotely interested in his amorous advances. Finally, the matriarch of the herd saw him off, the peace of the night being shattered by the noise of some ten elephant cows gathering protectively around this small cow, trumpeting their displeasure loudly. The bull withdrew to the far side of the waterhole, and when the herd left the waterhole he followed at a distance, no doubt hoping another opportunity would present itself later that night.

Giraffe, zebra, springbok and kudu appeared at regular intervals, and the whooping of hyena in the distance heralded the arrival of the first predator – a spotted hyena. Wary of this carnivore, the springbok snorted their alarm signal, ready to scatter. The hyena was only interested in slaking his thirst though, and once this was done, he slunk off into the dark. The hyena is mainly nocturnal and opportunistic in his hunting habits; no doubt he thought that his chances of a meal would be better away from a well-lit waterhole.

Having seen very little wildlife on our way to the camp, we discussed how much there was, and how this waterhole gave us the opportunity to see a variety of game, obviously coming here to drink after resting during the scorching heat of the day. As midnight approached we were all were starting to feel sleepy. Ian and Petrus had long gone off to their beds, but Gordon and I decided to stay up a little longer. We huddled together for some warmth, jolted out of our snoozing every so often when a faint noise signalled the arrival of more animals.

Suddenly, our senses were fully alerted by the faint but distinctive sound of a lion's roar, and then the answering roar of another lion in the opposite direction. We had no idea how far away they were, and listened intently, wondering if the faint roaring was getting louder or softer. Having not seen lion at all on this safari, we were determined not to miss this opportunity, even if it meant staying up all night. Minutes passed and the roaring stopped, only to start up again from another area. Wherever these lions were they were very obviously on the move – possibly a coalition of males marking their territory.

A quarter of an hour passed in silence, and then more roars broke the silence. The game at the waterhole was certainly not disturbed, but for me this was one of the most thrilling and exciting sounds I could possibly hear, symbolising Africa in all her glory. At about 1 a.m. the lion roars faded, and we were claimed reluctantly by sleep.

Beneath a wide-open window, I drifted off into a fitful sleep, only too aware that in a few days' time I would be back in England with no more game viewing for some time. Anything could present itself just a few feet away, which meant that I slept the kind of sleep I remembered after the births of my two sons – one ear open for any sound.

I awoke to the trumpeting of more elephants, and, nudging Gordon, we blearily made our way to the waterhole where a breeding herd was settling down to a good drink. On the opposite side, a herd of zebra were coming down to the water, and once the elephants had left, they too started to drink, their white and black stripes mirrored sharply in the still, inky black liquid. I took a few more photos and finally, we decided to retire to bed, determined to stay there unless woken by the roaring of lion at the waterhole.

Petrus roused us at dawn with a cup of tea, which we took to our bench, feeling distinctly jaded after such a short night's sleep. The waterhole was deserted; it was as though nothing had ever been there. We finished our tea and retired for a shower to revive us, before gathering with the others for another cup of tea and a rusk. Ann and Conrad had gone to bed much earlier than us and looked fresh and ready for a day of game watching, whereas Gordon and I got into the Landy feeling the worse for wear after only a couple of hours' sleep.

I dozed intermittently until Ian braked suddenly and announced that he had seen some lions. Instantly I was alert and peered into the distance, not seeing anything that looked remotely like a lion. Gordon gave me some guidelines as to where to look, then Ian added his input – but still they eluded me. Embarrassed, I searched the bleak landscape with my binoculars, wondering why everyone else was drooling over three large male lions, all with magnificent black manes, when all I could see was a grey and white lunar landscape with occasional tufts of scrub breaking up the monotony.

By now, everyone was incredulous that I could not see these three big cats, and the more I followed everyone's directions the more frustrated I became. Suddenly, I saw the funny side of the situation and started to laugh until tears were streaming down my cheeks. Gordon knew that when I started to laugh like this, it could only get worse, and he began to apologise to everyone. He knew me and my whacky sense of humour, blaming my lack of sleep for this near hysterical laughter. Best pull myself together I thought, otherwise Gordon would disown me and everyone would think they were harbouring a lunatic in the Landy, so I wiped away my tears, and returned to the task of finding these elusive cats.

Suddenly, to everyone's relief, I let out a whoop of excitement. There they were, lying under some scrub a few hundred yards away – how could I ever not have seen them! Three magnificent male lions, most probably the coalition we had heard last night, lay sleeping off their nocturnal activities – one lying on its back with its legs in the air, its full stomach revealing that it had obviously fed well recently. One of the other lions was staring in our direction in a bored sort of way, and the third was looking away from us, its thick black mane displayed.

Ian looked around with his binoculars, explaining that he was certain their kill was around somewhere not too far away. He started the engine and drove slowly up the track where, underneath a stunted tree, he spotted the partially eaten carcass of a zebra. As we drove up to it, the lion that was looking at us got up, and slowly the other two lion rose from their slumbers. We watched these three, huge male lions in their prime, stride slowly but purposely towards their kill, sitting down to guard it right in front of us.

This was a photographer's heaven! I shot photo after photo, and we settled down to observe them. They resumed their slumbers, every so often adjusting their positions to ease the pressure from their full stomachs. We watched what lions do for about twenty-two of the twenty-four hours in a day. Slumber peacefully! Even I felt my eyelids drooping. Before long other vehicles drew up beside us, and realising that there was not going to be any more excitement for the rest of the day, we decided to drive back to camp and leave these three beasts to sleep off their latest meal.

We spent the rest of the day recovering from lack of sleep, and observing the waterhole, whilst Ian and Petrus prepared the last braai we would share with them. The following day we would drive out of Etosha to Okonjima, a sanctuary for cheetah and home of the Africat Foundation.

We reminisced over our exploits of the last couple of weeks, going through the highlights and laughing at the mishaps. I realised just how much I would miss these two lovely men – Ian with his vast knowledge and passion of his beautiful country, and Petrus with his broad grin and ever helpful attitude.

Between them they had worked so hard to ensure that we had experienced the safari of a lifetime in a desolate, enchanting country, which was so totally different from any we had previously visited. We toasted them with more than one bottle of iced Amarula, Ian claiming that he did not want to take any back to Windhoek. Finally, we weaved our way unsteadily to bed.

The lack of sleep and, no doubt, the elimination of excess supplies of the remaining alcohol, meant that there were no nocturnal trips to the waterhole. I doubt that anything other than lions making a kill right in front of our bedroom window would have disturbed our sleep, and we were woken at dawn by the now familiar 'knock knock' on our door announcing the arrival of Petrus with reviving cups of tea.

We set off for Okonjima in the early morning, nursing our hangovers, but thankful that the further south we travelled the smoother the gravel roads became. I dozed fitfully, occasionally opening my eyes to see yet more scrub and bush stretch endlessly to the horizon. I woke with a start as Ian announced that we had a puncture. We all clambered out of the Landy and Ian and Petrus set to work, climbing onto the high roof and untying one of the two huge spare tyres. Somehow, they manhandled it down to the ground, politely refusing all offers of help from Conrad and Gordon.

The Landy was then jacked up, the offending tyre removed, and the spare one fitted in the space of a few minutes. I watched in amazement as they hauled the removed tyre onto the roof. They had obviously had a lot of practice in doing this and were as impressive as a Formula One team changing tyres at a pit stop. 'More so,' said Gordon, his voice full of admiration, 'when you think there are only two of them and they had to lift such a weight.' Praise indeed from a car fanatic!

We drove on, sweat pouring down the faces of Ian and Petrus, only to stop after a few miles. Ian jumped out of the Landy and went to look at the replaced tyre, returning with a reassuring grin on his face. 'Only checking it was okay!' There were we wondering if we had another puncture! I ruminated on how we had travelled thousands of kilometres over infinitely rougher road and I had never even thought about punctures.

Ian talked about our next and final stop before flying back to England. He had been to the Africat Foundaton at Okonjima many times, and we chatted about the cheetah, leopards and lion we would see there. Mentally, we prepared ourselves for the opportunity to take photos of these cats. What a great contrast this would be to Etosha, where we had driven for hours before seeing those elusive lions. Not only had I to brace myself for the return to civilisation, but also the realisation that these were the last few kilometres we would all be driving together. I looked at Petrus – as usual fast asleep, and then at Ian, concentrating on his driving. All journeys must come to an end. I just wished that these partings were not tinged with so much sadness.

Although these lion were in captivity at Okonjima, they still provided an unusual opportunity for some good photographs. These magnificent felines were living out their days in a vast enclosed area with their every need catered for. However, I get greater pleasure seeing lion in their natural environment even if this means an absence of any photographs.

Chapter 16

Cheetahs, Lions and Leopards

We arrived at Okonjima, the home of the Africat Foundation in the early afternoon, and said goodbye to Ian and Petrus who were travelling back to Windhoek. They would collect us in a couple of days' time to take us to the airport. We settled into our bedroom at the lodge, again revelling in the comparative luxury of king-sized beds and a large shower. Peering out of a window, I caught a glimpse of a cheetah strolling up and down a fenced-in enclosure. *This* is what we had come to see!

We went off to a lecture about the work of the Africat Foundation, learning how they rescued injured or orphaned cheetah and leopard with the intention of releasing them back into the wild when they were able to fend for themselves. Gradually, the farming fraternity were being educated with regard to Africat's work to preserve these endangered cats. Farmers were encouraged not to shoot them, but rather lure them into baited cages and notify the Foundation, who would then collect the trapped animals and relocate them where they wouldn't attack the farmers' livestock. We could see that this was going to be a long-term project, as who could blame the farmers for protecting their livelihood?

We were invited to go to a hide where we might see a large male leopard named Tyson coming down to eat, so armed with cameras, we joined several other visitors and were shepherded into a hide overlooking a rocky area. There on the rocks some meat was laid out, and we were told that Tyson would probably come down to feed. We were warned not to start taking photos until he was down off the rocks, as we would disturb him. This was certainly not what I was expecting.

Perhaps the many experiences we had had in the wild had made me rather cynical about this zoo-like set-up with the kill already provided, but I reminded myself that as this leopard had no opportunity to make the kill itself, what alternative was there? As dusk approached, Tyson duly appeared, only for someone to start taking photos with a flash, whereupon Tyson promptly disappeared. Shamed-facedly, the culprit busied himself with his photographic equipment as we waited to see if the leopard would re-appear. After half an hour, a wary Tyson made his way down from the rocky outcrop and grabbed the meat. He leaped up onto the top of the rocks and for a perfect second he stood still, silhouetted against the darkening sky before disappearing from view.

On our way back to the vehicle, I reflected on how different this experience was compared to the one a couple of days ago when the leopard had strolled past us in the dusk, off, no doubt, to hunt for his kill. Saddened and thoughtful we went to supper with Ann and Conrad, each of us voicing our concerns that perhaps this part of the trip was too great a contrast. It was difficult enough to acclimatise ourselves to socialising with other visitors after being in our close-knit little group, but seeing animals in enclosures was almost too difficult to bear, however honourable the intentions of the Foundation.

Determined to make the most of the next day, we set out in an open vehicle to see some of the rescued cheetahs, which were too habituated to humans for them ever to be safely released into the wild again. We were driven to a large enclosure and almost immediately several cheetah approached the vehicle. The ranger got down from the vehicle and unloaded some meat for them.

I watched in amazement when one cheetah came up to him and was fed by hand, the others approaching more warily. The ranger placed a few pieces of meat in a large metal dish, and returned to the driver's seat, telling us that we were safe and would get a good photo opportunity, as he would place the dish on the bonnet of the vehicle and an especially tame cheetah would come and eat there. I took a photo of Gordon sitting in the front passenger seat with a cheetah eating the remains of a springbok just a few inches away from him. However close the encounter, I would much rather have spent a day searching for a wild animal.

We decided to spend the rest of the day at a hide overlooking a small pool, looking at the varied bird life that was free to come and go as they wished. The ranger walked us to the hide, warning us that often there was a caracal there, which had been raised by the staff from infancy. Although used to humans, this small cat did not like men, although women presented no problem. Fascinated by this introduction we entered the hide and sure enough, there was a caracal, Africa's version of a lynx, lying peacefully in the corner.

Gingerly, I approached this elegant feline, and was immediately struck by its long tufted ears. Encouraged by the ranger, I stroked its tawny coat, looking at the dark markings on its cheeks, and noticing how the white markings above its eyes stood out clearly. I had never seen one before as they are rare and mainly nocturnal. No doubt, I would never see one again – certainly never as close.

The caracal is the heaviest of all the small cats, and whilst I sat stroking it, Gordon took out the camera and started to take some photos. He attempted to get a better close-up but the caracal immediately became wary and tense – a graphic warning that it certainly did not want him to come any nearer. No one knew why it was so wary of men, but it was clear that Gordon was not welcome to approach any closer, and it hissed fiercely until he retreated.

Once certain that this strange man was far enough away to present no danger, this graceful cat settled down with its head in my lap, purring contentedly. Gordon went to the other side of the hide, intent on doing some serious bird watching, whilst the caracal and I remained together, enjoying half an hour of mutual grooming. Its rough tongue rasped over my arms as I stroked its coat and stored memories of a precious time spent together.

Eventually, Gordon gently called me to come and see some birds, and the caracal's long tufted and unique ears twitched. Its tail started to swish from side to side. Even the sound of a male voice seemed to disturb it. It stood up, stretched, and elegantly strolled off into the far, dim interior of the hide whilst I, somewhat reluctantly, went off to join the humans.

Early the following morning, we set off for a vast enclosure where three rescued lions were living out the remainder of their days. We climbed up a few steps and peered over some stout wooden railings only to see two enormous male lions and one lioness strolling towards a ranger, who was carrying only a stick, which apparently was armed with an electric charge. The lions were disciplined with this if necessary, although it was rarely used.

Obligingly, the three lions climbed up onto a sandy hillock and Ann and I took reel after reel of photos of these magnificent cats. Again, I was saddened to see such majestic animals in captivity, but their existence here was at least infinitely better than those in many zoos. They had acres of bush in which to roam, acacia trees under which to shelter from the fierce sun, food supplied at regular intervals and all their medical needs taken care of.

In all probability, they would survive to a ripe old age – far longer than in the wild. However, they would never satisfy their natural instincts of the chase, the dynamics of living in a large pride, and rearing and protecting their young. That they are essentially lazy creatures, and sleep for the majority of the day in the wild, went a little way to lessen my concern. Again, I cast my mind back to the lions I recently had so much difficulty seeing in Etosha, and had great trouble in coming to terms with the whole concept of animals in captivity.

I had been fortunate enough to experience the satisfaction of searching, sometimes for hours on end, in the stifling heat for a glimpse of a wild animal, rather than have them presented to us for an instant photo opportunity. If nothing else, I hoped that people seeing these animals here would then support the numerous efforts worldwide to ensure that wild animals were able to roam free in their natural habitats, living out their natural lives as they were born to do. No doubt, this will inevitably become more difficult with the explosion of the human population producing ever-increasing pressure on space for wildlife.

Ian collected us after breakfast, Petrus staying in Windhoek to prepare a late lunch for us. Once on our way, Ian promised Ann and I a visit to a local market a few miles outside Windhoek, and our eyes lit up with the promise of a bit of retail therapy. I would much rather buy souvenirs from the locals and support them directly than buy in the sterile duty-free area of the airport. We chatted about what we wanted to buy, at which point, the faces of our men folk took on a glum expression. It was necessary to remind them that for the whole of the three weeks we had been touring we had bought nothing at all!

We reached the main tarred road that goes virtually the complete length of Namibia, and breathed a sigh of relief, albeit tinged with a bit of nostalgia. All the rattling, jolting and dust ceased, and we motored on, able to hear clearly what everyone was saying without having to resort to shouting. It felt as though we were gliding along in a Rolls Royce as the miles sped by, only for an ominous squealing noise from under the bonnet to break the comparative silence. We slowly drew to a halt, all power gone, and Ian was just able to pull off the road onto a wide stretch of scrub. Out jumped the men and disappeared under the bonnet whilst Ann and I sat awaiting developments in the increasing heat.

Ten minutes later came the diagnosis that the dynamo had failed, and we would have to wait for alternative transport to get us back to Windhoek. Unfortunately, Ian had unloaded the emergency radio telephone when he had unpacked the Landy, as the journey to and from Okonjima was not on remote rough roads, As Sod's Law would have it, we were in a patch where there was no mobile phone coverage.

We would just have to wait for a passing motorist to transfer a message for us when they got a signal. We waited, and waited and after half an hour, a bakkie travelling north pulled up and took the message and mobile number Ian gave him. Twenty minutes later, a lorry travelling south stopped and the same procedure was repeated. Now all we could do was sit and wait for rescue.

As the sun reached its peak, virtually all shade disappeared, and we had to unpack some of our luggage and rig up some shade with a few T-shirts draped over the open doors, so that we could crouch beside the Landy on the rough ground in this scant shade. Every quarter of an hour or so, a car or lorry would stop and ask if they could be of any help, and each time Ian gave the message and telephone number for them to phone, in case, for whatever reason, the previous motorists had failed to get through.

Thankfully, we had ample water, so we sipped the now lukewarm fluid to keep hydrated, chatting quietly about how lucky we had been that the breakdown had happened on a main road and not when we were driving in the remotest parts of Namibia. An hour passed and then two, and by now Ann and I realised that in keeping ourselves hydrated we would have to get rid of the excess fluid!

Once again, we bemoaned the fact that this exercise was so much more convenient for men than women, but decided that desperate times call for desperate measures. We went off a couple of yards into the scrub, stamping heavily to warn off any lurking snakes, and there at the side of the main arterial road of Namibia – the equivalent to our M1 in England, albeit with less traffic, we squatted!

Seeing a grin on our relieved faces, Ian decided that now was the time to break the news that our trip to the market would no longer be possible. Gordon and Conrad tried to stifle their relieved expressions. We were rapidly running out of time to make our flight home, let alone indulge in any retail therapy. All the plans of a refreshing shower at Ian's home and a leisurely lunch cooked by Petrus before catching our flight had also gone for a burton.

Ian was his usual optimistic self, assuring us that he would make sure that we would catch our flight. As if to confirm his optimism, our rescue transport arrived and the men sorted out a towrope. Gordon went with Ian in the Landy to keep him company, and the rest of us climbed on board the rescue Landy to begin the final part of our journey.

We travelled slowly towards Windhoek, passing a vibrant market at which Ann and I could only longingly gaze, when we were stopped by some traffic police. Apparently, the towrope was too long and it was illegal to carry a passenger whilst towing. After abject apologies from Ian, we continued on our way, Gordon now sitting in the rescue vehicle with us, and arrived in Windhoek for a hurried lunch with Petrus before we said goodbye to him. Hopefully, Ann and I did not embarrass him too much with the bear hugs we gave him, but he ran out into the road, following the Landy with his face wreathed in smiles and his arms waving frantically like windmill sails until he disappeared from our sight.

I wiped away my tears thinking how much I would miss that hard-working man with a lovely grin who gave his all to make our safari so comfortable. Finally, we reached the airport and it was time for one final goodbye. I hugged Ian with yet more tears in my eyes – thanks seemed so inadequate after all he had given us. He had shown us his Namibia and I had fallen totally in love with it.

Gordon and I had travelled from the southernmost part to the northern border, and nothing had prepared us for such a desolate, unforgiving, dusty yet spectacularly beautiful country. All the long hours of bumping up and down on the roughest of roads, adapting to the searing heat of the desert, the swirling fog and cold of the Skeleton Coast, long-drop loos that collapsed, and showers that failed to work – all these discomforts were remembered with laughter, and became some of our most treasured memories.

The beauty of the scenery, its rarely sighted wildlife and its fascinating people would remain in my heart and make me yearn for Namibia long after I had left. They say that you should never return to somewhere you have loved, that you would only be disappointed, but never is an unforgiving word, and whatever the future holds, my memories of Namibia will always continue to delight and enchant me.

My first glimpse of the Ngorongoro Crater in Tanzania was one of those iconic moments that I will remember forever. This massive caldera stretched below us as far as the eye could see. Slow moving dots, viewed through binoculars, materialised into elephant and buffalo. The descent was a hair-raising journey, matched only by the ascent. Groves of fever trees and the salt lake with flamingos provided unusual splashes of colour. Our 'over the top' accommodation overlooked the crater!

Chapter 17

Tanzania: Kilimanjaro, Plains and Craters

Where are we going to get our next African fix? Within a few weeks of getting back to our Derbyshire home, this was the question on our minds. We were ready to plan next year's safari, much to the wry amusement of our two sons. No amount of re-assuring would convince them that once Mum and Dad retired they would settle down and stop this annual migration to somewhere in Africa.

The word 'migration' suddenly rang all sorts of bells, and we instantly knew we must go to Tanzania to see the annual migration of the wildebeest. Therefore, after a few months' of planning with our patient African travel agent we found ourselves back in Africa, landing at Kilimanjaro Airport just as night was approaching.

As if by magic, our transport materialised in the midst of the usual chaos of an African airport, and we motored through the countryside in the dark for an hour or so, seeing nothing but trees on either side of the track. It felt as though we could have been anywhere in the world until we drew to an abrupt halt. There, out of the pitch black night walked a large giraffe across the track. We were back in Africa! It was nearly twenty-four hours since we had left home, so all we wanted was to go to bed and sleep, but on arrival at our small rustic lodge, we were greeted by the staff who had stayed up, ready to serve us an evening meal although it was well past midnight. It was impossible to disappoint these hospitable black faces however much we wanted our sleep, and soon we were tucking into a delicious meal, realising that we were ravenous. Replete, we retired to our bedroom to recover from the journey.

I woke as dawn was breaking, and drew back the curtains to catch my first real sight of Tanzania – a herd of buffalo quietly grazing. Towering above in the distance was Mount Meru, Tanzania's second highest mountain – a stratovolcano of nearly 15,000 feet, about seventy kilometres west of its more famous relation Mount Kilimanjaro. I peered around to see if I could see Mount Kilimanjaro, but the dawn mist was too thick.

I grabbed my fleece and ventured outside. I sat on the small rock wall separating the lodge's garden from the bush where the buffalo were grazing, and soaked in the sights, sounds and smells as a new African day emerged. What was it that was so enthralling about Africa that had me relentlessly in its grasp? Maybe it was its timeless quality. However fast the world was rushing into the 21st century, so much of the African bush remained resolutely unchanged.

I ruminated on how we were near to what has been called the Cradle of Mankind. In fact, we would be visiting an archaeological site where fossils of early hominids were first discovered. Was it possible to carry in one's genes some echo of the long distant past that resonated so strongly within the core of my being whenever I was in Africa? I got up from my seat, smiling at these many unanswered questions, and returned to the task of waking up my still slumbering husband. Our guide would be collecting us in an hour for our first full day in Tanzania.

As we were only spending a day in the Arusha area before flying into the Serengeti, our two guides, Erasto and Mohammed, took us to explore some of the Arusha National Park. Before long, I was in my element, photographing troops of shaggy, black and white colobus monkeys swinging effortlessly from treetop to treetop, and large blue monkeys with their extremely long tails, neither of which species had we seen before.

Dik-dik, a miniature antelope with a pointed, mobile snout and enormous dark eyes was another animal that was new to us, and we learnt that these tiny antelope mate for life. Where there was one, the chances were that another one would be close by. We stopped for a picnic lunch, and I asked where Mount Kilimanjaro was as I was longing to see this famous mountain. I would be disappointed if we couldn't catch a glimpse of the 'Roof of Africa', but it still remained overcast and our guides were doubtful if Kilimanjaro would be visible through the high clouds.

We continued on our journey to the Ngurdoto Crater, a mini volcanic crater about three kilometres in diameter and four hundred metres deep. Unlike the more visited Ngorongoro crater, this one was closed to visitors, but there were ample viewing areas where we stopped to gaze into its depths. I felt as though I was gazing into a Jurassic Park. Herds of buffalo and elephant were grazing on the green marshy area on the caldera floor, and birds swooped over our heads, soaring effortlessly down below us to feed off the insects the grazers were stirring up.

It was a peaceful, undisturbed scene, which had remained virtually intact from human interference since the caldera had sunk many thousands of years ago; how the animals got there was anyone's guess, but it was a delight to see them in their natural habitat with no vehicles to hinder their existence.

We travelled on until we reached the Momella Lakes where flocks of flamingos were feeding in the shallow alkaline water, which we learnt was continually topped up by underground streams. The individual honking sound each flamingo made blended together into a soft babbling noise, and the pink of their feathers and the richer pink of their bills were reflected in the water, providing a picturesque scene for some photographs.

We could see that dusk would soon be approaching as the sun was sinking rapidly, when our guide pointed into the distance, exclaiming that we were very fortunate as we could now see Kilimanjaro. I looked into the horizon, not seeing anything that resembled a mountain until my gaze was directed straight up into the sky. I gasped – there, high above a layer of cloud, I caught my first sight of the snow-covered peak of this iconic mountain. I was astounded at its height, and seeing the snow, now tinged pink with the glow of the setting sun was a surreal experience.

Quickly, we took a few photos before the light faded, and then spent the remaining few minutes just savouring the scene. Our guide suggested that if we hurried back to the lodge we might well see Kilimanjaro again before night descended. Unfortunately, we had to leave the park before sunset, and on our arrival back at the lodge we managed to snatch a few precious moments looking at Kilimanjaro fade into the dark. At least we had managed to see it, and now knew where to look the following morning.

The clouds were once again covering Kilimanjaro when we left for Arusha airport, but we consoled ourselves that we had at least been able to see it in all its glory, and how lucky we had been that the clouds had parted to give us this sighting. We boarded our light aircraft with a few other passengers, none of whom was going to the same camp in the Serengeti, but we were assured that we were on the right flight. After several drop-offs, which meant that we had many more take-offs and landings on dirt strip runways than I had anticipated, we landed in the middle of nowhere with two other passengers. We taxied up to a game vehicle that was waiting under the shade of an umbrella acacia, and hauling ourselves out of the narrow door, jumped down onto the Serengeti earth.

The driver of the vehicle greeted us, but our names did not match up with his passenger list to go to a nearby lodge. Our guide and vehicle was somewhere in this vast wilderness, but where was anyone's guess! I looked around hoping for someone to materialise, wondering if we were going to be left under the tree, but was assured that we would be transported to the lodge where they would radio our tour operator.

Clambering up into the Landy with our small amount of luggage, we set off, only to come across a pride of six lion within a couple of minutes. No wonder we were not going to be left to fend for ourselves! After taking some photos of these big cats lazing in the shade of some bushes, their only movement being the angry twitch of a tail when flies descended on them, we drove on to arrive at an opulent lodge perched on top of a hill. We were welcomed with a cool drink and wet hand towels to refresh us, and Gordon provided details of our itinerary with the vital telephone numbers of our tour operator in Arusha.

A few minutes later, we were told that everything was in hand and our guide would be with us in half an hour, as he had been delayed by a puncture. I was most impressed with the speed everything was sorted out. Never before in all our African travels did we have to resort to phoning anyone over anything, and this proved to us how important it was to keep safe these vital telephone numbers.

We relaxed on the veranda with drinks in our hands, staring out onto the vast Serengeti plains spread below us. Each dot transformed into an elephant, wildebeest or zebra with the help of our binoculars. We declined the kind offer of lunch as we were sure that our guide would have arranged something for us, such was our faith in our UK travel agent. Half an hour later, our guide for the next part of our safari arrived and we introduced ourselves, shaking hands with Rowland who was full of abject apologies and highly relieved that we had taken his late arrival in such a relaxed way.

We thanked the lodge staff for their hospitality, and set off with Rowland into the wide open spaces of the Serengeti. Once clear of any signs of civilisation we pulled to a halt under the shade of some acacia trees, and Rowland pulled out three canvas chairs, and a picnic table complete with tablecloth. Out of a large cool box, he produced a sumptuous lunch, served with iced beer and chilled white wine. We toasted each other and I thought how much nicer it was to dine alfresco in the middle of the bush rather than in the dining room of a lodge. We chatted to Rowland about the previous few hours, the stresses of the flight and his plans for us over the next week. His late arrival faded into insignificance as we relaxed into the gentle tempo of the bush.

We continued on our journey to where we would spend the next three nights – a lodge in the north-west part of the Serengeti, close to the Grumeti River. It was late afternoon when we reached our accommodation – a large tent standing on a shaded wooden deck overlooking the savannah plains and some high granite kopjes in the middle distance. What a magnificent vista! We quickly unpacked what little luggage we had, and after grabbing a hasty shower in the en-suite shower room at the back of our tent, we made our way back to the bar area for a G and T.

Another couple introduced themselves to us and we spent the next half hour before supper talking about their experiences in the bush. They had arrived the previous day and were on their honeymoon, so I assumed that they would want a bit of peace and quiet together at supper. Apparently, all the guests were like us and had their own guide and vehicle, enabling everyone to go off in their own time to view whatever took their fancy. Thankfully, there were no notorious mini-vans packed full of tourists around here.

The loud beat of a drum summoned us to supper, and we made our way to the dining area, drink in hand. Disaster struck when I tripped over in an unlit area going up some roughly hewn steps, and landed heavily, smashing the glass. I realised that not only was the glass broken, but I had also cut my wrist, which was now bleeding heavily. First aid training and my nursing experience came in handy and I held my arm up and squeezed my elbow tight as everyone rushed to help. I was ushered into the light of the dining area and sat down to recover and examine the damage. The honeymoon couple followed me and offered to help. They were both doctors, and we examined my wrist to make certain that was no remaining glass in the wound. Firm pressure helped control the bleeding, and I was relieved that there appeared to be no nerve damage. It was a question of what to do next as my wrist obviously needed suturing.

The lodge manager said he would organise emergency air evacuation to Arusha to get medical help. This seemed an horrendous idea to me, as flying in the bush during daylight hours was terrifying enough, and the thought of a night-time take-off was really more than I could face. He attempted to assure me that they would light up the dirt runway with flares and that it would be safe, but I was adamant that I did not want to do this. Another suggestion was that we could strap up my wrist and wait until the morning to fly me back to Arusha, but this would mean that we would miss at least one day of our precious time in the Serengeti – something I was very reluctant to do.

It was obvious that they had a very determined, if not bloody-minded and bloody-handed patient on their hands! The doctors asked if the lodge had a comprehensive medical kit, as they could suture up my wrist if I would let them. Would I let them? I would do anything to avoid an extra flight back to Arusha! I nearly hugged them, and then suddenly remembered that we had an emergency first-aid kit which, if my memory was correct, included sutures and suturing needles.

I asked Gordon to go and get it from our tent, telling him not to run and fall down in the dark. One injury was enough! Accompanied by the manager with two torches, Gordon returned unscathed, and the doctors opened the first-aid kit to find that there was indeed enough to do some emergency sewing repairs.

A casualty station complete with makeshift sterile area was set up in the middle of the dining room. The guests valiantly tried to ignore the situation and enjoy their meal whilst one of the doctors prepared to stitch my wrist. Unfortunately, there was no local anaesthetic available, so I just had to grin and bear it as the poor man inserted half a dozen stitches, sweat pouring from his brow. Finally, he declared that he had finished and the stitches ought to hold the wound. His wife bandaged me up, asking me if my tetanus injections were up to date, and that she thought I should have a course of antibiotics if I had brought any.

Thankfully, all my jabs were up to date, and I always carried a supply of antibiotics, as I have a heart murmur and need them to hand in case I had to have any dental treatment. We decided that a one-off hefty dose would probably do the trick and kill off any bugs that might have entered my system.

We had a belated dinner together, and I promised that we would not disturb their honeymoon from tomorrow onwards, although over supper we discovered that we were all going to be at the same lodge later that week when we were visiting the Ngorongoro Crater. I fell into bed that night, totally exhausted, my only worry being whether I would be able to hold my camera. I drifted off to sleep, Gordon's snoring and the sounds of some hyenas whooping somewhere in the distance, providing a discordant lullaby.

Dawn never ceases to be a magical time for me when waking up in the middle of the bush. I listened as the first sounds of birds began their pre-dawn chorus before the sun welcomed the bush to a new day. A troop of baboons started their early morning greeting ritual, and there was a pause for half an hour or so as the rest of the bush roused itself, before a cacophony of bird song and animal sounds announced that they had survived the night and all was well with the world.

I wrapped a plastic bag round my wrist and attempted to shower holding one arm up out of the water. By this time, Gordon had woken up, and enquiring about my injury was relieved to find that it was not too sore and that I was ready to carry on as normal. Rowland greeted us after breakfast, his kindly, shining black face full of concern. Obviously, the bush telegraph had been working overtime! He solicitously helped me into our vehicle as though I was the Queen. I decided that somehow I had to let him know that my injury was relatively minor, and that I was a tough, but not too old a bird who was going to forget about her stitched wrist and get on with the safari.

I found it strange that in Tanzania the safari vehicles were not open-topped but had their roofs raised on hinges, so we could stand up and look though the space between the top of the vehicle and the collapsible roof. I much preferred the open top Landys, but over the days we adapted, finding the one major advantage was that we could stand up whenever we wanted, and ease our numb bums, as we did not break the outline of the vehicle and disturb the wildlife.

The only unpleasant part of our safari in the Serengeti was the notorious tsetse fly. These vicious little blighters became the bane of our lives, as they seemed to adore both of us and whenever we were on the move, they zoomed into the Landy with unerring accuracy. We were soon nursing several bites, which swelled up into red-hot bumps, developing into the size of saucers, and reluctantly, we had to close the windows and roof when driving along. Thankfully, the attacks were fewer when we were stationary. It seemed the movement and exhaust fumes attracted them.

No amount of insect repellent seemed to make any impression to deter these horrible critters, even though our arms and legs were covered. Little wonder when they were able to pierce the hide of cattle. This was illustrated graphically when we were sitting down on camp chairs having a mid morning coffee break. Gordon leapt up, exclaiming angrily that the damned tsetse flies did not play cricket – one had even stung his behind through the canvas!

Rowland seemed immune to these pests, and said that if one did sting him, his usual retort was to thank the fly as it meant that the wildlife were safe from cattle taking over the Serengeti, as cattle did not survive in a tsetse fly area. Whilst driving along, we made vain attempts to ignore them, and resorted to waving a wildebeest tail fly swat that Rowland thoughtfully provided. Some light relief came as darkness fell, and they disappeared, only to renew their attack as morning dawned. At least the tsetse fly in the Serengeti did not carry the dreaded sleeping sickness.

We soon became used to raising the roof quickly whenever we came across any wildlife, and spent the first day amongst herds of wildebeest on their annual migration. Nothing had prepared me for the unending streams of these animals, sometimes galloping, sometimes stopping for a brief time to graze on the sparse vegetation, their incessant croaking, mewing sounds obliterating any other sound. No one in their right mind can say that these are beautiful animals, but their occasional idiotic behaviour of galloping round in circles after their tails, only to look round to make certain that no one had seen their antics, endeared them to us as the clowns of the savannah.

Rowland pulled up at the top of a riverbank, where for over an hour we watched as hundreds of wildebeest rushed down the steep banks, only to haul themselves up the opposite bank and continue on their journey, innately guided by their instincts to find better pasture. Interspersed amongst them were zebra, and I took photo after photo of this great trek, the red dust swirling up in atmospheric clouds, coating the shrubs, trees and us with a fine powder.

We gazed down into the river bed, and spotted a single wildebeest struggling in the water. However hard it tried to move, it seemed anchored to one spot. Eventually, we realised that it had trapped one of its legs in some rocks, and the more frantically it struggled the deeper it sank into the water. We watched for ten minutes, willing this poor animal to free itself. Unable to watch it suffer any longer, we asked Rowland to drive off.

We returned later that day to the same place. Herds of wildebeest were still pouring down the banks, but there was no trace of the trapped one. I wondered it had managed to free itself; this was very doubtful though, and I hoped its end had been rapid. In all our travels in Africa, we had yet to see an actual kill. We would frequently arrive after the event or witness failed attempts, and I wondered how I would react to seeing an animal brought down by a predator when I could hardly bear watching one wildebeest struggling for its life. I suspected that no amount of logical thinking about how predators need to eat and feed their young would ever make it easy for me to watch a kill happening before my very eyes.

Over a picnic lunch, we discussed what I would most like to photograph. Notably lacking in my photo albums was a leopard up a tree. I had leopards lying down, sitting up, walking alongside me, but my ultimate photo would be one of a leopard in a tree, its legs on either side of a branch with its tail hanging down. Of course, the light would need to be in the right direction and the leopard's face towards me! Rowland's expression told me that he had a tough job on his hands, but I reassured him that we were here for the total experience and he should not concern himself.

That afternoon as we were driving along slowly, swatting the tsetse fly, cursing the bites and somewhat reluctantly blessing the culprit as Rowland did, a lone male cheetah appeared in front of us. Bites forgotten, we spent the next half hour following this graceful cat, which frequently paused and called, chirping faintly – its call almost birdlike. Rowland thought it was one of a coalition of three males seen together the previous day, but there was no sign of its siblings.

On our way back to camp, we stopped at the foot of a large kopje, and there on the top of this vast granite outcrop was a pride of lions lazily surveying the plains below, no doubt thinking about supper. We counted eight lionesses and four cubs of about three months old, their coats still woolly with greyish spots, a reliable indicator of their young age. Engaged in a game of tag around their mothers, the cubs would occasionally stop their activities, and approaching a lioness, would nuzzle their heads against each other. Suddenly, one of the lionesses raised her head and stared in our direction, the others following her gaze.

I raised my binoculars for a close up, and the amber eyes of the lioness bore straight through me and then shifted slightly to the right. Glancing down in the direction of her line of sight, I caught the glimpse of a flick of a black tipped tail, and Rowland motioned to us to keep quiet and motionless. Another lioness appeared, strolling alongside our vehicle and swishing her tail gently against the side of the door, before she started to clamber up the steep slope of the kopje to join the rest of the pride. We watched quietly as she greeted her companions, the soft moaning and grunts quite audible as she settled down, only to be plagued by the attention of the boisterous cubs.

I find that time stands still when we are so privileged to witness such a close sighting, made all the more special by the fact that we were the only people there. I took a few more photos, and decided to simply enjoy the interaction of the pride. The more I travelled in Africa the more I learnt from absorbing what was going on around me, rather than concentrating on creating a photo with a sometimes intrusive piece of photographic equipment in front of my eyes. Through watching animals I found that I could often predict what an animal would do next which paradoxically, produced better photographs. Yes, I have some wonderful photos, many of which I have framed, and some that I've sold, but I often don't remember taking the photos; what is imprinted in my memory is the total experience of the sounds, smells and how I felt when I did nothing but just be there, letting Africa 'happen' in front of me.

The following day was our last one at this camp, and we set off after an early breakfast with a picnic lunch in the large cool-box. We did not want to miss one moment of our precious time by having to go back to have lunch in the dining room, even though in the heat of the day many of the animals would be quietly resting in whatever shade they could find. Our friends, the tsetse flies, were out in force to greet us with their vicious proboscises that resembled a hypodermic needle, producing a sting more painful than that of a bee, wasp and horsefly put together. It wasn't as though the pain of the sting went away after a few hours. If anything, for the next twenty-four hours it became more and more painful before gradually fading away. Perhaps Gordon and I were particularly sensitive to the sting, but even regular doses of antihistamine tablets taken in near desperation, failed to produce much relief. It was going to be a question of mind over matter as we swished away with the wildebeest tail, cheering when we actually managed to dispatch one of the blighters.

The wildebeest were still flowing past in an hypnotic stream, the never-ending noise of their bleating drowning out any other sounds of the bush. It was a relief to move away from the river crossings, leaving the herds to their frantic meanderings and once again, relax in the tranquillity of the vastness of the Serengeti plains.

Suddenly Rowland stopped the Landy and pointed to a tree a few yards away. Approaching it was a lone elephant, and then a large male leopard jumped down from a high branch and ran off into the distance. It must have been disturbed by the elephant, and I wondered how often we had passed a tree with an elusive leopard hiding unseen in dense foliage. One day, I promised myself, I would get that much wanted photo of a leopard in a tree.

On we travelled until Rowland pulled up and set up our picnic lunch. Never had we lunched with such landscape before us. As far as the eye could see, the golden Serengeti plains stretched from left to right, dotted with the occasional acacia tree. In the far distance, Gordon spotted a black dot – an ostrich, Rowland informed us. Even with binoculars we couldn't identify it. What a gift to have such wonderful eyesight and the knowledge that resulted from living in the bush. We talked about our different way of life, and how Rowland wanted to go to London to see some of the sights that we take for granted, but he was frightened and bewildered by crowds and large cities. We told him how we would love to go walking in the bush by ourselves as Rowland had all his life, but were equally scared that we would not survive there for long without a guide. We set the world to right over our lunch, content just to let this beautiful scene nurture our souls with its gentle balm.

We could have done with some of that balm when we set off for an afternoon of game spotting. The tsetse flies were out in droves, and I was reduced to getting some drink cans out of the cool box and put them on the emerging inflamed bites. Rowland was amazed at how quickly a bite turned to an angry wheal. They hardly affected him; no doubt a lifetime of increasing immunity helped.

The appearance of herds of elephant and a pride of lion resting in the shade helped as a distraction, and then we came across one of the most bizarre sights we had ever seen. There in the middle of an empty plain was an isolated buffalo turning round and round in ever more frantic circles. As we approached, we realised what was causing the animal so much distress. Somehow, it had managed to get one of its front legs hooked over its right large curved horn. How, we could only guess, as Rowland had never seen this happen in all his years of living in the bush. If only the poor animal would stop its futile struggling and lie down there might have been a chance that it could disentangle its leg. As it was, it became more and more distressed, frantically snorting and circling around on three legs, its fragile stability becoming more and more precarious.

We decided it would be better if we retired to a distance as our presence was only going to stress this frightened, angry animal even more, and there was absolutely nothing we could do to help it. In all probability, it was no real threat to us, although nearly a ton of one of the most dangerous animals in Africa could potentially be a real danger if, suddenly, it was to free its trapped leg. Rowland drove the Landy away and we settled down to watch the buffalo, willing it to free its trapped leg. Our departure did nothing to calm its desperate efforts, so we left it to its fate. Certainly, if the pride of lions we had seen earlier came across the scene there would be an easy kill.

As the afternoon wore on and we started to make our way back to camp, tiredness, pain from the tsetse bites and a sore wrist started to take its toll. The stitches pulled each time I flexed my wrist to balance the camera and take a shot. I sat back, cold cans of drink attempting to soothe my bites, whilst Rowland and Gordon chatted companionably together. I wished I could magic myself out of this tsetse fly belt, and feeling a bit of a wimp, I closed my eyes for an overdue siesta.

A few minutes later, there was the sound of excited conversation. Rowland had spotted a leopard and it was sitting in a tree! My photographic dream was about to come true. The late afternoon light was perfect and the nearer we got to the tree, the clearer the leopard became, posing elegantly over a branch as Rowland slowly positioned the Landy for the ultimate shot.

Silently, I hauled myself up to angle my camera through the open roof space, composed the shot and ... a nanosecond before I pressed the shutter, a tsetse fly stung me on the neck! All composure went out of the window, as I swore loudly and graphically, completely forgetting the cardinal rule of not disturbing the wildlife.

I managed a couple of shots of the leopard jumping down the tree, my long hoped for photographic opportunity disappearing into the bush. What an idiot I had been. It only remained for me to apologise to Rowland for my colourful language, and I spent the rest of the journey back to camp soothing yet another painful bite, and wondering how professional photographers cope with adverse conditions for hours on end.

We set off early the next morning for the Ngorongoro Crater by way of the Olduvai Gorge, the so-called Cradle of Mankind. I was longing to see where the famous archaeologists, Louis and Mary Leakey spent most of their working life excavating this unique site, and proving to the world that early hominids first walked here around 3.6 million years ago.

In the scorching heat, we walked to the edge of where they had started their excavations, staring in wonder at the multiple layers of strata, each change of colour signifying another era of time. At a small museum, Rowland showed us the casts of footprint trails found here. The Leakeys proved once and for all that these footprints were of early bi-peds. No knuckle traces were found, so these indeed were homanid, not ape prints.

I paused in front of the trail of three of our earliest ancestors who, some three million years ago would have passed not far from where we now stood. It was evident that they were in no hurry. These were clear, not scuffed prints, and for a short time, one of them stepped in the footprints of his companion. How very privileged we were to be able to visit such a truly awe-inspiring site. I imagined how my ancestors might have set off from here, and it was not the first time I felt I was on some sort of a pilgrimage, visiting the very source of my roots. We travelled yet further on our own personal journey of discovery until Rowland pulled off the road, informing us he had a surprise.

We jumped out of the Landy and walked a few yards down a dusty track together. Rounding a corner, I gasped. There below us lay the Ngorongoro Crater. For once, I was dumbstruck. I had never expected such a vast, spectacular scene. I gazed down into the world's largest unbroken caldera, formed some 2–3 million years ago when the volcano exploded and collapsed into itself. The far rim was just visible, a light haze softly fading its edges until it merged with the light blue sky.

Way below, black dots moved slowly – elephants, buffalo and wildebeest just discernable with the aid of binoculars. In the distance a salt lake spread in front of us, tinged a faint pink hue in places. They were flocks of flamingos, Rowland informed us. He pointed to where our next stop would be, and travelling on along dusty roads, we glimpsed the occasional Maasai in their vivid red cloaks, carrying long wooden clubs, and providing a startling splash of colour against the pale, arid landscape.

No amount of hyperbole from our travel agent could have prepared us for where we were to spend the next couple of nights. John had advised us to go really upmarket and spoil ourselves, not that we had been exactly slumming it so far! We would probably never visit the Ngorongoro Crater again, and he felt that we would really appreciate some luxury in the middle of our safari.

We were ushered to our suite and there waiting for us was a charming man who introduced himself to us as our personal butler! Now this really was going over the top, but glancing at Gordon, we decided to go with the flow. Our butler showed us round our accommodation, and treated us like royalty. In front of a large fireplace were two high-backed easy chairs full of cushions. Apparently, it would get cold enough to light the log fire each evening.

In between the chairs, an antique side table hosted a selection of drinks in silver-labelled decanters together with crystal glasses. An enormous bed was placed in front of large French windows, which opened out onto a wooden balcony overlooking the crater in all its glory. In another room, under an elaborate Venetian glass chandelier, a Victorian bath stood in solitary splendour overlooking the crater. Piles of fluffy white towels were placed on stools beside one side of the bath, and on the other, a table with champagne flutes and a wine cooler provided the ultimate touch to this decadent luxury. A double shower and a separate lavatory with windows on three sides provided yet more views of the crater. Yet another definitive loo with a view!

We sat out on the balcony, and watched as dusk slid gently into darkness over the crater, reluctantly moving inside when it got distinctly chilly. The butler had lit the fire and drawn a hot bath for us, complete with red rose petals floating on the surface and a bottle of bubbly on ice waiting to be consumed whilst we soaked away our aches and pains. We clambered into the bath, and cracked open the bottle, toasting each other amongst the rose petals. Unfortunately, this romantic interlude was short-lived, and quickly turned into a French farce. The only thing that became inflamed was our tsetse fly bites, and it was soon a mad dash to reach the shower and stand under a soothing cold stream of water.

Suitably calmed, we made our way to the dining room where our butler was waiting to serve us an exquisite meal accompanied by French wine. No wonder this establishment was nicknamed the Maasai Versailles. We retired to our suite to sit in front of the log fire, and wallow in all this luxury. I was becoming increasingly ambivalent over the opulence we were experiencing in a country where there was so much abject poverty. I could rationalise this to some extent by telling myself that our money helped to provide income to some families. Nonetheless, I was disturbed.

Camping whilst on safari, albeit in relative comfort, seemed to be less of a contrast between the 'haves' and the 'have nots', but realising that all the ills of this world were not going to be solved overnight by my musings, I decided I would be stupid not to enjoy our two nights of such opulence.

The following morning the butler woke us with a gentle verbal 'knock knock'. He placed our early morning tea on the bedside table before drawing the curtains to reveal the crater, shrouded in a soft pre-dawn mist. This was a perfect prelude to spending the day exploring the crater.

Before long, Rowland was driving us along the rough, steep track down the side of the crater wall. I breathed a sigh of relief when at last we were driving on the floor of the crater, no longer trying to ignore the precipitous drop of our descent. Almost immediately, we were rewarded with the sight of three black rhino emerging from a thicket of trees. We watched them amble round some bushes, browsing on the vegetation before they snorted angrily and trotted off into the distance. Thankfully, there was quite some distance between them and us, and we avoided becoming the focus of attention of these rare but notoriously bad tempered animals.

We meandered gently along towards some giraffe nibbling the leaves off some acacia trees, and passed a thicket of magnificent fever trees, their striking yellow bark lit up by the early morning sun. I could now see the crater walls towering all around us and the further we got to the centre of the crater, the more we could appreciate its vastness. The small specks we had seen at the top materialised into buffalo and zebra, and before long, we came across a breeding herd of elephant. The faint rumbles emitting from their stomachs reminded us that we were getting hungry.

Rowland drove to a freshwater stream and unpacked the table and chairs before he cooked us a full English breakfast on a small camping stove. We gazed at the scene before us and soon were fending off flocks of glossy starlings, which had decided to mob us for their breakfast.

Our peace was destroyed when six vehicles, full with tourists arrived. They began unloading themselves before queuing up to be issued with a paper bag containing their snack breakfast. I felt so sorry for them, being packed into a vehicle with some of them not even having a window seat, and the looks on their faces said it all when they saw us sitting down to our cooked breakfast, as they strolled around, easing their cramped limbs. One of them came over to us and asked who our travel agent was, as the next time he went on safari he wanted none of the packed vehicle rigmarole. We gave him the details and wished him well for the rest of his trip. Once again, we blessed our travel agent for making our African travels so special.

Picnic over, we motored towards some vultures Rowland had spotted circling high in the sky. Within a few moments, we were watching them descend on a carcass. I decided the smell of a rotting carcass of a buffalo would have guided us to this kill without the need for vultures to direct us! We searched for any sign of predators, but apart from some mangy-looking hyenas lying replete in the bush, there was no sign of any cats.

We continued to the lake and saw two more hyenas trying to catch a flamingo, causing an uproar amongst the large flock. Pink feathers floated down from the sky when the birds took off in a blur of frantically flapping wings. We got out of the Landy and walked a few yards down to the lakeside, the salt crystals crunching under our feet. Rowland pointed where our lodge was in the far distance, high up on the rim of the crater.

The morning passed in a haze of game viewing and attempts to avoid the numerous vehicles that sped off from one sighting to the next. If I had been on my first safari, no doubt I would want to do the same, so I tried to be more empathic to these tour vehicles packed to the brim with camera clicking tourists, reminding myself that I too was a tourist. My sympathy ran out when we came across a pride of lion and were quickly surrounded by a dozen mini buses, all revving their engines and following the lions when they moved away a few feet, no doubt to seek a bit of solitude.

However much potential the photo opportunity might yield, I saw no point in disturbing these magnificent beasts just to get a photo of them with a vehicle in the background. Gordon and I decided to call it a day, and asked Rowland to drive us back to our lodge. Like us, he admitted to being relieved that he didn't have to spend the whole day chasing after photo opportunities and avoiding the human race.

We spent the return journey to the lodge talking about the next part of our safari when we would be camping far away from any signs of mass tourism. We drove slowly to the gravel road and the Landy groaned up the steep slopes of the crater in first gear, with us yet again clinging to anything that gave us a modicum of support. I peered down the unprotected side of the crater, grateful that neither of us suffered from vertigo. We arrived in time for a late lunch and a welcome siesta, before spending the rest of the day on the balcony overlooking the panorama below us. We agreed that some things are better viewed from afar, and watched the sinking sun and darkness creeping over this most famous of all craters.

Tarangire National Park was very special and our tented accommodation sheltered by acacia trees was idyllic. It was a great contrast to the opulent luxury at Ngorongoro, and a haven of tranquility. Game viewing was spectacular, and we spent a couple of afternoons seated at a spot overlooking a river where hundreds of elephants came down to drink and bathe. We relaxed and recharged our batteries here before flying off to the Selous – our final stop in Tanzania.

Chapter 18

Tarangire and the Selous

The next morning we left the opulent magnificence of the 'Maasai Versailles'. I was glad that I had experienced it once in my life, but more excited about the prospect of camping in the bush. En route Rowland told us more about Tarangire National Park where we would be staying for the next three nights. We were lucky enough to be camping in a concession area far from the madding crowd, added to which Tarangire offered magnificent but quiet game viewing in its 1,000 square miles.

The three of us were in complete agreement that this was just what we needed after Ngorongoro. Gordon and I both agreed that it would suit us down to the ground to just sit and stare, rather than chase around after wildlife. Rowland's enigmatic smile was promising, and when we motored through the Park gates, and ventured further and further into what seemed to be pristine bush along a narrow dirt track, we knew our wishes would be granted.

We turned a bend, and there was our camp, especially set up for us. Our tent was placed away from the mess tent, and behind some bushes a few yards away, was the kitchen and where the staff of five slept.

A large double bed screened with a mozzie net, and oil lamps standing on the two bedside tables greeted me. No bath with rose petals, just an entirely adequate en-suite bush shower, a bowl and water jug, and a long-drop loo. Heaven! I came out of the tent to see Gordon sitting on one of the canvas chairs underneath the front awning, a gin and tonic in his hand and one waiting for me on a side table. This certainly deserved a toast!

Gordon explained that Rowland had shown him where the drinks were kept in the mess tent, and we were to pour ourselves whatever we wanted if there was no staff around. Rowland would join us for dinner in a couple of hours, but in the meantime, we were to relax and enjoy our surroundings, and if there was anything we wanted, we were just to shout. No shouting was required as we had everything we could possibly need.

In the distance, we could hear some elephants trumpeting, and around our tent, the prolific birdlife kept us entertained. Slowly the heat dissipated and having finished writing my diary, I sat back drowsily, smiling when I remembered the phrase 'sometimes I sits and thinks and sometimes I just sits!' I was more than content just to sit – no rushing about – no crowds of people – just another day in Africa gently coming to an end.

We woke up early the next morning just before the sun surfaced over the horizon. Before long, Rowland was driving at a slow pace and we came to a bend in the Tarangire River. This river is the only source of water in the Park, and as we were nearing the end of the dry season, it was a mere trickle, but more than enough to provide the vital water for all the wildlife.

Rowland parked the Landy underneath the shade of a magnificent baobab tree. We sat down on our canvas chairs and relaxed, allowing Africa to unfold before us. For the next couple of hours we sat in an amicable silence, as first one breeding herd of elephants came down to drink and then several others followed. After counting over fifty, I lost count of how many elephants sauntered down the sandy bank opposite us, all eager to quench their thirst. The calves played with each other in the water whilst the adults retired with dark watermarks on their bodies to spray dust over themselves to protect their skin from parasites.

The occasional zebra and giraffe appeared at the river, followed by a herd of buffalo. It was as though we were watching the screening of a National Geographic film. This was such a contrast to the Ngorongoro Crater. By the time we arrived back at camp, we had yet to see another vehicle.

A hearty brunch awaited us, and inner man satisfied, we retired for a siesta in the heat of the day before going out for another game drive in the late afternoon. The heat slowly yielded to the cool of the evening and the shadows lengthened. We drove to another viewpoint overlooking the river, and with sundowners in our hands, we relaxed and watched yet more elephants come down to slake their thirst. I decided I could never tire of such a scene as we motored back to camp for our second night under the stars. In the mess tent, we ate a delicious three course meal, chatting with Rowland about our plans for the next day. This was to be our last full day with this charming, knowledgeable man. We decided that another relaxing day in the bush, not travelling too far was just what we needed. The following day we would be travelling to Arusha and then flying out to the Selous National Park, our last stop on our safari around Tanzania.

I awoke as dawn was breaking, and listened to the sounds of the bush waking up. During the night I had heard lion roaring somewhere in the distance, but now there was only the sound of the birdlife, interspersed with the occasional sound of an elephant trumpeting and zebra barking. A discrete 'knock knock' heralded the hot water for our morning wash, and after grabbing a mug of tea and a couple of rusks, another day in Africa began. Rowland had also heard the lions, and after a brief discussion, we decided to spend part of the morning seeing if we could find them, as he was certain they would not be too far away.

Slowly and painstakingly, Rowland drove though the bush, stopping to examine spoor every so often, until, with a broad grin on his face, he pointed to three large male lions in the distance, all lying out in the open. They had feasted well as they were on their backs with their legs raised in the air, their bulging stomachs sagging down onto the parched earth. These cats were going nowhere in a hurry, and seemed totally disinterested in us as we edged closer, parking the Landy about twenty feet away. The only movement was a twitch of a tail and an occasional grunt as, one after the other they adjusted their position to ease the strain of last night's feast of a zebra, the remains of which lay a short distance away.

The appearance of a vulture with others following soon disrupted this peaceful scene. Ever protective of their kill, the lions took it in turns to defend the carcass, but gave up after a while, staggering to the shade of a nearby acacia tree where they thumped down with resigned grunts, as if regretting their over-indulgence. We watched as the flock of vultures demolished the remaining flesh and reduced the carcass to a skeleton, seeing first-hand how these scavengers acted as essential garbage clearers of the savannah. No doubt, hyenas would soon arrive to demolish the bones. Nothing goes to waste in the bush.

We left the cats to sleep off their nocturnal banquet, and drove down to the river. We spent the rest of the morning watching processions of elephant come down to drink and bathe. Once again, we were content to relax and enjoy the scene unfold in front of us before the heat of the African sun became too intense. We drove back to camp to have a shower and a hearty brunch before retiring to our tents for our now obligatory siesta. only surfacing for a cup of tea and slice of cake before we set off for our evening game drive.

I decided I just had to go and visit the kitchen where all the delicacies were prepared, and Rowland introduced me to the cook and his helpers. Apart from a fridge running off batteries and a generator that was only switched on when we were out of camp to ensure we had peace and quiet to enjoy our surroundings, the cook relied on a large open fire and a pit which served as his oven. How he managed to produce a perfect Victoria sponge for our tea and freshly baked bread for each meal was beyond me. I had yet to master the art of bread making, and my cakes would never come up to the standard he set in his bush kitchen. I was shown around with obvious pride, and thanking them for all their hard work left them to prepare our evening meal whilst we went off to enjoy ourselves in the bush.

In all the time we had been here, we had yet to come across a single vehicle, but this time we went on a different route and came across a large lodge in the distance before veering off to avoid its inhabitants. Tanangire was obviously large enough and thankfully less known to swallow up any tourists, and Rowland told us that our next and final stop in the Selous National Park was even more remote and isolated. With a smile on his face, he assured us that we would not be so bothered by the dreaded tsetse fly there. Thankfully, our time at Tarangire offered some respite from their attack, and those bites received in the Serengeti and Ngorongoro were at last calming down.

I took photo after photo of the ancient baobab trees, never having seen so many in one place. Sundowners yet again in hand, we gazed at hundreds of buffalo coming down to drink before making our way back to camp for our last night of camping under the stars. Retiring to our tent after yet another delicious meal, I lay in my bed, saddened that this would be our last night under canvas. I drifted off to sleep, listening to the sounds of the bush.

Unfortunately, this was soon to become a very disturbed night, as a couple of hours later I was woken by Gordon staggering to the loo. This was repeated at regular intervals throughout the night, accompanied by grunts and groans. 'Just leave me to die in peace,' was the retort when I offered to help. I wondered how we were going to proceed with the final part of our safari, as we had a rough journey back to Arusha, and then a flight to the Selous. Gordon certainly didn't sound as if he would be fit enough to undertake any journey. As dawn broke, I looked at his wan face, pale underneath his tan, and suggested that he should take sips of water, and I would mix up some rehydrating fluid once I got some more water from the mess tent.

Rowland was already up, organising the packing up of the camp. I explained that Gordon had been up all night with an upset stomach, and I was concerned he would not be well enough to fly to the Selous. It was pointless asking for another day in camp, as all around me the staff were packing the camping equipment away in a large lorry ready to return to Arusha.

Rowland brought my breakfast to our tent, and enquired about the invalid who yet again, had retired to the loo. Gordon staggered out to come face to face with Rowland who solicitously asked him if he was still 'diarrhoea-ing.' I tried to keep a straight face whilst Gordon said that he didn't think he had anything more inside him to be 'diarrhoea-ing'. Re-assured, Rowland departed, leaving me to hastily pack our luggage, whilst Gordon dressed and then sat outside sipping his rehydrating mixture, and grumbling that he couldn't even go to the loo without an audience. The fact that he was actually able to crack a feeble joke was, I felt, a step in the right direction, and before too long we were ready to leave camp.

The camp staff lined up to bid us goodbye, and shaking hands with each of them, we thanked them profusely for looking after us so well.

Gordon settled back in the Landy to try and get some rest, occasionally opening his eyes when we went over an especially deep pothole. Rowland and I chatted as we went through villages en route to Arusha, and we decided that if Gordon were no better when we arrived, we would take him to a doctor. Sipping the magic mixture seemed to be doing the trick though, as some colour came back into his face, but insisting he should drink large volumes had the inevitable effect of us needing to halt for wee-stops. Gordon moaned at me for making him drink so much, but I was now in nurse mode. He was to do as I said, as the only way he was going to feel better was to sip copious amounts to rehydrate his system and to flush out whatever bug he had managed to pick up.

Eventually, after a nightmarish journey, we arrived at Arusha Airport where Rowland ushered us into a waiting room and went to find the pilot for our light aircraft flight. As usual, our travel plans materialised seamlessly, and we were soon saying our goodbyes and thanks to yet another wonderful guide.

On board the tiny aircraft, our pilot explained that our flight would take us first to Zanzibar where we would transfer to another plane for the final leg into the Selous Game Reserve. Ours was not to reason why we were flying two sides of a triangle to get to our destination, but I decided that it would be interesting glimpsing Zanzibar from the air. Gordon did not share my enthusiasm however. Although he was on the mend, the thought of being in the air for an indeterminate amount of time without access to a loo brought little comfort. Added to which I had 'forced' him to drink nearly a litre of rehydration fluid at the airport, and I was now the cause of all his misery and discomfort. The only thing I could do was to ignore his mutterings and hope that this flight would not last too long, otherwise our marriage would be in severe trouble.

As we flew low over the Indian Ocean, leaving the coastline of Tanzania behind us, I gazed down at the clear turquoise water, watching dhows sail across the straits to Zanzibar – a scene that could hardly have changed in thousands of years. We swooped down to land at the tiny airport, and scrambling out of the tiny plane, were assaulted by the humid heat and aroma of spices. I gulped in the sweet perfume of nutmeg, which amazed me as we were on the tarmac of the airport. However, there was no time to stand and stare – or sniff.

Our pilot grabbed our bags and we followed him at a trot to our next plane, which was a slightly larger one and contained several fellow passengers, obviously waiting for us in some discomfort in the heat and humidity.

Before boarding, Gordon requested a loo break, but it was explained to him that there was just not enough time. I suggested to my now nearly crossed legged husband that maybe there was a loo on board, and he would just have to grin and bear it, as it was obvious that we were holding everyone up. We embarked and sat down on the nearest two seats, hardly having time to fasten our seat belts before we were taxiing down the runway. No amount of frantic looking around for an onboard loo helped one to materialise. We sat in silence, trying to ignore the calls of nature by entertaining ourselves with the unfolding scenery of the bush below us.

We circled the dirt runway once and as we came into land, Gordon came to life. He insisted that the pilot was making a grave error of judgement by landing with a tail wind with the ground sloping down in front of us. We hung onto our armrests as the brakes were applied, gently at first and then with increasing severity until, finally, we screeched to a halt. Climbing out of the aircraft, we saw our transport materialise out of the bush, and looked with amazement at the end of the runway only a few feet from where we had screeched to a halt.

Our ranger for the next few days strolled over to us and greeted us with a wry grin, exclaiming 'Well ... that was a novel way of landing. I've never seen that approach before!' After a hurried introduction, we simultaneously announced that we had to have a pit stop before we even thought about getting into the Landy. We dashed off to the nearest bushes for some blissful relief without a moment's thought to the potential hazards of any wildlife that might be lurking. On our return, I apologised profusely to a somewhat bemused ranger who remarked that he didn't realise it had been quite such a bad flight, before we told him briefly about our tribulations over the last twenty-four hours. Inside the Landy, we waited until the plane had taken off with its remaining passengers – a safety measure we had never observed before.

With an enormous sense of relief, we motored through the bush, arriving at our lodge, situated on the banks of the Rufiji River. Our rustic room had the most beautiful view over this vast river, and leaning over the wooden balcony, we gazed at pods of hippo and watched as grey herons picked their way along the shore line. We had decided to visit the Selous Game Reserve for various reasons. It appealed to us, being Africa's largest but the least visited game reserve, named after Frederick Courtney Selous, the famous hunter turned conservationist. Selous had been a fellow explorer of Africa with Gordon's grandfather in the late nineteenth century, and was shot by a German sniper during the First World War. He was buried close to where he fell here in the Selous. We wanted to visit his grave if possible, and over drinks that evening, arranged our itinerary for the next three days with our ranger, Toby. We also wanted to make the most of the river setting, so opted for boat trips in the mornings and driving in the Landy in the late afternoons.

At dinner that evening, we were introduced to a larger than life American lady who had visited here before. She was on safari with her son who was game hunting in a concession area on the other side of the river. She abhorred hunting so spent the time here at this lodge waiting for her son to appear. We discussed the thorny subject of hunting, how the income from it helped preserve this pristine wilderness, probably yielding more money for conservation than photographic safaris, but we agreed that trophy hunting was not for us.

This fascinating elderly woman, who every so often would go out onto the veranda to have a cigarette, regaled us with stories of the bush and her life in America where she was a theatre nurse to the first American heart transplant surgeon. We retired to bed knowing this was going to be an interesting and special few days, and looked forward to the mutual sharing of African adventures.

Early the following morning, we set off up river in our small boat. The outboard motor chugged noisily, disturbing the calm, but providing an efficient warning for the hippos. I sat at the bow, clinging on, trying to forecast where the next pod of hippos might appear. These enormous creatures were soon surfacing all around us, and with a series of noisy grunts and splashing would veer away from us, only for the next pod to surface a few hundred yards downstream. Nowhere had we seen such a quantity of these ugly, ungainly 'sea horses'. I recounted briefly our narrow escape from a hippo charge, and that they are not my favourite creatures. Toby assured us that he would do his utmost to keep us safe.

I asked how he could avoid motoring over a submerged hippo, only for it to surface and upturn the boat. He explained that as he had got to know the river, he had also got to know the hippos' favourite places. There was one place where he would not venture. An aged bull hippo who was notoriously bad-tempered and territorial, ruled that stretch of the river – and everyone gave him a wide berth.

I balanced precariously against the side of the boat and took photo after photo of hippos dosing, swimming, fighting, yawning territorially, and rushing down to the water, making a huge bow wave, which would then rock the boat violently. After counting over two hundred hippo I gave up, and started counting the crocodile lazing on the bank with their jaws agape, soaking in the warmth of the early morning sun.

It was just as well Gordon and I enjoyed being on water, as potentially this seemed much more dangerous than a walking safari. If we were to capsize then not only had we the hippos to contend with but also large quantities of gigantic crocodiles. I decided to relax and enjoy the experience rather than fantasise over something that might never happen, hopefully!

Every so often Toby would turn off the outboard and we would drift along, able to hear the sounds of the bird life clearly. We were watching some grey herons and Goliath herons pick their way slowly along the shoreline a few feet away from us, when Toby picked up his binoculars and pointed towards the shore. There, climbing stealthily over the huge boulders was a large leopard. Every so often, he would disappear into the thick tree line, only to reappear a bit further along the shore. Finally, he disappeared and we resumed our journey towards the picnic spot for breakfast.

Toby beached the boat on a narrow sandy beach sheltered by tall cliffs, with a few giant boulders towards the back of the sand. These, he explained, would provide privacy for anyone needing a loo break. Gordon helped him haul the bow of the boat clear of the water to make it easier for me to get out and just as I was preparing to swing my leg out over the side, Toby shouted, 'Stay still!' I looked up towards the boulders and there was an enormous hippo shaking his head and staring at us. He then rushed towards us, veering off past the boat and with a violent splash, disappeared into the river.

I sat down in the boat to recover whilst Toby took his rifle and went to see if any more hippos were lurking about. He returned to declare the coast clear. We were soon safely sitting down and tucking into our breakfast – bacon and eggs in large rolls, fruit and yoghurt and a thermos filled with aromatic coffee. Inner man satisfied, we make the return journey with no further incidents despite some close encounters with the numerous pods of hippos.

In the afternoon, Toby took us in the Landy to a magnificent viewpoint overlooking a bend in the river where elephants quietly grazed. He invited us to go on a short walk but I decided I would wait in the Landy whilst Gordon accompanied him. With strict instructions to remain in the vehicle, and if I needed to attract attention in an emergency, a couple of hoots on the horn would alert Toby, the two men set off and I settled down to enjoy some time to myself in the bush.

I stretched back in the front passenger seat to enjoy the warmth of the late afternoon. I realised that this was the first time in all my visits to the African continent that I had ever been alone in the bush. Savouring this thought, my senses tuned to the sounds of my surroundings. Here I was, without the customary ranger to protect me, and only a horn to attract attention if an emergency arose.

Downriver, I caught sight of Gordon and Toby striding off towards some elephants, and I willed them not to get too close. As if on cue, they halted and then crouched down on a termite mound to watch the herd proceed to the water. I too relaxed and watched the elephants, wondering if Toby would actually hear me if I had to summon help. He certainly would have a long run uphill to reach the Landy. Putting these concerns to the back of my mind, I listened to the sounds of the bush with one eye on my other half. A crack of a twig alerted me to something behind me and turning around, a couple of impala came into view, grazing delicately on the sparse grass. Some guinea fowl scuttled along past me and then a faint rumbling alerted me to something much larger approaching.

The rumbling got louder and I sat transfixed as a large bull elephant sauntered out of the bush. He stopped to feed off some vegetation a few yards from me, raising his head in my direction from time to time, in between his noisy munching. I was acutely aware that there was not much space for him to pass by the Landy and that he was probably making his way down to the river for his late afternoon drink. Using all the bush knowledge I had picked up over the years, I could see that he was relaxed and there was no streaming from his temporal glands, which would indicate he might be in musth. He was obviously aware of me, as he would raise his trunk in my direction for the occasional sniff.

So far so good, I thought. He knows I am here. At the moment he does not believe I am a threat to him. He moved slowly towards the vehicle. Was this what Toby meant as an emergency? If I tooted the horn, it would only alarm the bull and what could Toby do anyway? I looked down into the valley and saw the two men still perching on the termite mound, so I decided to sit out this close encounter.

I remembered our first walking safari in Zimbabwe and our ranger Shane standing his ground when an elephant was within a foot or so of us, but also remembered that he was armed and had many years of experience. Considering everything, I really did not have much option but to stay put, as I certainly was not going to get out of the Landy. Minutes passed and the rumbles of the big bull's stomach got louder as he drew nearer. Thankfully, there were no trees overhanging the vehicle, so I did not have to face the situation of branches coming down on top of me.

I held my breath as the bull drew up alongside the driver's seat, thanking my lucky stars that he had chosen that side. He ambled past the vehicle, and stopped a couple of yards in front of it, turning his giant head towards me. He raised his trunk in my direction and I could hear his intake of breath as he sniffed the air. Time stood still as he and I faced each other.

'Oh, you beautiful animal,' I murmured to myself, and with a gentle toss of his head he flapped his ears, the motes of red dust shining in the sun as he ambled off down the track. I sat back, savouring my close encounter, and relaxed once more in the late afternoon sun, which was losing its fiery heat.

Sometime later Gordon and Toby arrived back, hot, puffing but smiling, telling me that they had had to make a detour as they had seen a large bull elephant and wanted to give it a wide berth, but they had got very close to some other elephants down by the river. I explained that the bull had passed by the vehicle and I could have reached out and touched it. The moment I saw the amazement and concern on Toby's face, I decided to play down my experience and savour it as one of those precious moments no one could really understand or share.

That evening we shared a table with Daphne, the American lady. We enjoyed her tales of the bush, and her experiences as the senior theatre nurse during the first American heart transplants fascinated us. We warmed to this larger than life woman who had packed so much into her life and who in her seventies still travelled the world, delighting everyone with her sense of humour and enthusiasm for life. She was leaving the lodge in the morning after a brief boat safari, so we said our goodbyes before going to our room.

The following day we spent a couple of lazy hours on the river, avoiding the hippos and enjoying the prolific bird life, before returning to the lodge for brunch. As we sat having coffee on the deck overlooking the river, we were amazed to see a very wet and bedraggled Daphne being helped from a boat. She strode up to the deck dripping water everywhere. She explained that a hippo had got too close and her ranger was obliged to take avoiding action. Daphne lost her balance when the boat swerved violently, and she toppled over, doing a backwards summersault into the hippo and crocodile-infested river. Thankfully, it was not too deep, so standing, chest high in water, she waited for the ranger to do a rapid u-turn to pick her up. Being a buxom lady required a difficult and inelegant manoeuvre to haul her over the side of the boat to safety. She recited all this with hoots of laughter, whilst her ranger stood close to her, still looking shocked at the narrowly averted loss of a much-valued client.

She emptied her soaking pockets to find her passport now reduced to a few pieces of wet, disintegrating paper, but her main concern was her sodden packet of cigarettes. This was her last packet of cigarettes and there was no opportunity to buy anymore until she got back to the airport at Arusha. 'Sod the sodding passport, I'll find some way to get back to the US of A,' she boomed. 'But how can I possibly survive without my nicotine fix?' The ranger disappeared for a few minutes, arriving back with a handful of assorted cigarettes he had managed to scrounge from the staff. Quickly lighting up, Daphne's equilibrium was soon on an even keel, and we said yet more goodbyes to this extraordinary woman as she went off to change before rushing off to catch her flight.

We set off the next morning with Toby to visit Selous' grave. On the way we talked about how Gordon's grandfather had come to know him, this famous big game hunter turned conservationist, and records showed that at least on one occasion they had travelled back together on the same boat to England. We considered it strange that Gordon should be travelling through this vast tract of pristine bush over one hundred years later to pay his respects to a friend of his grandfather. Toby stopped the Landy and jumped out. He had seen some acacia blossom that had just come into bloom. Cutting off a few sprigs, he gave them to me to place on the grave.

A few minutes later, we arrived at the place where Selous had fallen, the victim of a sniper's bullet. We walked slowly to his final resting place – a slightly raised mound of earth surrounded by a small moat to stop vehicles driving over the grave. Gordon took some photos and shot a brief video of the grave and the surrounding area to show his mother back in England, before placing the small spray of yellow acacia blossom on the red earth.

As we walked back to the vehicle, Toby stopped us and in amazement showed us the fresh tracks of a leopard, sharply imprinted over the tracks of our tyres. How had we not seen this elusive cat? We had only been a few yards away and in the brief time we were standing at the graveside, a leopard had passed behind us, unseen and unheard. We drove off in silence, each of us deep in thought. Some things cannot be explained. Probably better that way.

Back at the lodge, we had a refreshing shower, rinsing off the dust of the long, tiring drive, before making our way to have a pre-lunch rock shandy. We had just sat down to lunch when Toby appeared, looking excited. There had been a radio call to tell him that a pack of wild dog had been sighted. Would we like see if we could find them? All thought of lunch and a leisurely siesta disappeared as we hastily grabbed our cameras, binos and sunhats, before hoisting ourselves into the vehicle we had only just left.

Wild dog were the ultimate sighting as far I was concerned, and the prospect of seeing a pack banished all my aches, pains and tiredness of the morning's journey. With the midday sun blazing down on us, Toby drove for over an hour before he slowed down and started to scour the arid bush with his binos. A few minutes later, we had found the pack sheltering from the scorching heat under an acacia tree. On either side of the tree there were a few bushes and drawing up as close as was practical without disturbing these painted wolves, we settled down to some quality time with some of the most endangered mammals on earth.

To my absolute delight and amazement, after a few minutes, we saw six pups emerge from the undergrowth. The alpha female nuzzled them as they flopped around, moving from one place to another trying to get some much-needed shade. Once the pack got used to us, Toby thought we could drive in a bit closer, so turning on the engine, we edged nearer.

The adult dogs ignored us completely, but one of the pups decided that he would exert his authority, and standing up he faced us, letting out a warning growl followed by a brief high-pitched yap, before retiring to the shade to sleep off his exertions. We watched the pack for over an hour, before deciding we would have to leave them. They were obviously not going to start off on their evening hunt for some time, and we had a long drive back to the lodge. The next morning would see the start of an even longer 24-hour journey back to our home in England.

The photos I took that day are some of my most treasured, my favourite being one of that plucky little pup facing me head on and growling his warning. What a wonderful leaving present the Tanzanian bush gave us, and despite travelling back with many unwelcomed tsetse fly bites and a sutured wrist, we would remember our experiences of this beautiful country and welcoming people with great affection.

A hippo charge and the sight of its pink belly above me was one of the reasons we decided to stop wandering around sub-Saharan Africa. Why not buy a second home somewhere in Africa where we could regularly get our wildlife 'fix' from the safety of our own car? The thought of having our own home worked out fine, but ten years later, we were still getting into scrapes with African wildlife!

Chapter 19

Walking in Zambia

Over the next few months, our thoughts not only turned to our next holiday but also to our future retirement. What we had originally planned as a winding-down process into full retirement had actually developed into two nearly full-time second careers, and it became increasingly difficult to take time off together at the same time. As Gordon had a lecturing commitment in Singapore, we decided this presented us with an ideal chance to travel on to Australia for a fortnight's touring holiday.

The downside was that we could only squeeze in a week's safari somewhere in Africa. It was unthinkable that we should go without our annual 'Africa Fix'! Lengthy discussions followed and the first seeds of an idea started to germinate. What if we spent anything up to half a year somewhere in Africa? Should we buy a place of our own and perhaps rent it out for holiday lets to help the finances?

Suddenly my view of retirement took on a completely different aspect as we planned a walking holiday in Zambia. We wanted to feel Africa under our feet again, and visit another African country. After all, we could well be settling anywhere in this vast continent and the more countries we visited, the better informed we would to be in order to make our decision as to where that might be.

In late May we boarded our flight to Lilongwe in Malawi, and who should we meet on the plane but Patrick Mavros, the Zimbabwean jeweller who was travelling back to Zimbabwe where we had an hour's stopover at Harare. The usual boring time between boarding and take-off was filled very pleasantly with catching up on all his news. His silver jewellery and ornament business had taken off in a big way since we last met him, and he now commuted between his show room in London and his Zimbabwean home. It was good to hear of one success story in a country that was on its knees and struggling to survive.

After a night of fitful snoozing, we landed at Harare and said our goodbyes to Patrick, wishing that we too were returning to that lovely but beleaguered country. The sight of the ramshackle little airport brought back so many fond memories and I felt ashamed we were not brave enough to even consider a holiday in Zimbabwe, let alone the possibility of buying a home there sometime in the future.

Perhaps we were just being prudent, but deep down in both our hearts we yearned to be back where we had so many fond memories. The Zimbabwean bush had nurtured my soul and touched something previously unexplored deep inside me. I looked out of the small window and said goodbye to the dusty, neglected tarmac as we took off for Malawi, another African country we had yet to visit, but unfortunately one we would only see very briefly at the beginning and end of our week's safari.

We landed at Lilongwe, Malawi's International Airport, a miniscule place reminiscent of Harare but with a much more cheerful atmosphere. We were shepherded through immigration and into the departures area. Here we met up with our walking companions for the next week – Bob, Sally, Nigel and Anne, and we chatted amongst ourselves as we waited for our plane to Mfuwe in Zambia. A pilot came up to us and explained that one light aircraft was unfortunately out of action and we would have to travel in two separate groups aboard his plane.

It is in situations like this that I place myself in an enormous quandary. Do I go on the first or second flight? It seems like a version of Russian roulette to someone with my fear of flying. Gordon sorted things out – we would take the second flight.

We had about two hours to wait for our flight, and ordered a snack lunch at the small restaurant overlooking the runway. We saw the other two couples walk out onto the tarmac and waved them goodbye, before watching their tiny aircraft disappear into the blue sky. At least we had an hour or so to relax over lunch and people watch, observing the families that came and went. They sat down on the balcony overlooking the runway, hoping for some activity to amuse their impeccably behaved children who sat quietly in their Sunday best, and smiled shyly at us when they caught our glances.

In the mid afternoon, our plane returned and I clambered into the rear seat whilst Gordon was invited to sit in the co-pilot's seat. Donning some earphones, the pilot started to chat to him and I mused on the fact that male dominance seemed rampant on this continent. There was no question that I might be invited to occupy the co-pilot's seat. I might be able to relax a bit more if I could chat to the pilot during the flight.

As it was, I strapped myself tightly into the seat and holding on to an armrest, practised deep breathing and relaxation exercises as the plane's single engine revved up. The flimsy fuselage shuddered before we shot off down the runway and became airborne for 50 minutes of high adrenaline flying. It soon became obvious we had drawn the short straw, as the sun had done a good job of heating up the air and we lurched from one bumpy thermal to another.

A distinct smell of kerosene seemed to get stronger and stronger. I poked Gordon's shoulder, signalling to him to take off his earphones, before asking why there was this distinct smell. He asked the pilot and then turned to re-assure me that the pilot said there was nothing to worry about – it sometimes was rather smelly! Not re-assured, I tried to distract myself by looking down at collections of thatched rondavels surrounded by highly cultivated areas of subsistence farming. I glimpsed the tail end of a large range of mountains as we flew over the border and entered Zambian airspace.

I breathed my usual sigh of relief when we touched the runway at Mfuwe, thankful that now our speed was no faster than driving down a motorway and I might just survive. We taxied up in front of a small building and I waited for that blissful sound of silence as the propeller spun slowly to a halt.

On our arrival at the bush camp that was to be our home for the next week, we were greeted warmly with cold towels and a welcome drink, and the news that we would be setting off for our first evening drive in half an hour. I hardly had time to admire our thatched hut overlooking the great Luangwa River as we rapidly sorted out our safari gear.

I climbed aboard a Landy, my camera, binos, sunglasses and sunhat strings getting into the usual tangled mess around my neck as we set off into the bush. There is nothing like a mutual love of wildlife to gel a group quickly together, as we were introduced to two species of animals none of us had seen before – herds of puku, a small, sandy-red coated antelope, and Thornicroft's giraffe, a sub-species found only in this area.

We stopped for sundowners, and once again I felt I had come home. In the darkness I gazed up into the clear African sky and saw the Southern Cross. Hippos grunted in the distance, and to complete the scene, a large bull elephant trumpeted. Driving back to camp, a sub-adult male leopard strolled into view, and obligingly sauntered down the track in front of us for a few minutes, its white tipped tail swaying from side to side, before he veered off into the bush. What a sublime start to our week!

We tucked into a dinner of roast beef and all the trimmings, and were given a briefing about our walk tomorrow. Afterwards, we were escorted to our hut where I spent the next half hour attempting to unpack and put things in order – not an easy task as the only illumination we had was a paraffin lantern and our torches. Exhausted but happy, we slipped into our beds, draping the mozzie nets around us. Gradually, I relaxed into sleep, surrounded by the sound of Gordon's snores and the deafening noise of the African night, waking only to briefly register the roaring of two lions.

Our early wake-up call was the beating of a drum. It began with a soft thud, which escalated into a frantic rhythm, signalling in no uncertain terms that it was time to get up. After a hurried shower, we appeared for a steaming cup of tea and some toast with honey, before climbing on board the Landy for the short drive to the entrance of the South Luangwa National Park.

I was interested to see how the Zambian system of guiding worked. Our armed ranger Simon, was an employee of the Park and responsible for the ultimate safety of the walkers. The trained guide, Doubt, concentrated on informing us about the flora and fauna, liaising with the ranger on safety issues, and lastly the assistant, Robert, known fondly as the tea boy, brought up the rear, carrying the vital refreshments. This arrangement seemed to work extremely well, as all the time the guide was talking to us and we were examining spoor for example, I was aware that we had two other pairs of eyes keeping an ever alert watch over our surroundings.

We walked in dense bush for much of the time, having to be careful to negotiate the deep potholes and ruts made by the animals churning up the thick clay soil during the rainy season, but which now was as hard as concrete. I was certainly glad to have my walking pole with me, and Gordon found his video-cam tripod made a handy walking stick. The others in the group were soon using stout branches as sticks to enable them to walk safely over this rough terrain, and avoid a sprained ankle or worse.

We watched in amazement as a herd of puku fled in front of us, seemingly flying over the treacherous surface, and I wondered how many animals came to grief when fleeing from predators over these deep craters. After a couple of hours, we stopped for a tea break in a shady ebony grove close to the grave of Norman Carr, conservationist and founder of walking safaris in Zambia. We chatted softly, sipping tea and enjoying thick slabs of home-baked fruit cake, and I thought how peaceful this place was, hoping the great man would approve of the future generations of walkers seeking shade near his final resting place.

All too soon, it was time to get up and walk for another couple of hours in the increasing heat, stopping frequently to identify birds, and observe giraffe, puku and elephants in the distance. Reaching the Landy at the Park gates, we drove for twenty minutes, sipping water and looking forward to the ice-cold beers waiting for us at camp, together with the now customary cold damp towel to wipe our hands and faces. These little touches of luxury made all the difference and as the week passed, we all began to fantasise about the cold towels waiting for us at the end of four hours' walking. After a delicious cold buffet lunch, we made our way to our tents and I stretched out on my bed for a blissful two hours' siesta before setting off for an evening drive.

These evening drives provided another aspect to our game viewing. We were acutely aware that we did not want to come across anything that might charge, attack or bite whilst we were on foot, whereas, in the Landy, we were only too keen to come across any of the Big Five. We were content for the first couple of evenings to see civets, scrub hares, a pair of mating monitor lizards, giraffe and elephants, the latter being a bit too close for comfort for Nigel. Both he and Anne were on their first safari and were understandably nervous. Over the week, despite everyone's effort to help them relax, they seemed to become increasingly apprehensive.

I guess our gallows sense of humour did not help when, over sundowners and at mealtimes, the rest of us recalled all the excitements and near misses we had had on previous safaris. This had always been an essential part of the pleasure of being in the bush – the reminiscing and sharing around the campfire, the stories getting more outrageous as the night wore on and the alcohol intake increased. We concentrated on encouraging these two 'safari virgins' to enjoy the bush in the hope that they might return to Africa on subsequent safaris and be able to share more of the banter with their fellow companions.

That evening I found to my dismay that I had what looked like the beginning of a blister beetle bite on my ankle. I remember Iona talking about these beetles on our Zimbabwean safari at Mana Pools, and how she landed up in hospital with some bites, as she had managed to get some of the fluid in the blister into her eyes and was very lucky not to have been blinded.

There are several hundred types of this species, all secreting the poison cantharidin, and it seemed I had been unlucky enough to have come across one of these which was producing a nasty blister that was intensely painful. I covered the blister with a plaster, as the last thing I wanted was to have the blister burst when I was asleep, producing even more blisters with the toxic fluid.

The blister became unbearable painful, and after a disturbed night, I decided the only thing to do was to burst it and get rid of the irritating fluid. I set about this operation, being scrupulously careful not to spread any of the poisonous fluid, and covering up the wound with a sterile dressing sealed with tape and some tea tree oil. This is something I always travelled with, finding it a panacea for virtually everything. The relief was immediate, but the following afternoon I found that these beetles had struck again, and by the end of the safari I had been attacked by these vicious beetles five more times, each blister requiring the same treatment to give me some relief.

The weather was getting hotter, as we set off for our now usual walk, this time crossing the Luangwa River in a large but rickety boat. As it was the end of the dry season, the water was shallow so we could easily see where the crocodiles and pods of hippos were and gave them a wide berth. The terrain on the other side of the river was much more open. Consequently, we were not in a continual state of alert, but the disadvantage was that any plains game was instantly aware of us. If we were not careful, they would stream away from us before we had a good sighting. The scenery reminded me very much of Mana Pools and I relaxed into the slow walking pace, relieved that we didn't have the head high 'adrenaline grass' to wade through.

We managed to get close to several giraffe, which stared at us with their usual imperious, inquisitive look, before strolling off to find another tree to browse on. In the distance, we heard the distinct but faint roar of a lion, but it was far enough away for us to merely relax and enjoy the sound, exchanging smiles of pure joy at this shared experience. Stopping for the now usual cup of tea and slice of cake at a lagoon, I perched on a fallen tree trunk, taking in the sights and sounds of Africa. Saddle billed storks soared above us; a lone hippo surfaced in the lagoon with a grunt, the trails of waterweed adorning his head making him look like a rather blowsy bridesmaid. Once again, I fell in love with this continent.

Mine was an up and down love affair and I realised how fickle I was when an hour later we were in thick bush, avoiding deep ruts and I was coping with sweat running down my face in scorching temperatures, and swearing to myself that never again would I put myself through this torture. My companions looked equally shattered, and I wondered how much further I could stagger, as Doubt ploughed through the undergrowth, urging us to keep up and telling us it would be worth it.

What 'it' was had yet to be explained, but just when I thought I could not put another foot in front of another, the bush thinned out and we arrived at a shady grove overlooking the river. The camp manager appeared from behind a bush, together with two helpers, and offered each of us an ice-cold towel to refresh us, before leading us to where a sumptuous lunch was laid out on a table covered with pristine white tablecloths. All the time we had been walking, this hardworking group of people had been ferrying a gourmet lunch, table, chairs and the all-important restorative drinks over the hippo and crocodile-infested river for our surprise al fresco lunch.

I sank down into a canvas chair, drink in hand and began to cool down. We discussed how tough the last half hour or so had been, but, like childbirth, all the pain was soon forgotten as we recovered our equilibrium. Doubt apologised for what we were now calling the 'forced march'. He had been afraid our lunch would spoil!

As our three-course meal was served and wine poured, Simon, rifle in hand, was ever watchful for any wildlife that might interrupt our banquet. We fantasised over the worst-case scenario of a pride of lion or a herd of buffalo or elephant coming across this decadent gathering, and jokingly planned our escape routes – some up trees, others into the boat moored down the bank in front of us. Doubt jokingly reminded us that we would obviously do exactly what he told us to do, as the last thing he wanted was six guests scattering in all directions and making it impossible for him and Simon to ensure our safety. As we relaxed, enjoying this delicious meal and good company, little did we realise how prophetic his words would be the following day.

We set off on our penultimate morning walk assured by Doubt that it would be a gentle stroll with no forced marches! Again, we saw large quantities of plains game and concentrated on studying the bird life and spoor, including that of a lion, encased in the dried mud some time ago. Putting my hand over these pug marks graphically brought home to me how big a lion's paw actually is. The morning passed peacefully, and by 11 o'clock, the heat was intense so we decided to make tracks for camp, enjoying the shade of the trees as we walked along a narrow track bordering the riverbank.

On each walk, we alternated the position we walked in, and this morning Gordon was walking directly behind Doubt, followed by me. Bob and Sally came next and Nigel and Anne came last, with Robert bringing up the rear. Simon alternated his position depending on what was happening in the bush and the first intimation I had that anything was amiss was my vision of him flying past me yelling, 'Hippo!'

He halted, raised his rifle over me, and aimed into the thick undergrowth. The next thing I was conscious of was Doubt flinging his arm out, sending Gordon sprawling, which resulted in me falling underneath Gordon, and Doubt landing on top of us both. As I lay on my back, with two men on top of me squashing all the remaining breath out of my body, I glanced up and said to myself, 'I never realised hippos had such pink bellies!'

An enormous hippo had been grazing in the dense bush bordering the river, and most unusually had not gone back into the water in the heat of the day. Disturbed by us, he dashed for the safety of the river, actually thundering over us in his attempt to escape from the perceived danger. With a deafening splash, he landed in the water as we began to examine the damage he had wrought.

Simon cautiously went deeper into the bush, rifle at the ready to make certain there were no more hippos, and once Gordon and Doubt had rolled off me, I slowly sat up, regained my breath and looked around.

Bob and Sally were attempting to untangle themselves from some vicious looking thorn bushes, having stayed in their walking position but flinging themselves into the bushes to try to avoid a collision with the rampaging hippo. Robert was still holding Nigel and Anne by the scruffs of their necks as apparently, they had attempted to run back down the path to distance themselves from all the chaos.

Gingerly removing Gordon's tripod from my shins, I examined my legs, which already were starting to become very painful. Mercifully, I did not seem to have broken any bones, and there was a general sense of amazement when we realised all of us had managed to escape being trampled on by the enraged hippo. Not one of those flailing tree trunks of legs had touched us as he launched himself over us, and the only thing that registered with me was that shiny pink belly flying over my head. Thankfully, everyone else was uninjured although we were all extremely shaken.

Once the ranger had made certain I was capable of walking, a somewhat subdued party arrived back to the safety of the camp to be greeted with great concern by the manager, who immediately organised cold towels and drinks all round. It is amazing how a bit of alcohol cheers up a party, and soon we were going through an informal de-brief which, in retrospect was the best possible thing we could have done.

We realised now the importance of following in single file closely behind the guide, as Doubt knew instantly where we all were and had acted instinctively, knocking Gordon and me flat, thus not only preventing us from getting in the way of rifle fire, but also avoiding the gaping jaws and razor sharp tusks of the hippo.

Bob and Sally had done the right thing and stayed in the same position, albeit in a thorn bush, and Nigel and Anne learnt a salutary lesson: Never run away from the ranger in the bush unless instructed to. They listened somewhat shamefaced as the guide explained that if Robert had not caught them, he would have had no idea where they were and they could have run into even greater danger without a guide and ranger to protect them.

Gradually we started to relax and laughter erupted, with jokes about an English woman landing up under two men in the bush helping to release our pent-up emotions. I rolled up my trouser legs to examine my shins. Immediately, ice bags were produced to help reduce the emerging bruises, and I put my legs up on a stool sipping the best G and T of my life.

We were alerted to the arrival of a couple of elephants who were browsing around the back of the camp. The others went off to take some photos whilst I decided to go back to our hut and have a shower. Under a stream of refreshing, tepid water, I reached for the shampoo and realised that my hands had suddenly started to tremble uncontrollably. Maybe the stiff G and T had not been such a good idea and probably a strong mug of sweetened tea would have been the wiser treatment for delayed shock. Deciding that I was going to take the rest of the safari quietly, I made my way back to have lunch with my fellow survivors.

The evening drive was a welcome rest from the morning's drama, and at long last, we came across a pride of lion, which were very obliging. After walking towards us, they lay down and gave us some good photos. A breeding herd of elephant with some very young calves provided the next sighting, and I sat gazing at the peaceful scene of one female and her calf, her milk-filled breast outlined against the setting sun. I thought how lucky we were not only to observe this intimate scene but also to have survived a hippo attack. I now had first-hand knowledge as to why hippos had the reputation of killing more people than any other animal in Africa

As the early morning wake-up drums sounded, I hobbled to get dressed, determined to enjoy the last full day of our safari, despite five blister beetle bites and vivid bruises from kneecap to ankle on each leg. I was offered a morning drive rather than a walk, but decided I just had to go on a bush walk; otherwise, I doubted if I would ever attempt one again. It was the equivalent of getting back on a horse after being thrown. Everyone else was of the same opinion and we were assured that it would be an easy and short walk.

I soon found that my aches and pains eased with a bit of gentle exercise. Thankfully, we avoided the riverbank and walked in the open bush along a raised bank straddling some beautiful plains on either side. Puku grazed peacefully; in the mid distance there was a herd of buffalo, and giraffe browsed on some trees in the far distance – an idyllic scene and one that helped heal the psychological wounds of the previous day. It was slightly overcast which made walking very pleasant. We paused for our customary cups of tea and hunks of home-made cake, sitting in peaceful silence, and drinking in the sights and sounds of the bush. I was all too aware that the next day we were returning to the UK and had no idea when we would be returning to Africa.

We came across a hyena with a couple of pups on our way back to camp, and walking quietly and slowly, we managed to get close enough to take some photos without disturbing the nursing mother. Leaving this peaceful scene, we strolled along the open track when Robert whistled softly to Doubt.

We turned around to see a hippo ambling along the same track a few hundred yards behind us! Immobilised by surprise and apprehension, we waited for instructions. Calmly, Doubt motioned for us to turn off the track and walk at right angles to the hippo. After a few tense moments, we had left the hippo behind. It was all very well walking along game trails, but we always ran the risk of coming across the users of these well-worn tracks.

Whilst we paused for breath, we talked with Robert, who suggested that we might like to go and visit his village. We discussed this with the camp manager over lunch, and transport was arranged for us, so instead of our usual siesta we were soon bumping along a dirt track road, before arriving at a small compound, which was Robert's village.

He was obviously very proud of his home as he showed us around, introducing us to his extended family and friends. His wife appeared from the inside of their thatched rondavel, and shyly came towards us to shake our hands. She was very obviously heavily pregnant, and with Robert interpreting, I found out that this was their first child and that she would give birth here with a traditional village midwife attending her.

Children started to gather round Gordon who had asked if he could film the village. Robert was only too delighted to have him film, so Gordon spent some time entertaining the children, playing back to them their antics, which produced riotous laughter once they had overcome their apprehension. I was shown where they grew their vegetables and told that the women have to walk over two miles to collect water in the dry season.

Apparently, the camp where we were staying funded basic medical care and education for the children, and we all were determined to contribute to this fund before we left for England. Bidding everyone goodbye, we set off back to camp, only to find that a doctor was there on a routine visit to tend to any ailments the staff might have.

I chatted with the doctor and found out that he was a locum from England, working in Zambia for six months, and struggling to come to terms with the lack of facilities. I suggested that maybe he could make use of some medicines we had in our first-aid pack, which thankfully we had not had to use. I went round to the other rondavels, and before long had a collection of medications donated by our fellow travellers. The doctor received them with effusive thanks, saying that we had no idea how useful these would be, and they would actually save lives. It was good to know that these donations would be put to good use. This was the first time I was personally involved in giving aid face to face with the recipient, knowing that red tape and corruption would not hinder it going to the right people.

It turned out to be a busy and unusual afternoon. We were alerted to a bloated dead hippo, which had drifted down and was now lodged in the middle of the river in front of our camp. Some villagers had followed its movements and asked if they could be taken out to the hippo by boat, so that they could retrieve some of the flesh, which apparently was a local delicacy. Several crocodiles were circling around the hippo, but none had started to rip it up, so the boat was prepared and a couple of rangers with three villagers set off to the hippo.

It was a difficult operation avoiding the crocs to bring the boat alongside the inflated carcass. We watched as the boat was steadied, and the pangas prepared to start the gruesome task of butchering the decaying flesh. The first strike produced a resounding hiss as the gases were released, and one of the rangers put his head over the side of the boat, his retching clearly audible. He was obviously overcome by the noxious smell. Thankfully, we were up wind and not affected.

Soon the villagers were transporting hunks of meat back to shore. Their happiness was evident at the thought of feasting on this haul for several days. We continued to watch as the crocs circled the half-submerged hippo, wondering if there would be photographic opportunity of the crocs thrashing around in a feeding frenzy. I waited for some time, but apparently, the crocs were still in semi hibernation mode at the end of the winter, and would not feed with much enthusiasm. A few nibbled at the carcass as we prepared to go on our last evening drive, and eventually they started to feed in earnest, grabbing a mouthful and then twisting and turning in the so-called 'death roll' in an attempt to detach the flesh from the carcass.

I relaxed and enjoyed the luxury of being driven instead of walking. My bruises were now coming out, and to add insult to injury more blister beetle bites were erupting into painful blisters on top of the bruises. Chatting quietly to the others, we all agreed that this walking safari had been very special and not just because of the hippo attack. The beautiful areas we had walked through, the exquisite setting of the camp with our huts overlooking the Luangwa River, and the hospitality of the camp staff with nothing being too much trouble all went to create an unforgettable experience.

Our animal sightings had exceeded our expectations for a walking safari, and as if on cue, a small female leopard appeared out of the bush in front of us. She gave us a nonchalant glance, and with a flick of her white tipped tail, she strolled down the track in front of us, every so often stopping to sniff the air, before disappearing like a ghost into the undergrowth

We stopped when Doubt spotted three hyenas standing underneath the branches of a huge tree. Looking up, we could just make out the body of a puku draped over a stout branch and assumed that the kill belonged to this leopard. What a herculean task it must have been for such a slight leopard to drag its prey so high up, graphically proving the strength these cats have to remove their kill out of the way of other predators.

We hoped the leopard would return to its kill, and sat in silence, enjoying the sounds of the bush starting to prepare itself for the oncoming night. Birds flew about in seemingly frantic efforts to catch the last of the insects. In the distance a lion roared, its subsequent grunts decreasing in volume until after a few moments of silence the sequence began all over again, preparing the predator for a night of hunting and alerting the plains game for a night of disturbed alertness.

Doubt picked a magical place to have our last sundowners – a small open area surrounded by a glade of trees. Venus, the Evening Star, shone brightly despite the full moon rising, and although the emerging stars were robbed of their brilliance by the bright moon, the Southern Cross soon became visible. The setting sun was directly opposite the moon, and sipping my G and T, I wondered when we would be back in Africa again. For us it was more than just coming back to Africa. We needed to decide whether we might settle somewhere on this vast continent, and spend six months of each year living here rather than just visiting.

A braai was waiting for us on our return to camp, and as we were going to have a leisurely start in the morning before we flew back to Lilongwe and then back home, we stayed up far later than we had during the week, chatting over nightcaps as though willing the safari not to end. Eventually, we dragged ourselves away to our huts, and I spent the next twenty minutes dressing my blisters, before jumping into bed for our last night's sleep beside the Luangwa River.

Sleep was a somewhat arbitrary term as I was woken at 1 p.m. by the intense itching of yet more blister beetle attacks and Gordon's snoring. Just as I was losing my sense of humour and wondering why I ever had set foot on this wretched continent, let alone marry a man who snored, some lions started to roar. I drifted off to sleep listening to this and thinking how I would miss this most evocative of sounds.

The following morning after a full English breakfast, and the usual last minute flinging of clothes into our small canvas bags, we said our goodbyes to the camp staff, with smiles on our faces, but with an underlying element of seriousness. It was important to thank Doubt, Robert and Simon for saving our lives from marauding hippos! Soon we were in the Landy, bumping along the dirt track road, catching glimpses of giraffe, puku and baboons before passing Robert's village. We managed to avoid numerous rickety bicycles, goats, cattle and over-laden bakkies, and arrived at the airport for our transfer flight to Lilongwe.

As we had half a day to spare, our travel agent had arranged for us to have a guided tour of the onetime President Hastings Banda's State House, which had recently been converted to house Malawi's Parliament. We entered this enormous building with increasing incredulity. No expense had been spared in fitting out this vast building with what only can be described as vulgar bling – marble bathrooms, satin swathed window drapes, and lush fitted carpets, with everything possible being adorned with gold.

At least it was no longer the exclusive preserve of one man, and as we discussed this obscene luxury, I remembered Robert's wife in Zambia, close to giving birth in a village where there were no modern facilities. I fervently hoped that the work done here in Malawi's Parliament would alleviate some of this country's abject poverty, which no doubt was similar to that we had witnessed firsthand in Zambia.

At the check-in desk at Lilongwe airport, the staff took one look at my bruised legs and thankfully, gave us four seats between the two of us. We sprawled out in relative luxury, and yet again I contemplated how I could ever adapt to living in a continent where there were so many contrasts between the 'haves' and 'have-nots'. Here were we flying back to good medical care and even contemplating buying a second home somewhere in Africa, and I kept returning to the picture firmly engraved on my mind of Robert's pregnant wife outside her rondavel.

However much I had come to love our holidays in Africa, I could see that it would take a giant leap of faith to take the next step of living there. Gordon seemed more pragmatic about the situation, as we chatted together over trays of airline food. I wondered what our sons would say when we arrived back home, their mother limping, with her legs black and blue and covered with plasters, and I looked forward to our family reunion as we settled down to spend yet another overnight flight in fitful sleep.

For three very special minutes, we watched as the Zambian bush descended into night in the middle of the afternoon. The birdlife came home to roost but all too soon, daylight and normality returned. We returned home from Zambia via South Africa, where within a week we had bought a plot of land. Six months later, our African home named Jabula, was built, and we were spending six months of the year at Jabula.

Chapter 20

Total Eclipse and Our Very Own Piece of Africa

Our sons were there to greet us on our return to our Derbyshire home. We settled down to a meal together, and we regaled them with our stories of the walking safari. Suffice to say, the hippo incident was the last straw as far as they were concerned.

'You are far too old to be doing this sort of thing,' number one son, Shaun exclaimed, sighing heavily.

'You really ought to stop all this safari lark and think about settling down in Africa as you obviously love it so much,' retorted number two son, Michael. 'Besides which,' he continued with his banking hat on, 'you'll be saving money in the long run. If you have a house out there, it could be an investment.'

'And we'll be able to come and have holidays with you,' added Shaun, remembering his honeymoon with Caraline in South Africa, and eager to return.

Well, that was easy! Gordon and I exchanged amused glances; we didn't even have to mention that our thoughts were already way ahead of theirs!

Michael's comments about having a home in Africa were beginning to make some sort of financial sense to us – at least as much as it was possible to in a mainly Third World continent. We could spend half the year there and half the year in Derbyshire, renting out the African home on short-term lets when we were not there, to cover some of our running expenses. But where, in the whole of the African continent were we going to put down our roots?

Our instinctive first choice was Zimbabwe. We had been there more often than anywhere else, adored the country, loved the people and had made several good friends there. However, the winds of change were sweeping through the country. On our last visit, the Zimbabwe dollar had started its final fatal decline and the land seizures were well under way. We decided we couldn't risk investing in this beautiful country, which was being systematically ruined by one man.

We had to try to be sensible. Our dream was to have a home in the bush, but realistically this was entirely impractical. Our retirement looming, it is hard to imagine two English pensioners coping with isolated living and shops hours away, let alone any other services. This would be a huge mistake and a disaster in the making. We needed a country that met most of our needs. The first and foremost need was easy access to the bush – those wild open spaces we had come to adore.

The bush nurtured our souls in a way nothing else could. If we couldn't live in the bush, then we had to be able to drive ourselves there whenever we wanted. We needed a First World economy, or as near to this as possible in Africa, good medical care, and easy international airport access. English would have to be at the very least a second language and our potential home should be in an area that was attractive to people wanting a holiday let. Everything pointed to South Africa.

We first visited South Africa the year after apartheid ended, and it was there that a young woman game ranger called Kathy nurtured our love for the bush. Her enthusiasm and love for the bush and her ability to make even the smallest insect or bird, let alone trees and plants, fascinating, encouraged us not only to search for the 'Big Five' but to rejoice in finding anything the bush had to offer. The director of the travel firm that had booked most of our safaris had become a trusted friend over the years, and we had given him a brief all those years ago. 'We want to visit South Africa, and you had better make the trip a good one, as it will be the only trip we will ever make to Africa.'

Little did we know that umpteen trips later we would be deliberating where to make our second home. But *where* in South Africa? The obvious choice was Cape Town, but this was just too cosmopolitan for us, had few wild open spaces, and we never really felt we were in Africa when we visited the 'Fairest Cape'. Most importantly, there was nowhere where we could get our wildlife fix easily, however lovely the Cape scenery is.

Just as we were ruminating on this, a friend who lived a couple of miles away from us and whose husband worked for a South African firm, got in touch with me. They had just decided to build a holiday home on a golf course in Kwa Zulu Natal. She had no idea we were travelling along the same path, as we had decided to keep this to ourselves until we knew what we were doing. There must be something in the Derbyshire air! This news couldn't have come at a better time and it galvanised us into action. Someone we knew had taken this step. It wasn't impossible or crazy! They mentioned that they had visited a golf estate in Mpumalanga, the old Eastern Transvaal, and stands were still available there if we were interested.

We knew the area well. In fact, we had stayed at a wonderful lodge just a few kilometres up the road on our first trip to South Africa, and had revisited the area several times. Shaun and Caraline had also stayed there for part of their honeymoon. It was in a sleepy backwater of the Lowveld, a small town called White River. There was a connecting airport at Nelspruit, the nearest large town, and most important of all, the Kruger National Park was half an hour's drive away. Our dream of living in Africa was starting to develop an air of reality..

We decided to combine a week in White River looking at plots of land for our potential house build with a safari in Zambia where we would observe the first full solar eclipse of the twenty-first century. Our excitement was intense as we joined a party of 20 like-minded travellers at Heathrow at the beginning of our ten-day safari in the Zambian bush. I could not think of anywhere I would rather spend those precious three and a half minutes of total eclipse than in the seclusion of the bush.

The beginning of our safari got off to an unexpected and very welcome start when we were upgraded not just to business class but first class. Apparently, the airline was heavily overbooked due to the unprecedented interest in the eclipse, so for eleven hours I experienced the luxury I had previously only dreamt about.

Onboard the aircraft, we actually enjoyed the tedious wait for take-off whilst sipping glasses of champagne. After a couple more glasses and a silver service dinner of lobster followed by steak, fresh strawberries and a cheese board, I settled down to watch a film on my own large screen. My enormous seat converted into a full-length bed, complete with sheets, a duvet, and a jumpsuit to change into. Ironically, I was excited as a child in a sweet shop and hardly slept a wink all night. After all, this was the first and probably the only time I would ever experience such luxury, and it seemed a shame to waste the experience asleep! So I whiled the night away looking at whatever film I wanted to order, interspersed with hot and cold drinks, finally snoozing fitfully just before breakfast was served.

As dawn broke, we landed at Lusaka and were soon being transferred to a lodge on the outskirts of this sprawling, busy capital city. We came across a BBC news crew filming in the lodge grounds. Apparently, much of the world's media were interested in reporting this iconic eclipse. Our group congregated on a large veranda to relax and enjoy the surrounding grounds of the lodge, where kudu, impala and giraffe strolled right up to where we were sitting.

The main topic of conversation was how we were going to cope with the meagre luggage allowance of 10 kilograms. We all had strict instructions that under no circumstances were any of us to exceed this limit, as we had several light aircraft flights in order to get us in and out of the special bush camp that was being set up for us in the middle of the Kafue National Park. Most of us had decided to wear several layers of clothing and our heaviest walking boots as our camera equipment, which had to be included in the ten-kilo allowance, was much more important than our clothes. Those of us who had been lucky enough to be upgraded joked together when we realised that we were all wearing multiple layers of well-worn safari gear and boots in the first class cabin. So much for the belief that one had to dress smartly to get a treasured upgrade!

Thankfully, our bush flights the following morning were uneventful and soon we were in a Landy taking us from the dirt airstrip to our camp, traversing a stream by way of a bridge made of wooden planks, which wobbled alarmingly as the driver made certain he had aligned the vehicle correctly. Half an hour later, we arrived at our camp, where a Union Jack flew proudly from a flagpole in the middle of the area where we would congregate around the campfire. We unpacked our meagre luggage in our small tents before having the first of many briefings by John Parkinson, a charming man who was our expert astronomer, supported ably by his wife Jan. Soon we were all buzzing with excitement as John bought the whole experience of an eclipse to life, explaining what we would be seeing and how we should prepare our cameras and viewing equipment.

Over sundowners round the campfire, I relaxed into the bush once again, and having identified the Southern Cross, knew I was finally back in Africa. A delicious three-course meal was served in the large mess tent, and we were all full of admiration for the organisation that enabled us to enjoy such superb facilities. The only thing we now needed was clear weather in two days' time. The possibility that it might be overcast was too distressing to contemplate.

The following morning, a discreet verbal 'knock, knock', announced the arrival of our shower water. Drowsily I got up to sample yet again the delights of a bush shower in our adjoining shower tent, fervently hoping that I did not succumb to any of my previous mishaps. This time, my ablutions were totally uneventful and very satisfactory. The bucket strung up contained more than enough hot water as long as I was careful not to use too much shampoo and shower gel. My breath was clearly visible as we all started to congregate round the fire and warm our hands around mugs of steaming tea, and I realised just how cold the early mornings were in mid winter.

The morning and afternoon game drives passed pleasantly and uneventfully, the bird life being especially beautiful, and we spent the intervening time wining, dining and chatting to our fellow travellers about the forthcoming eclipse. The weather forecast was good, and round the campfire that evening all talk was on what we could expect and where we were going to position ourselves. We were shown pictures of how to create eclipse patterns with makeshift pinhole cameras. Even the flickering light through the leaves of trees would form spectacular images of the eclipse that we could photograph.

Sleep came slowly on the eve of the eclipse. The sounds of the African night eventually lulled me off – the cry of a hyena, the faint sawing sound of a distant leopard and the warning barks of baboons.

Morning dawned somewhat nosily for us, as the man carrying our shower water tripped and fell over the guy ropes. Quiet cursing and louder profuse apologies were followed by a replacement supply of hot water, which arrived a few minutes later. After breakfast and a short game drive, it was back to camp for final preparations of cameras and eclipse viewing equipment.

Lunch followed, after which we scattered over the surrounding bush area in small groups, watched over by our ever-vigilant armed rangers. It is only in retrospect that I wondered what would have happened if a pride of lion had strolled into this area. Probably, any self-respecting lion would have given us a wide berth! Bizarrely, game spotting was the last thing on our minds.

The moment of first contact came gently and unseen, but soon it was possible to see a minute black mark on the sun. This area of black increased and with it, our excitement. The light quality softened and became greyer. Gradually, the hot African afternoon became cooler and cooler. We experimented taking photos of eclipse patterns silhouetted on the ground under trees and on our clothing – our own unique record of a unique event.

Birds came home to roost and plains game stopped grazing and adopted that alert aware look they have at dusk. Suddenly, the light changed dramatically – the moment of totality. It had happened!

We hugged each other and our newly made friends. There was just too much to take in. On one horizon, it looked as though dawn was approaching. The opposite horizon looked like midnight.

Jupiter was visible, low on the horizon. Just in time, we managed to take a few photos. Suddenly, with a flash of light, the sun started to emerge and the strange grey daylight reappeared. I looked down realising the front of my shirt was damp. Tears were streaming down my face! Nothing could have prepared me for such an emotional few minutes.

Gradually, the temperature rose, the birds and animals resumed their normal activities and we went for a walk in the Zambian bush during the final part of the eclipse and the return of normality. It was difficult to know what to do after such a beautiful and surreal experience. We walked slowly back to camp and did the typically British thing – we had a cup of tea! We watched in silence as a spectacular sunset descended over the plains of Kafue that evening – the second setting of the sun in one awe-inspiring day.

We left Kafue in a light aircraft to Livingstone, the border town on the Zambian side of Victoria Falls where we spent three nights recovering from a week in the bush, soothing our tsetse fly bites with frequent showers. These wretched flies had attacked us once again, with the bites swelling up into the size of saucers, thus re-enforcing our decision not to build a home in Zambia. After a week of bush showers, I enjoyed the bliss of getting into a shower attached to a mains water supply.

Our three days of luxury, combined with several soaking visits to the Falls which were in spectacular full spate, sped by. All too soon we crossed into Zimbabwe to travel to the airport there for our flight to Johannesburg. As we drove on the long road out of Victoria Falls, my heart sank. A few years ago, this road was humming with activity. Now the roadside stalls had gone and all that remained was a road full of potholes, the rich red soil swirling around in the wind. The remains of stumps of trees stretched as far as the eye could see, with a few forlorn figures gathering wood. How could a once vibrant community be reduced to this in so short a time? How could we contemplate settling in South Africa when its next-door neighbour had so quickly been reduced to this?

Depression set in, emphasised by the departure lounge in the airport. The shelves of the duty-free and souvenir shop were empty, and a battered ancient fridge contained no more than half a dozen cans of cold drinks. A thin young man was sweeping the floor, and caught my eye when I got out a packet of mints. Instinctively I went over to him and gave the sweets to him, receiving the most gracious and heartfelt thanks for something worth only a few pence. 'Thank you, mam. I give these to my children.'

On the flight to Johannesburg, I wondered if I could ever come to terms with living on a continent with so much poverty. Going on safari and being insulated against it was one thing. Living amongst it was quite another.

It was only a fifty-minute flight from Johannesburg to Nelspruit in a small twin-engine plane. At least it had two engines, unlike the small planes we used for our bush flights. The approach to this particular airport had always made me grip the sides of my seat and breathe several prayers for a safe return to terra firma.

High rolling hills surround the airport on three sides. Consequently, the landing approach is steep and the short runway ends close to where a spectacular escarpment falls several hundred feet. We have heard the locals suggest it is similar to landing on an aircraft carrier! Coming into land, my feet pressing on imaginary brakes, my fingers were white with the effort of clinging on for dear life.

We landed safely, and walked to the tiny terminal surrounded by a few small round thatched shelters for spectators and departing passengers to shield themselves from the fierce African sun. Alas, this tiny, picturesque airport has now been replaced by a larger modern one with a much longer runway, just outside White River, so visitors no longer have a glimpse of what must rate as one of the most spectacular and terrifying airports in the world. The local flying school has taken it over, so trainee pilots should be getting a good grounding in take-offs and landings in stimulating conditions.

We collected our hire car, and started out on the forty-minute journey up to White River. The journey is upwards because Nelspruit is about 500 metres below White River. The short journey out of the airport to Nelspruit is a lovely introduction to the Lowveld, with umbrella acacia trees spreading their branches high over the road. Soon, Nelspruit has to be negotiated, with its numerous traffic lights, known as robots. Robots often seem to be only advisory by the local population, which makes all the intersections a trial of nerves.

Nelspruit is the commercial hub of the Lowveld and no one can say its centre is particularly attractive, although the surrounding hills are spectacular. It is also several degrees hotter than White River, and the humidity in summer can make it a place to avoid. We avoided traffic lights and drivers with death wishes, and half an hour later, we had passed through White River and arrived at the Country Estate.

The golf professional's wife who was renting us a small apartment for the duration of our stay greeted us. I'm sure we were somewhat of a disappointment to her when we confessed that neither of us were golfers. Gordon had given up when he found he could hit divots further than the ball, and the only game of golf that I had ever played was the result of a bet with my mother and father, both keen golfers. When I was somewhat dismissive of the game, they suggested that I couldn't get round their local course in less than 150. The challenge was all I needed, and I won £10 for playing what appeared to them a game of hockey, before finally deciding that golf was not for me.

Yet again, doubts were surfacing. If we were to come and live here, would we fit in? Why choose a golf estate when we don't play golf? Would all our neighbours be keen golfers? To have to learn to play golf in order to fit in was not on our agenda. We wanted the security of a 'lock up and go' house, which the estate provided, but would I have to adapt my game of hockey and Gordon learn how to hit a ball further than a bit of grass? Our host re-assured us jokingly that golf was not compulsory, and that there were many non-golfers living here, although a glint in her eye suggested that she had hopes of converting us.

We spent the next few days walking round the estate looking at several plots of land, and soon becoming used to the local terminology. If we were talking to English-speaking residents, a plot was a stand. Afrikaners referred to them as erfs. We finally narrowed down our choice to a plot bordering the perimeter of the estate with forestry behind. It had houses built on each side, which to us was an advantage, as we knew what was already there and wouldn't have any potentially nasty surprises with someone building a house where we least expected it.

The plot seemed ideal. It had magnificent views over the river and was on a slope giving us privacy from the access road. It also faced north-east, which would give us the all important shade. We were already adapting to the Southern Hemisphere and thinking about keeping out of the sun and remaining cool. Water was an issue. It was the middle of the dry season but the plot seemed to be a somewhat wet one.

We realised that the whole of the Lowveld was still recovering from the disastrous flood when Mozambique suffered incredible damage, and the flooded Kruger Park made international news. After a shower of rain, we noticed that water streamed down onto the road in front of the plot. Unusually, the soil seemed to be sandy rather than the heavy red soil that covered most of the estate.

All sorts of doubts started to surface. If we built here, would the house be flooded in the wet season? In the dry season, would the foundations hold as the soil was so light? Indeed, were we crazy to attempt to build here in the first place? The land was a re-sale, so obviously someone wanted to get rid of it.

Just as we were looking despondently at the soggy bit of Africa we hoped might just be ours, a car drew up and a man rolled down the window and greeted us. This turned out to be the first of so many occasions when we found South Africa turned up trumps and delivered the goods. Don turned out to be a well-respected local builder, but to us he became a guardian angel. He listened to our fears about the site, and offered to do a soil survey and exploratory dig at no cost to us to see if it was a viable site.

Just as we were saying our goodbyes, another car rolled up and out jumped a larger than life man, full to the brim with laughter and good humour. He turned out to be Tom, an architect who had been used by Don's building firm on several projects. We instantly took to both these warm-hearted men and arranged to meet them in a couple of days for an exploratory meeting. When they left us, we looked at each other in bemused amazement.

'I don't believe this has just happened,' murmured Gordon. 'It looks like we might just have found ourselves a builder and an architect without even trying!'

'For heaven's sake, Gordon, we have yet to find out if the plot is suitable to build on,' I retorted. Things were moving rather faster than I had anticipated.

Off we went down the road to the Casterbridge Centre, a conglomeration of small shops and restaurants built around a large Italian style courtyard and shaded by large mango trees. To Gordon's amazement and utter delight, he discovered there was a vintage car museum there. Now this was like winning the lottery as far as he was concerned. Vintage cars had been his passion since he bought his first one in his late teens, and throughout our married life, there has always been at least one ancient car in the garage, either in bits or ready to be stripped down and rebuilt. Not just in our garage either; when we got married, a spare bedroom was an overflow for the garage, housing large pieces of a vintage Alfa Romeo.

Walking around this Lowveld Museum, I saw that nothing could persuade Gordon to settle anywhere else in the universe. He managed to find out the name of the owner, and quickly phoned him, all thoughts of architects and builders forgotten in the excitement. Ten minutes later Hans appeared on the scene, and we settled down to a drink and talk with a man who not only owned the museum and most of the vehicles inside it, but appeared to know virtually everyone in White River and most of the Lowveld too. We had met the fountain of all knowledge, and he shared this with largesse and a wicked sense of humour. Little did we know that Hans and his wife Jeanette were to become two much loved friends, and over the years share so much of their life with us with generosity, laughter and affection.

Several drinks later, followed by a leisurely lunch, Hans phoned a builder friend, who quickly arrived, and over a few more drinks, we talked about building our house. He gave us an indication of how much per metre we should expect to pay, and confirmed that Don was the owner of a well-respected building firm, and was someone we could trust to do a good job. Gordon then spent the rest of the day drooling over vintage vehicles with Hans, whilst I engaged in a bit of retail therapy at a boutique.

That evening we sat sipping wine and ruminated on our experiences so far. We were struck by the friendliness of everyone we had come across and were already beginning to feel we could integrate into Lowveld life; the laid-back atmosphere was weaving its gentle spell. We were starting to become captivated, understanding why the Lowveld is sometimes called the Slowveld by those in more cosmopolitan cities in South Africa. To us it was like going back thirty years or so, the pace of life slowing down to a gentle stroll rather than the frantic rush in England.

There was only one more thing to do to convince me that this was the right place for us. It was the weekend and nothing more was going to happen on the house front until Monday. We had to take ourselves off into the Kruger National Park. I needed to convince myself that I would be satisfied with this sort of a bush experience. To be driven in the bush by experienced game rangers was one thing. Driving ourselves was quite another, and then there was the fact that we would not be able to drive off-road in the Park. I wondered if this might prove very frustrating, as we were used to being able to drive a Landy anywhere over pristine bush. I wanted to spend a day by ourselves there, and see if the Kruger National Park would work its magic on both of us.

We got up before dawn had broken, packed up a picnic breakfast, and set off for the Park. The journey took exactly half an hour although the road was full of potholes and in the process of undergoing major repair work. We passed through the sprawling townships where thirty years ago, there was nothing but open countryside. Wood smoke drifted from the homes, some no more than a shack, others built with concrete blocks or even bricks.

People were transporting water containers in wheelbarrows; children were herding goats and cattle; babies swaddled in blankets were hitched snugly onto their mothers' backs. Women dressed in white and blue robes were making their way to the local church, and men were having haircuts in small shacks next to the road. African life was going on all around us. We smiled at a sign written on a piece of wood urged passing tourists to 'Buy gifts for your lovely ones', and another version stated 'Buy presents for your beloved ones'.

We were in the minority here, and however much I tried to put it to the back of my mind, I felt vulnerable. Local warnings flashed through my mind. 'Don't stop in a township, it's not safe'. We were visitors passing through a foreign world. I was somewhat ashamed of myself even suspecting I was at risk in any way. This was the beginning of a long journey of self-discovery. Building a house in Africa could well be the easiest part of this journey.

In a thoughtful frame of mind, we approached the Park gates and completed the entry formalities. Rapidly, the bush claimed us. We unpacked the binoculars and camera and prepared ourselves for whatever came our way. We were not disappointed. The dry season is always spectacular for game viewing. The grass has died down and the wildlife tends to congregate at waterholes. Thus, game viewing is made relatively easy, and soon we were rewarded by a breeding herd of elephant crossing the road in front of us, giraffe reaching for foliage in the almost leafless trees, and a herd of buffalo slowly grazing on the meagre remains of the previous season's grass.

We went off the tarmac roads onto the gravel tracks, exploring with the help of the Park map. We rarely got lost and adopted the attitude that all roads did eventually lead to another signpost. I soon realised that the experiences we had already had on safari in the bush guided by rangers were invaluable. The pressure was off to find lions, leopards and cheetahs – in fact anything at all. We already had numerous of photos of the Big Five, and were able to relax and enjoy nature at its finest. It would be a real bonus to see any of the cats, but in the meantime, we could revel in anything that strolled, galloped or just grazed in front of us.

We knew that wild animals need their space, and I found that the best photographs offered themselves when we turned the car engine off and waited. So much more could be gained from observing animal behaviour this way, and over the years, I enjoyed anticipating what the animal might do next.

We had our picnic breakfast overlooking a dam, watching a herd of zebra warily coming down to the water's edge. Several impala joined them, and a hippo snorted in the distance. Waterbuck, with their unmistakable white ringed rumps, sauntered past us, followed by a couple of kudu rams with magnificent horns. We sat entranced when a fish eagle cried its unmistakable call. If any birdcall could symbolise the African bush, it would have to be this haunting cry. With all this beauty on our doorstep, we knew without a doubt that we could live here.

Off we drove to Skukuza, the largest rest camp in the Park to stretch our legs and answer our own calls of nature. We passed large tourist buses on the main roads with tinted windows that could not be opened, and wondered how the tourists sealed inside these air-conditioned monsters could possibly have an authentic experience of the bush. How could you learn to love nature if you were unable to smell the odour of a herd of buffalos kicking up the dry earth, a bull elephant in musth, the sweet smell of a shower of rain on the parched grass or hear the bird cries and hippos grunting like old men laughing at a risqué joke?

I hope their experience was not too disappointing. If it were, I would put a large percentage of the blame on some travel agents who mass market package deals around South Africa. We've seen the advertisements selling tours, detailing the highlight of a ten-day holiday being a day 'searching for the Big Five in the Kruger National Park'. Search they might, but what the small print never reveals is you can spend weeks visiting the Park and never see all of them. If they were very lucky and came across any of them, how could they enjoy the moment with camcorders and cameras whirring, trying to get a photo through tinted glass? We realised how very blessed we were to have been able to have all our bush experiences and hoped that those not as fortunate as ourselves might be able to return to Africa for a more rewarding experience.

We left the bustle of Skukuza, and drove along the banks of the Sabie River, astonished by the debris of branches of trees and grass draping the bush. The floods a few months earlier had reached far higher than we had ever imagined. Enormous trees had been uprooted and lay on the sides of the banks, yet the river bed was virtually dry. How there had not been greater loss of animal life was incredible, yet here was nature being left to sort itself out after a once in a century natural disaster.

Vervet monkeys scampered about, and troops of baboons watched us pass by, hoping no doubt for an illegal tasty morsel to be flung out of the car to them. If only visitors to the Park realised that once an animal is fed by a human, its death warrant is signed. Baboons demanding food soon become aggressive and have to be destroyed, all the result of thoughtless human behaviour, something we later learnt first-hand with near disastrous consequences during one of our subsequent stays in the Park.

Soon it was time to wend our way homewards. The heat of the afternoon meant that the wildlife was sheltering in whatever meagre shade they could find, and we found that driving with the windows closed and the air conditioning on, isolated us from the sounds of the bush. We wanted to hear the crackle of branches warning us of any impending encounter with a large mammal, not to mention the barking of baboons or the snorting of impala, which might signal a carnivore approaching.

I put my camera away as we approached the Park gates. Suddenly, we saw an animal saunter across the road. We could not believe our eyes. Here, in broad daylight, was the most elusive nocturnal cat of all – a large male leopard. Turning the car around we followed it for several minutes, watching it mark its territory before disappearing. So much for getting a photo, with my camera tucked up safely on the back seat of the car. We learnt another lesson – never pack the camera away. Not only this, some wildlife is best enjoyed when not struggling to get the ultimate photograph. Yet again, the bush reminded us that nothing is certain and surprises lurk around every corner. Such excitement called for a loo stop, and when we arrived at the loos at the Park gate I found three ladies in staff uniform hiding behind the only door that could be locked.

'Eish mam, you see animal? I's so scared. You brave to get out of car. Where it now?' said one trembling lady in broken English. Despite assurances that the leopard had disappeared into the bush, nothing would convince them to leave the security of the loo block. Apparently, the leopard had walked straight in front of the gates and strolled past without a care in the world, creating mayhem amongst the staff.

As we left the Park, I knew we would cherish the memory of such an amazing sighting. We still had smiles on our faces when we arrived back at White River half an hour later. We both knew that we had made up our minds – this was the place for us. Our faces confirmed it!

Monday dawned and we were up with the lark, or rather to the raucous cries of the hadedahs, large dark birds with long beaks and a cry that is certainly not very melodic. Don and his workforce were already on our plot, having arrived at half past seven, not like your English builders drifting into work whenever the mood takes them. We watched the excavator digging deep into the soil and after a couple of metres down it came to water, but we were assured that this was normal and wouldn't be a problem. Don walked round the plot with us to make sure that there were no obvious signs of large boulders, which would put up the price of building there.

Don advised us that a reinforced concrete base would guarantee secure foundations, and if we were worried about it being a damp plot, a French drain at the back of the site would ensure that excess water would drain safely away. His advice seemed sound, so we arranged to meet him later that week with Tom the architect. This meant that we would have time enough to think things through. To give us an idea of his workmanship, he invited us to view some of the houses he and his team had built.

Our next stop was Nelspruit to meet a lawyer who had been recommended to us. Geraldine turned out to be just the person we needed. She was experienced in both property and international law, and filled us with confidence that she could handle all the legal aspects of buying our land. She also led us gently through all the issues connected with this, including the making of our South African wills. After this, we had to open a bank account, which was by no means as simple as it sounded.

We joined a queue only to be advised to join another one after half an hour's wait. At least we could entertain ourselves by people watching. Smartly dressed black businessmen mingled with Afrikaner farmers in their tackies and shorts. Black women with babies slung on their backs, dressed in clothes that were obviously cast-offs from their white madams waited patiently, chatting and calling to their friends across the many queues, adding to the cacophony of sound all around us.

Luckily, we could provide the paperwork needed, but this took a lot of time to finalise. Geraldine agreed to make sure that all our funds from the UK went through the right channels so that if we wanted to repatriate the money at any time in the future, she would hold the correct records. Gordon and I had already discussed the future worst-case scenario of South Africa going the way of Zimbabwe. We had satisfied ourselves that we could walk away from our investment however distressing this might be in the knowledge that this would not be financially catastrophic.

Facing this issue head on now meant that we could allow the future to unfurl as it might. Without Geraldine's help and infinite patience and kindness, we would never have been able to negotiate all the formalities as smoothly as we did.

Somewhat-shell shocked, we then went to the estate agent and signed the contract for our South African 'erf'. We were now owners of our own tiny piece of Africa! What had started as a pipe dream was slowly but surely beginning to turn into reality.

The meetings with Don and Tom took place over several days. We were confident that they were the right people for us. We instinctively trusted them and liked their work. Tom asked us to supply a wish list to work from, and he would submit his initial drawings by e-mail to us in England. We could keep in touch by e-mails and telephone calls until we had finalised the plans, and we agreed that a turnkey project would work best for us. This guaranteed that the build would be finished on time and to budget, plus or minus five per cent to make allowance for fluctuations in the cost of building materials.

We would pay in instalments as each stage was finished, and an agreed date of January 2002 was set for the beginning of the build. We prayed that the next rainy season would not be as dramatic as the last one. All being well, we would be able to move in at the end of June that year. This would be six months from start to finish!

As for a contract, all that was required was for us to sign off the detailed architect's drawings, which would be couriered to England once agreed and finalised by us. In retrospect, this might sound terribly naïve, but we felt happy with this. Perhaps we were taking a chance, but there was mutual trust on both sides. We shook hands on this gentlemen's agreement and arranged to come out to White River in late November to finalise all the finer details of finishes and fittings before the building work commenced.

Back in England, it was fascinating to see the reaction of family and friends to the news that we were going to build a house in South Africa. By far the hardest thing for me was to tell my mother. She was frail, living in a nursing home a few miles away from us, and five minutes away from where my brother lived. She had become well used to our trips to the African continent, and enjoyed looking at the photos I brought to show her and hearing about all our experiences.

How was I going to tell her that we intended to spend up to six months away each year, albeit probably in three-month stretches? I need not have worried. She enthusiastically encouraged us. I owe an immense debt of gratitude to her that never once did she complain or try to dissuade us from embarking on this adventure. I know that she missed me terribly sometimes, and the guilt I felt was often horrendous. During the long years of my mother's decline, the staff became her extended family and it was their loving care in an exceptional nursing home that enabled me to let go of some of the guilt and follow her loving instructions – 'Go and live your own life!'

Shaun and Michael were supportive and enthusiastic if a little surprised that their parents had actually gone and done the very thing they had advised them to do. My brother's first comment was, 'But it's not safe out there, is it?' This was followed by, 'And what about all the bugs and animals and malaria?' No amount of reassuring would ever persuade him to visit us there in the future, as he firmly stated that he did not want to be killed either by the natives, the animals or the insects. I learnt to live with the disappointment of never being able to share with him all the beauty and joy we regularly experienced in South Africa, but I also owe him a big debt of gratitude as he took over the task of visiting my mother more often when we were away.

Gordon's elderly mother took the news in her stride. Maybe it helped that her own father had been one of the early explorers in the 1890s in South Africa. Her mother was a chorus girl on the stage in Cape Town, and caught the eye of her future husband there. They eloped and married somewhere in the wilds of South Africa, and Gordon's aunt had the dubious distinction of having both Cecil Rhodes and Leander Starr Jameson as her godparents. Gordon's mother was born many years later to this fascinating couple when they had returned to spend a genteel but impoverished old age in England, having made and lost several fortunes on the 'Darkest Continent'. We hoped that history would not repeat itself!

A few of our friends adopted the same attitude of my brother, but the majority were enthusiastic and supportive, and our closest friends started to think ahead in terms of holidays out there with us, which delighted us. This was just the sort of affirmation we needed. It was all very well being enthusiastic about building a house when we were in South Africa, but White River seemed very far away when we were back in Derbyshire. Not least, we had the exciting but daunting task of designing our new home virtually by e-mail.

We had only ever owned two houses in our married life, both built in the mid thirties. We altered these to some extent, but had never had the task of designing a house from scratch. We spent a week on our wish list before e-mailing it to Tom, and waited anxiously to see what would appear on our computer screen. The first design arrived within a fortnight, and we soon realised that we would have to go back to the drawing board.

The design was exquisite, but being a double-storey house meant that when we calculated the floor space, the cost would be way over our budget. We had set aside a specific sum of money and this would be financially impossible. We had also omitted to put on our wish list that we wanted a one-storey house, a somewhat basic mistake. Feeling very naïve and stupid, we e-mailed back explaining the situation. We had to try to see if we could get a four double-bedroomed bungalow, each with en-suite bathrooms on the site and within budget. Four bedrooms would be essential if all the family were going to be able to stay with us.

Tom seemed completely unfazed by this and a few weeks later, he supplied us with a completely new design, having re-visited our site to make certain there was enough room for a ranch style bungalow. His new design was near enough perfect, and he had even managed to include a double garage, somewhat overkill I thought, as Gordon had specified a mere single garage on his wish list. Tom was brilliant in advising us over issues we might not even have thought about. We ought to consider re-sale desirability and think like a prospective South African buyer. This was good advice when we recalled some of the vast houses and garages on the estate.

We measured the floor area, and established it came within budget. The stoep area seemed enormous and we thought we could reduce this by half. As usual, Tom was right. 'You can't have a stoep that is too large,' he bellowed over the phone. Suitably chastened we went along with his vast stoep. Thanks to this talented architect who is used to getting his own way, we have a wonderful area overlooking a stream running down from a dam, where we eat, braai, relax and, party, and the living area inside is barely used for much of the time.

One issue, however, I was determined to win over Tom's design. He had followed our instructions over wanting a light and airy design and enormous French doors spread across the front of the house. But where was our front door? Tom felt we could use one of these sliding doors. I didn't! Gordon decided to retire into the background and watch the fireworks whilst I battled it out with Tom.

Thirty-five years of married life had taught him that when I was determined about something, arguing the point was useless. I had fallen in love with the old sleeper wood furniture, made from the sleepers, which straddled the railways throughout South Africa, Zimbabwe and Botswana.

An enterprising firm had set up business in White River and I had persuaded Gordon that this beautiful furniture would be perfect in our home here. I found out that they also used this wood for doors, bookcases and fireplace surrounds, and I was intent on having a large front door made from this beautiful old wood. It stirred up stories of the old Africa. If wood could talk, what tales would it tell of early days of exploration and discovery? Tom, to his eternal credit let me have my own way, and whenever he visited us, he stroked the door and graciously conceded that I was right to stick to my guns!

We spent hours measuring the dimensions of the various rooms, pacing out these measurements in our Derbyshire home to give us a more realistic idea of the areas. It all seemed vast and we had to keep pinching ourselves that this was affordable. We would have to have spent over four times the amount in the UK to build anything near the design we had fallen in love with, and felt we were so fortunate to have transferred most of the money when the rand was so advantageous to sterling.

So far, everything was going as planned. One weekend Shaun and his wife Caraline popped in to see us. They were looking a bit sheepish, Shaun hiding something behind his back. They burst into happy laughter and announced that we were going to become grandparents in late January the following year. Shaun produced a bottle of champagne from behind his back. We could not believe we were hearing such wonderful news. They had been married for eight years and together from their early twenties, and we had all but given up on ever becoming grandparents.

After the initial excitement had died down I turned to Gordon murmuring, 'But we have just bought the land in South Africa. What will we do?'

He looked at me in utter amazement. 'What do you mean? We'll build our house there as planned, of course.' What a typically male response. We had just received the most wonderful news and now I was expected to live half the year missing out on many of the stages of our first grandchild's development. Here was the beginning of the biggest test for me, something that pulls at my heartstrings every time we leave England for South Africa. Leaving family and friends is hard, but leaving Beth who was followed by Louis two years later, is something that I still find incredibly difficult.

Paradoxically, I have learnt that this is a situation many South African parents and grandparents have had to adapt to with much heartache. Quite a few of our friends in White River and beyond have had to adjust to their children living abroad, and I remind myself that I am very lucky that I get to see our family for half the year, whereas they only see their loved ones for short holidays, sometimes years going by without any direct contact. When I get a low day, or what Gordon calls 'a hate Africa day', I have friends who know firsthand what I am experiencing.

Gordon attempted to cheer me up by saying that we will just have to try to have as many family holidays together as possible, and I thanked my lucky stars that our first grandchild would be born when we were in England and I would have several months of baby worshipping before our African house was built.

The whole world turned upside down on September 11th. Although the horrendous loss of life did not directly affect us, the world seemed a much less safe place. Some of my friends' reactions surprised me. 'At least you have a safe place to go to in South Africa,' said one, having previously asked us if it was safe there.

Michael and his partner Stephanie worked in London, and I used to turn on the news, fearful of another atrocity. In fact, they missed the subsequent London bombings by only a few minutes. Sleepy White River and the bush seemed such a safe haven from all this horror. We turned to the task of finalising our house plans and with the financial markets falling amidst all the chaos, decided we would have to wait to get the remaining funds out to South Africa. The bulk of the money was already out there, so we would just have to sit and wait for the markets to recover a little. Having booked our flights, we arranged to meet up with Don and Tom to finalise details and finishes three weeks before Christmas, not the most convenient of times, but if the build was going to start on time in January, then we had to get everything organised.

We left England on a cold, wet dark evening. I dozed fitfully during the flight before surfacing to enjoy the magic moment of dawn breaking over Africa. There is something I have yet to understand. Why do I feel I am returning home? Something deep inside me seems to stir whenever I return to Africa. Maybe some deep instinct is telling me this is where all of us had our beginnings. Perhaps I am just romanticising.

My mother would be horrified. I remember when, at the age of nine, my parents took me on my first trip abroad to Switzerland. We were on the boat deck, and as we approached Calais, my mother firmly told me, 'Now don't forget you are British.' What was I supposed to do? How was I to behave any differently? It was a complete mystery to me then, and now here am I, a middle-aged woman believing Africa is her home. With a wry smile, I soon faced the usual chaos of Johannesburg airport and presented my British passport for inspection.

After a day recovering from lack of sleep, we met Don and Tom who introduced us to Louis, the project manager of our build. If we thought Don and Tom were wonderful, then Louis was absolutely brilliant. Nothing was too much trouble, and his powers of organisation were phenomenal. Not only that, he and his wife Linda, together with their whole family have become some of the closest friends we have ever made. We have shared the ups and downs of life in South Africa with them, gone on many safaris and other holidays together, and with their friendship, love and generosity, our lives have been enriched beyond anything we could have ever imagined.

We sat down with Louis and planned what there was to be done before we returned to England in two weeks' time. He gave us a list of all the suppliers we would need to visit, together with a price guide. If we kept within the limits he had written down, we would be within budget. This at least would give us the control we wanted. Off we went to choose the tiles for the floors, the sanitary fittings, washing machine, microwave, oven, hob, carpets for the bedrooms, together with all the furniture and minutiae we needed to make our house a home.

I thought this would be the most awful task imaginable, as Gordon, in common with many men, regards shopping as a form of torture and will do anything to avoid it. Once in a shop he will yawn, fidget and generally project the image of a henpecked man in the terminal stages of acute depression. Thankfully, choosing the white goods went relatively smoothly; the tiles for the floors and bathrooms were chosen without too much trouble, and the sleeper wood furniture and fittings were ordered painlessly. The curtains, blinds and bed drapes were another matter though. We spent hours with a very patient interior designer, but after the first hour or so, I could see Gordon's patience sink to an all time low. I stopped going through sample after sample of the most beautiful materials, fearing our marriage would be severely threatened if we didn't take ourselves off to have lunch and a well deserved bottle of chilled white wine.

In a fortified frame of mind, I decided that the only thing to do was to get on with the job in hand myself and left Gordon to go and commune with the vintage cars. Several hours later, the task was completed and it is only in retrospect that I realised that I had chosen everything for our new home in a couple of days. Never before had I the opportunity of creating a home from scratch, and I really regretted the fact that it was necessary to do this so quickly. I would have adored to have had much more time, but as Gordon pointed out, there is nothing like a deadline to concentrate the mind. If we were to move into our home sometime in July next year, choices would have to be made now before we returned to England.

So, orders were placed, money paid, and promises made that everything would be in place by the time we came back, all coordinated by Louis, who was now the most important person to us in the whole of South Africa. I gave him several reels of film for his camera, with instructions to photograph each stage of the building of our house, and courier the prints out to us at regular intervals.

Reluctantly, we said our goodbyes, and boarded our flight, satisfied that everything we could have done had been done. We looked forward to a family Christmas and the birth of our first grandchild. Jabula, our South African home, half a world away, would be built in the New Year. But ... that is another chapter of my life and a completely different adventure!

CPSIA information can be obtained at www.ICGtesting.com
Printed in the USA
LVOW11s0135031113

359766LV00004B/816/P

9 781909 300224